A

N

I

DISASTER
AT
THE POLE

A SELECTION OF OTHER BOOKS BY WILBUR CROSS

+ History +

Zeppelins of World War I

Presidential Courage

White House Weddings

Challengers of the Deep

+ Self-Help and Inspiration +

Choices with Clout: How to Make Things Happen
by Making the Right Decisions Every Day of Your Life

The Complete Idiot's Guide to Grandparenting

+ Young Adults +

The Space Shuttle

Solar Energy

Brazil

Egypt

Portugal

+ Business and Industry +

Encyclopedic Dictionary of Business Terms

Small Business Model Letter Book

Amway: the True Story of the Company
that Transformed the Lives of Millions

+ In Progress +

Encyclopedia of American Submarines

DISASTER
AT
THE POLE

The Tragedy of the Airship *Italia*
and the 1928 Nobile Expedition to the North Pole

Wilbur Cross

THE LYONS PRESS

Disaster at the Pole is a revised edition of Wilbur Cross's book Ghost Ship of the Pole, which was published in 1960.

Printed in the United States of America

10 9 8 7 6 5 4 3 2 1

Library of Congress Cataloging-in-Publication Data
Cross, Wilbur.
    Disaster at the pole : the tragedy of the airship Italia and the 1928 Nobile Expedition to the North Pole/
Wilbur Cross.
            p.   cm.
    Includes bibliographical references (p.).
    ISBN 1-58574-049-7
    1.   Italia   (Air-ship)   2.   Nobile,   Umberto,   1885-
3. Arctic regions—Aerial exploration.   I. Title.
    G700 1928 .C72   2000
    910'.9163'2—dc21   00-031486

In cherished memory of
HENRY MELVILLE PARKER
lifelong friend,
former director of
the Massachusetts Audubon Society
and a dedicated explorer of our natural world.

CONTENTS

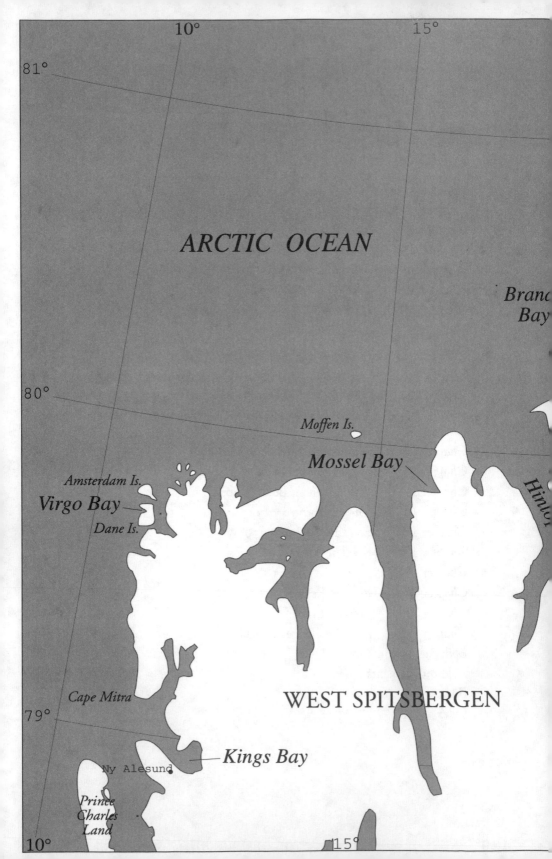

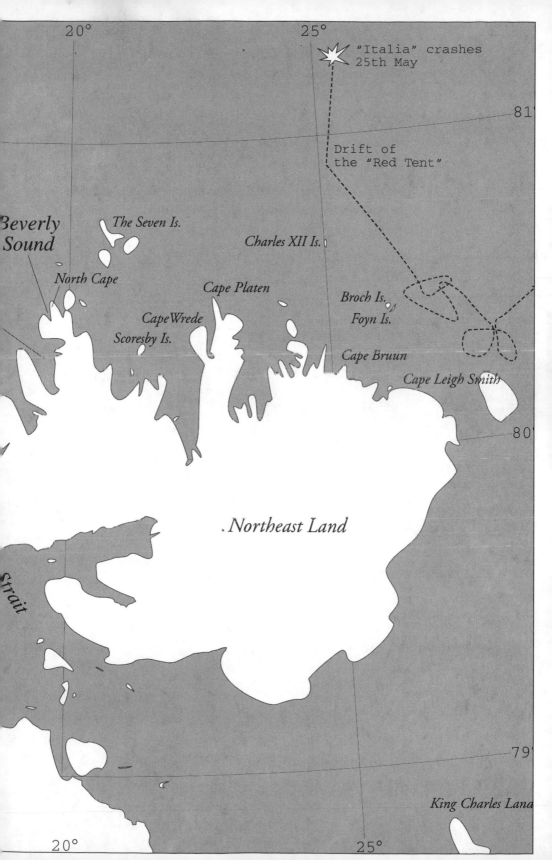

PROLOGUE

My interest in the *Italia* disaster dates back to the late 1950s, when I began writing a series of articles for *True*, the outstanding men's adventure magazine of its day, which published, among other features, stories about hazardous expeditions and disasters in far places. During a luncheon meeting with my editor, Don McKinney, I was asked if I knew anything about General Umberto Nobile and the ill-fated North Pole dirigible expedition of 1928. I admitted that I recalled little except that the Italian airship had crashed on the polar ice pack, and that the whole world had followed the radio and newspaper stories for months as searchers from many nations tried to locate and rescue the survivors. I told Don I was interested in taking on the proposed article assignment, and began researching one of the most remarkable—often unbelievable—exploits in the history of polar exploration.

What intrigued me most was McKinney's statement that after his rescue, Nobile, leader of the expedition and designer of the airship, had long lived under a cloud, accused of cowardice and put on trial by the Italian government. In my pursuit of the story I went far beyond *True*'s requirements and committed myself to a lengthy personal investigation of the allegations and character assaults on the expedition's commander.

I started by locating and interviewing two of the surviving officers of the doomed airship when they were visiting New York. I then contacted journalists I knew in Italy, France, Russia, and three Scandinavian nations to interview not only the remaining survivors of the fatal flight, but also some of the key members of the international search parties who had been involved in scouring the arctic regions after the airship crashed.

After that, I flew to Rome and spent several days with Umberto Nobile himself, who fortunately spoke English fluently. I later continued my contact with him through extensive personal mailings and by assigning one of my editorial researchers in Rome to conduct further interviews, in addition to the compilation of data and photographs.

At first glance, Nobile seemed to me anything but the image of a daring arctic adventurer. Slight of build, cordial and considerate, he personified his background as an engineer, scientist, and educator. It was his habit from earliest days to file data and keep meticulous accounts—even down to quoting people verbatim about events and circumstances relating to his work as an aeronautical engineer and lighter-than-air pioneer.

It was astonishing to me that he was able to make such records, often during flights when one or another of his airships was in the grip of a storm that threatened the lives of all aboard—and most especially during his ordeals in the polar regions. After the crash, he even wrote detailed instructions to his fellow survivors at a time when he was certain he was going to succumb to his injuries.

Although many years have passed since I first heard about the *Italia* disaster, the story remains as fascinating today as it was then. It is a classic example of courage and survival.

DISASTER
AT
THE POLE

1

PRELUDE TO DISASTER

ay 11, 1928. At 10:45 A.M., General Umberto Nobile looked up from the chart table of the semirigid dirigible *Italia* as the craft bounced and jerked in the glowering arctic sky like a rat shaken by a terrier. Slight of build and dark haired, the forty-three-year-old Nobile displayed a tense, haggard frown that contrasted with his otherwise youthful appearance. Around him in the long, narrow space of the frigid pilot cabin were half a dozen officers and men in leather flight jackets hunched over the control wheels, valves, and instruments that were their several responsibilities. But his gaze focused on the man who had just clambered unsteadily down the ladder leading from the airship's great bag overhead. It was foreman rigger Renato Alessandrini.

"What is it?" asked Nobile hoarsely over the roar of the wind and engines, as the figure lunged toward the chart table, grasping handrails and stanchions for support.

"Rudder cable . . . General, our rudder cable has frayed badly, just forward of the fin."

"How could it have?" Nobile's voice rang hollowly from the strain of the flight. "I gave orders before we left Kings Bay to inspect every line and cable on the ship."

"We did, sir. With meticulous care. I examined every inch myself. It is the wind. The cable has had great stress. I think you should see it." Alessandrini's voice displayed no sense of panic, but it had an urgency that was not characteristic of this usually placid airman from southern Italy.

"I will be up in a minute. Take Arduino. Start splicing a reinforcing cable along the weakened section."

As the foreman rigger hoisted himself up the ladder and disappeared, Umberto Nobile glanced back at the chart. The *Italia* was now cruising at an altitude of two thousand feet as she approached Cape North, a bleak and uninhabited land at the far tip of the Arctic islands of desolate Spitsbergen. She was about 150 miles northeast of her base at Kings Bay—or well over three hours out if the threatening storm should hit with the force expected. For Nobile, it was particularly galling to have this—the initial flight of a planned series of arctic explorations—cut short, for the weather report the evening before, from Tromsö, Norway, several hundred miles to the south, had been highly favorable. Avoiding dangerous weather would be crucial to an airship's success in the Arctic.

In a few minutes, Nobile lurched to the ladderway himself and scrambled up to the V-shaped keel of the airship, with its metal catwalk running fore and aft. Alessandrini and engine mechanic Ettore Arduino were already splicing a reinforcing section onto the frayed rudder cable. The danger seemed to be over.

"Inspect all other control cables," ordered the general. "There is little chance we can skirt the storm."

Around 11:30 the atmospheric pressure suddenly dropped, and the *Italia* was caught up in violent squalls that made the earlier trembling and shaking seem mild in comparison. Nobile was not worried about the buffeting winds that twisted the *Italia*'s great envelope as much as the ice that had begun forming on the skin of the ship, weighing it down. The magnificent silver shape, which had seemed such an indestructible mammoth when hovering over the rusty supply ship *Citta di Milano*, back at the Kings Bay base, was now a plaything of the sleet-heavy clouds and ice-fanged lunges of the arctic gale. The outside of her canvas-walled cabin was fast sheathing with frost needles, and her wooden propellers were being dangerously chewed by hail.

Nobile turned to Dr. Finn Malmgren, the expedition's meteorologist, at his station nearby, to ask how the weather was to the north.

"It might be better," replied Malmgren. "A change of course is worth a try."

"Left rudder," ordered Nobile, "hold course steady due north." Commander Adalberto Mariano, the first officer, supervised the shift in direction, and the airship rolled and pitched in protesting response to heavy hands on the rudder wheel.

"She does not feel right, General," said Mariano in a matter-of-fact voice.

Acknowledging this presumption without comment, Nobile turned to engineer Felice Trojani, who stood at the telegraph signal connected to the three 250-horsepower Maybach engines, located to port, to starboard, and aft of the control cabin: "All engines, ahead at full!"

The *Italia* had been in the air over the rocky wastes and scattered ice floes for less than four hours. She had plenty of fuel left, either for riding out the storm or for battling her way back to the base if the gale did not abate. It was Nobile's intention, therefore, to switch to an alternate plan and head north to clear the storm. If successful, he would then swing due west and explore the northernmost coast of Greenland. It was obvious that he would have to forsake—at least for several days—the flight eastward to the unknown territory of Nicholas II Land. But this was of little consequence. The big objective, after two weeks of preliminary exploration, was to be a dangerous and history-making flight—to the North Pole itself.

Trojani transmitted Nobile's order to the three enginemen in their cramped motor gondolas suspended below the giant bag. The *Italia* picked up speed with a lurch that almost threw the officers and men in the pilot cabin off their feet.

"I think we may soon be in the clear," said Malmgren, as the airship battled through dark, heavy clouds and into a brighter section where, through breaks in the undercast, they could make out scattered ice floes in ghostly ranks on the black waters of the Arctic Sea. But his hope was short-lived. The barometer continued to fall, and the diabolical force of subzero winds began to increase, rather than abate.

"Her response is very sluggish, General," reported the second officer, naval commander Filippo Zappi, who was standing near the elevator wheel.

Nobile noticed on the altimeter that the ship had lost some altitude despite the increase in engine speed. "Up elevators," he ordered. The bow tilted skyward, like an outboard that has too heavy a motor at the stern. It was an exaggerated position, but with the fins fighting the downdrafts of the wind and the increasing weight of the ice, the airship was able to maintain altitude.

Dr. Malmgren expressed his concern, however. "I do not like this combination," he said. "Despite the wind, slush clings to the envelope, and we are getting heavier every minute."

"All right," replied Nobile reluctantly, "we will abandon our present plan and turn back."

Shuddering violently, almost as though in protest, the *Italia* was swung about in the storm and pointed southwest, toward the shelter of the temporary hangar at Kings Bay. In her retreat she outdistanced the storm and made the base by 4:00 that afternoon. Though momentarily safe, her destiny lay in the dark, ice-laden clouds and subzero winds that swirled around the North Pole and the far reaches of the floe-specked Arctic Sea.

2

THE IMPOSSIBLE DREAM

Ten years before the *Italia* took flight for the North Pole, Umberto Nobile's career made the shift that would eventually lead to his historic expedition. In July 1918, Nobile and three other engineers—Giuseppe Valle, Benedetto Croce, and Celestine Usuelli—formed the Aeronautical Construction Factory for the design and construction of lighter-than-air craft.

Nobile had long been intrigued with the work of aeronautical originators like Count Ferdinand von Zeppelin of Germany, whose giant monsters of the air were to terrorize British civilians during the Great War. Born near Naples in 1885, Nobile graduated from the University of Naples *cum laude*, with degrees in both electrical and industrial engineering. In 1911, after five years in the state railway system, where he helped to develop electrified power lines, he entered the new and largely untested field of aeronautical engineering. When Italy entered World War I in 1915, the short, slight Nobile, then twenty-nine, was rejected three times by the army as physically unfit. By chance, however, he was eventually assigned to the Ministry of Public Works and attached to the Establishment for Aeronautical Construction in Rome. Thereafter, he was taken into the army because of technical ability alone and given the rank of lieutenant colonel.

Although construction on Nobile's early airships began during World War I, peace arrived before they could be put into combat service like Germany's zeppelins. In any case, Nobile, who had pacifist leanings, was more interested in the use of dirigibles for peacetime transportation. They could travel much farther than the airplanes of the day, carrying passengers and freight, and they could land on tiny airfields close to the heart of cities and ports, their only requirement a landing mast and a crew of ground handlers.

Nobile was not only a pioneer in airship design, but one of the top aeronautical engineers in the field of lighter-than-air craft. After having gone on hundreds of flights in many types of airships, he obtained a test pilot's license so that he could command his ships under a wide range of flying conditions. He was also well qualified as an instructor, and was a lecturer in aerodynamics at the University of Naples. During this period he authored *Elementi di Aerodynamica* (Elements of Aerodynamics), which became a classic textbook in its field, as well as numerous theses on this subject.

While the mighty zeppelins and other airships of the day were largely of a type referred to as rigid, Nobile was a firm believer in a "nonrigid" design. The former utilized an aluminum skeleton that stretched from bow to stern in the shape of the airship, whereas the latter design had a keel from end to end but rounded metal skeletons only at the bow and stern. The semirigid's central portion was more like that of a blimp, with the interior gas maintaining the form of the skin, or outer fabric. His theory was that a semirigid airship 300–400 feet long was flexible enough to bend and give in strong winds, whereas the rigids, at 600 feet or more, were known for breaking up when gusts hit the long, unyielding bag in different places at different strengths—as often occurred during a thunderstorm. One danger common to all airships was the highly volatile hydrogen gas that gave them lift. Helium, which is nonflammable, could also be used, but the United States had the only supplies of it.

When peace came in his early thirties, Nobile had already proved that he could be successful in a field of aviation that was notable more for its failures (often tragic) than its successes. However, the company's first airship, the T-34, never made its expected mark in aviation history, a planned record-breaking ocean flight, because a few days after its completion, on July 6, 1919, the British dirigible R-34 sprinted into headlines by flying from Scotland to Long Island, New York, and thus completing the first dirigible Atlantic crossing. Also, Nobile broke with his cofounders Valle and Usuelli, who disagreed with Nobile's theories about the superiority of semirigids and wanted to build bigger airships. Nobile's company flourished nevertheless, becoming one of the most important producers of airships in the world, with nearly 1,200 employees. The young engineer's talents, fanatical energies, and time were directed more toward exploring markets in North America than in Italy, however, in part because of the hostility he faced in his own native land as fascism began to flourish there.

Nourished by unrest, disorder, and dissatisfaction with weak government, fascism began to invade civilian life, soon overrunning military and naval areas as well. But Nobile, who, like many scientists and inventors, tended to have little interest in politics, was far more absorbed in the problems of lifting capacity per cubic foot, the stress factors of metals, and the horsepower of aircraft engines than in supporting the Fascist Party. This error of omission was to find him, in years to come, far out of favor with the Mussolini dictatorship at a time when he would need government help for his very survival.

Although Nobile knew that the once tiny Fascist Party was evolving in Italy, he was not aware of how much it had grown in power until a fateful day in June 1919 when the door to his factory office opened and Colonel Giulio Costanzi strode purposefully into the room. Costanzi was an acquaintance of long-standing, an engineer, and a man who enjoyed the freedom of the plant, where he could roam casually about and watch the giant airships taking shape. From the moment he entered, however, Nobile sensed that something was wrong. And when his visitor began suggesting that the young engineer "give up the big struggle against private enterprise" and sell the plant to the government so he could focus on engineering problems alone, the light began to dawn: Constanzi, a rising young star in the new administration, had been expressly sent to talk Nobile into relinquishing his factory.

"You will be well paid for the plant," promised Costanzi, after he had launched his arguments against the astonished Nobile. "A figure something like ten million lire should cover it, don't you think?"

"Ten million lire!" Nobile had heard that the Fascists were trying to strong-arm businesses into becoming party property, but he could not believe this was happening to him. The supplies in his warehouse alone were worth ten times that amount.

In the end, Nobile all but physically ejected Colonel Costanzi from his office and left word that the man's courtesy pass to the shops and hangar was to be immediately cancelled. For a man of less perseverance, and without Nobile's incessant energy, this rash action could have meant economic suicide and professional ostracism, but Nobile's technical brilliance and personal sacrifices had won great respect. There were few government officials in postwar Italy who had yet gained enough of a foothold to risk taking on, unnecessarily, an aeronautical engineer who had won respect from aviation experts not only in Italy, but in England, France, and the United States as well.

Moreover, Nobile had a few staunch friends in the government who were advocates of his lighter-than-air program and interceded on his behalf. One of these was General Moris, an Italian aviation pioneer greatly respected by airmen in every branch of the service. Another was Filippo Turati, president of the Parliamentary Group for Aeronautics and hence in a highly influential capacity in all matters pertaining to aircraft production and operation.

For the next two years, however, Nobile was so harassed by incidents like the Costanzi affair that he hardly had time to devote to his profession. Finally, in 1922, to some extent dismayed by the unhealthy political climate in Italy, he decided to accept an offer to go to the United States, to whose navy he had sold two airships, on an extended absence to fulfill a contract as a consultant with the Goodyear Company for a dirigible of his type for the United States Army. The air attaché of the American Embassy in Rome, Colonel John Chaney, intervened with the Italian government so that Nobile's request to leave the country would be granted. If not for that, his enemies might have prevented the trip, hoping to stifle his company's production activities to such an extent that he would be forced to close his plants and sell all of his holdings to the government for a pittance.

Nobile embarked for the United States in the summer of that year, but by October the situation in Italy had reached a point of crisis. On October 28, 1922, the Fascist Party swept its way to power when King Victor Emmanuel III turned his government over to Benito Mussolini to form a ministry and granted him dictatorial powers. The king was all but forced into this "lesser of two evils" because of rising unrest throughout Italy and the threat of communism, which was feared by business owners at every level. Immediately after that date, dramatized by a march on Rome by the Fascisti, party members, known popularly as the Black Shirts, began intensifying the scanning of the country's industries for money-making ventures into which they could hook their tentacles. Umberto Nobile's Aeronautical Construction Factory was a prime target and would have been a great plum for the new Italian administration.

> *My dear Umberto,*
> *It is with the utmost urgency I ask you to hasten back to Rome before it is too late. Your enemies are more active than ever laying plans for sucking the blood from ACF . . .*

> *My dear Umberto,*
> *Your life's work is endangered by the ambitions of certain Fascists. I think you know their names without my listing them here . . .*

When letters like these began arriving at his residence in Ohio, imploring him to return, Nobile had no choice. He arrived back in Rome in January 1923, to face an opposition whose strength he could not have guessed while he was in America. One of the anti-Nobile leaders was a general, Arturo Crocco, whose determination to prevent Nobile from achieving success was fueled by his personal ambition to dominate the airship industry. Nobile had designed and constructed a new nonrigid airship, designated the N-1, and was about to test it in a series of long, strenuous flights. This project was of particular concern to Crocco, who had long held the belief that rigid dirigibles like the zeppelins were superior to the nonrigids. He was afraid that if the N-1 proved to be more maneuverable and reliable in the air, than were the larger dirigibles, she would disprove his own engineering theories and thus lower his prestige in the new regime.

Nobile completely ignored this obvious challenge and began testing the new airship on his own initiative and without obtaining certain permits or authorizations that the new government was trying to impose on all industries. That he succeeded in his mission is in itself remarkable. The new government's agencies were so invaded by the *squadristi*, or Fascist undercover watchmen, that organized opposition to anything at that stage of affairs was practically impossible.

In the tumultuous, uncertain political world of Italy in the early 1920s, where rivalries and jealousies dominated personal and business life alike, Nobile was something of an odd cog, a man who had risen to his position by reason of intellect rather than braggadocio. He possessed a restless curiosity and a deep sensitivity that were not always easy to discern behind his natural reticence. He was extremely considerate of others, self-effacing, and a stubborn perfectionist in his work.

General Crocco's campaign against Nobile in 1923 seemed like the final threat to his aircraft factory. And it might have been if Nobile had not found courageous support in the person of a man with unusual technical insight, General Uselli Guidoni, the chief of Military Aeronautics Engineering. In March of that year, Nobile sent a memorandum to Guidoni deploring the fascist attempts to take over his factory and buy him out.

It was at that point that Guidoni sacrificed his own career by adding his support to Nobile's cause. As an engineer, he openly opposed the "abuses and brazen-faced corruption of the Fascist Air Force" by initiating, at the end of 1923, a special competition for admission to the Military Aeronautical Engineers Corps, a competition in which Nobile was invited to participate, and that he passed with honors.

For six months Nobile survived the barrage, fending off those who tried to seize the plant. He managed to retain his facilities intact because the greedier and more important state officials were kept under control by Guidoni. But Guidoni's position was greatly weakened when, in the summer of 1924, an influential senior officer became chief of the general staff, with full control in all matters relating to aviation. The officer was Italo Balbo, twenty-eight, a large, handsome man with a copper-colored beard and a hearty personality. Balbo was a self-serving individual despite the jovial demeanor and objective nature that made him popular with fellow officers and with the public. He was competent, courageous, and in certain areas instrumental in the development of Italian aviation. His great weakness was an intense personal ambition, which drove him not only to accomplish impressive deeds but also to resort to any method to eradicate the men who stood in his path.

In one incident, Balbo instructed the editor of the government-controlled newspaper *La Tribuna* to publish an editorial, which appeared in the issue of September 28, 1924, about Nobile's construction of his new airship, N-1. The airship was described as an engineering blunder and "so incompetent it could not even cross the Apennines."

This editorial was followed by other disparaging, Balbo-initiated commentaries, both in print and in speeches. In December of that year, a serious accusation was leveled at Nobile—one that could also be traced back to the chief of the general staff. It took the form of a report to the chief of aeronautics, General Bonzani, charging that Nobile was a professed socialist, a man who filled his factory with Red laborers and who had resisted the government's offers of assistance in building lighter-than-air craft because he was afraid his anti-Fascist underground would be exposed. The man who filed the report was Captain Giuseppe Valle, Nobile's former colleague who repeatedly lent himself as a tool of the rising young strong-arm politicos.

THE IMPOSSIBLE DREAM

Once again, only a stroke of good fortune saved Nobile from downfall. Unaware of any charges against him, he was going to the Ministry building on business, ordered there with several other officers by General Bonzani. Just before he set out, however, a lawyer named Tucci, who worked in the Ministry, phoned him and suggested he stop by on a personal and highly confidential matter.

In the corridor, Nobile came face to face with Valle, who smiled, offered his hand, and commented that it was good to see him and that he should not be working so hard. Nobile accepted this with the polite response that he really had not been working hard enough and asked where he could find Tucci's office. Valle guided him down the hall, waved him inside the lawyer's office with another ingratiating smile, and departed as though Nobile were one of his dearest friends.

It was only after he sat down with Tucci that Nobile discovered the outrageous charges against him and learned that the perpetrator was the same man who had ushered him down the hall not realizing his underhanded tactics were about to be revealed.

Forewarned by Tucci, who explained his actions by saying that he was increasingly concerned about the legality of some of the Fascist Party's proceedings, Nobile went immediately to General Bonzani, before any official charges had been made public. He was thus able to demand an investigation and a chance to vindicate himself and his conduct as an officer. This was granted, and General Guidoni, fortunately, was selected to conduct the inquiry. The results were not only favorable to Nobile, but also condemnatory of Valle. There was nothing General Bonzani could do but order a second investigation, to be conducted by persons supposedly impartial to both sides. The report of this investigation was long, confused, and filled with meaningless detail. The results were the same as the first investigation and were announced in an official document dated November 7, 1925, which read in part:

> The conclusions listed above and founded on unassailable documents, show that Lieutenant-Colonel Nobile's morality is perfectly clear and above reproach. Delighted to find it thus, I order the Commandant of the Third Territorial Airforce Zone to communicate all the above to Lieutenant-Colonel Nobile during the report, at which all senior officers of Air Force, Aeronautical Engineers and Air Commissariat are ordered to be present.

The report of the second investigation included one additional recommendation, which had not appeared in the first report and which libellant Valle had not expected: that he, Valle, be punished with three months' arrest in the military fortress for conduct unbecoming an officer and for false testimony.

Although Nobile had triumphed, he had once more placed himself squarely in the limelight as an antagonist of the blackshirted Fascisti.

3

AN AMBITIOUS
UNDERTAKING

Toward the end of 1925, Nobile was thoroughly absorbed in a daring new project. Its focus was that most bizarre objective of mankind: the North Pole. In 1909 Robert E. Peary had become the first man to reach the Pole, but the first bid to get there by air had actually occurred in 1897, when Dr. Salomon Andrée had disappeared during a failed polar flight in a balloon, *The Eagle*. Several more recent attempts by aviators in other countries to reach the North Pole by airplane had failed, largely because the crafts did not have enough range, and adding extra fuel tanks limited the number of people and surveying equipment that could be carried on exploratory missions that would have any scientific purpose. An airship, Nobile reasoned, would proceed more slowly but would be able to stay aloft much longer and allow its officers to make meteorological observations above the jagged wastes of the arctic ice. Cruising along at airspeeds of fifty miles an hour or more, the airship offered an intriguing alternative to the arduous foot or dogsled travel that had claimed the lives of so many arctic explorers.

Little might have come of the idea had not the same thought crossed the mind of a man about as different from Nobile in personality and talents as it was possible to be: Roald Amundsen. At the age of fifty-four, the celebrated Norwegian explorer had an impressive list of achievements to his credit. He had started his polar career as first mate on a Belgian expedition that was the first to winter in the Antarctic; he had been first to sail from the Atlantic to the Pacific through the Northwest Passage; and, most famously, he had, in 1911, become the first man to reach the South Pole.

Amundsen was one of the explorers who had recently failed on an aerial expedition to the Pole, in collaboration with an American polar explorer, Lincoln Ellsworth, and four other crew members. In the spring of 1925, they had flown to within 150 miles of the Pole in two amphibian planes, only to make emergency landings because of bad weather. The men became stranded for thirty days without radio contact and were given up for lost. They finally managed to carve out a takeoff field on the rough ice pack, after which one plane, overloaded with the total party of six, managed to get airborne and return to the base at Spitsbergen.

The experience left Amundsen with the idea that an airship might succeed where heavier-than-air craft had failed, and he contacted Nobile to ask about purchasing one. Amundsen's conclusion was based mainly on what he had read in articles published by Nobile and conversations with Ellsworth, for he had absolutely no working knowledge of dirigibles, and had no concept of how difficult they could be to control and maneuver, especially in typical arctic winds. Nobile had always acknowledged these facts; he maintained that, to be successful, airships depended a great deal on reliable weather information and should always have an experienced meteorologist on board.

Amundsen's decision to participate in the expedition was largely at the urging of Ellsworth, who wanted to shed his reputation as a wealthy adventurer by allying himself with the pioneer who had the most formidable standing in the field of polar exploration. Another factor in Amundsen's decision was the fact that he was constantly short of money and, at this time, had no funds to mount an expedition of his own. His hope was that a successful flight—another first on his estimable record—would put him back in the money through endorsements, publishing contracts, and speaking engagements.

There were personality and social complications as well as monetary ones. Amundsen had a prickly, competitive temperament. Another complication was that, while he had great respect for his fellow Norwegians, Finns, and other Scandinavians, he had little understanding of, or use for, Italians when it came to polar exploration. But he had little choice. While it was true that the Italians had made far fewer forays into the Arctic than the Scandinavians, the fact of the matter was that they were the ones with the most advanced airship for this kind of purpose. The Germans were no longer building dirigibles; the British had cut back on production because of a series of tragic accidents; and even the Americans had turned to Italy to order two airships for their navy.

Nobile, for his part, was enthusiastic. He had an excellent ship in the N-1, which had taken her first trial flight in March 1924. The N-1 had two distinct advantages over most of the airships of her day: first, the keel was designed to maintain the streamlined shape yet was, like a vertebra, flexible enough to twist and bend under heavy stress without causing any damage; second, the ship was relatively short, at 348 feet, and not as subject to being broken in half as were some of the larger airships, like the zeppelins, which had suffered more disasters from storms during World War I than from enemy action. Despite these qualifications, the Italian government was reluctant to give official backing to the expedition, certain that the flight would come to an inglorious end and reflect badly on the prestige of the regime.

Italian backers finally advanced 25 percent of the money needed for the expedition. But it was the Aero Club of Norway that made the venture possible, contributing the greater part of the funds to purchase the N-1 from the Italian government, which had actually bought the ship from Nobile's company a year earlier. The club also directed the preparation of landing fields and advance bases in Norway, and at Kings Bay, Spitsbergen, which was to serve as the springboard for the stab at the Pole. Lincoln Ellsworth was a partner in the expedition and contributed one-sixth of the funds needed.

Thus, when the N-1 was rechristened *Norge* (*Norway*), Umberto Nobile—though far more experienced in judging when, where, and how to proceed once underway—was forced into a secondary position, and his title remained vaguely that of pilot. To make sure that there was no misunderstanding, the Norwegians titled the project the Amundsen-Ellsworth Polar Expedition, with no mention of Nobile. Nevertheless, Amundsen at that time had great respect for Nobile, despite what he thought about the Italians countrymen, and went along with a joint vote of confidence, expressed later in the American version of his book, coauthored by Ellsworth, *First Crossing of the Polar Sea*, wherein it was stated: "As captain of the *Norge,* we secured the best possible man to be procured, Colonel Umberto Nobile . . . and we congratulated ourselves and all agreed that we had found the right man. On his appointment, Nobile threw himself heart and soul into the enterprise."

The men selected for the flight were experienced and highly skilled. Two of them would later play eminent roles in Nobile's life: Finn Malmgren, a Swedish meteorologist who had been associated with Amundsen earlier, and First Lieutenant Hjalmar Riiser-Larsen, of the Norwegian Navy, who would serve as one of the two pilots.

Though most of the crew members, at Amundsen's insistence, were Norwegians, it was appropriate that five Italians, "among the finest mechanics in Italy," were selected to man the three 250-horsepower engines: Natale Cecioni, thirty-nine, with fifteen years' flying experience as an engine mechanic; Ettore Arduino, who had been flying for more than ten years and had been decorated in the war; Attilio Caratti, thirty-nine, an experienced airship mechanic; Renato Alessandrini, experienced as a rigger in the assembling of airships and the man who perhaps knew the N-1 better than anybody else on the flight, having helped to build her; and Vincenzo Pomella, a motor mechanic who was not as experienced as his flight mates but was from southern Italy and so well liked, especially as an optimist when the going got tough, that he was a joy to have on any long, arduous flight.

Nobile informed each of his countryman crew members, along with dozens of others who applied for, but did not obtain, positions aboard, that the *Norge's* unprecedented journey could be a dangerous one. But that was no deterrent. Neither was the sudden deluge of editorializing by the press—particularly in Germany, home of the giant zeppelins—that the airship was totally inadequate, both in size and power, to reach the North Pole. About the only effect the critics had on the expedition was to dissuade a number of journalists from taking a press flight in the *Norge* before she left Italy.

Inadvertently, Nobile once again managed to offend the Fascisti politicians. By expressing his belief that an airship was far better suited to conquering the polar regions than an airplane, he was refuting the bombastic proclamations of Italo Balbo, the Fascist chief of all air activities in Italy, that heavier-than-air craft would rule the skies and that dirigibles were destined only for minimal roles in the air.

Preparations for the journey began with an initial test flight of the N-1 in late February 1926. When recruiting potential crew members, Nobile had warned them that they had only a fifty-fifty chance of reaching the Pole and then returning to Spitsbergen. Instead, depending on the weather and other factors, the airship would likely continue past the Pole, with the prevailing winds, and land in Alaska. Amundsen had protested that he wanted to make a round trip and end the flight in his native Norway, but Nobile convinced him that his new dirigible had future possibilities for such a flight but was not yet properly equipped or modified in design to attempt a perilous return flight against strong prevailing headwinds. Besides, he added, the necessity for additional fuel would greatly limit the number of people and the amount of equipment the *Norge* could carry.

On March 29, 1926, the *Norge* was officially turned over to Amundsen and Ellsworth at ceremonies held at the Ciampino Airport near Rome. Although it was announced that the flight from Italy to the base in Spitsbergen would begin on

April 3, Nobile had to disappoint onlookers who had come to view the takeoff—including Mussolini—because a threatening thunderstorm necessitated a delay. It was a week before the airship finally lifted off and headed north. The planned route included brief stopovers in France, England, the Scandinavian capitals, and an airfield near Leningrad, where the *Norge* would remain until Kings Bay and the forward base at Vadsö were ready and the weather favorable. In the meantime, Amundsen and Ellsworth and an advance party had gone by train to Oslo to board a ship to Spitsbergen, where they would complete last-minute details and await the airship, leaving Nobile in sole command of the trip's first leg.

Nobile had anticipated that the flight over the polar wastes—vast stretches of nothing but melting floes, jagged ice, and a few desolated islands—would be marked by gusting winds and other hostile meteorological conditions, but he had not foreseen that the flight from Rome to Spitsbergen would be, if anything, even more strenuous and threatening. Because of dense fogs and a heavy overcast, his navigators had to admit on several occasions that they could not tell what their position was and that they would be virtually lost until the weather cleared.

It was a great relief when the *Norge* finally landed in Russia at Gatschina Airport, near Leningrad, on April 15. The 738-mile flight had taken seventeen of the most anxious and exhausting hours in the air in Nobile's memory. This was not the end of the ordeal, however. It was not until May 11, after many delays in organizing the base at Kings Bay, and after a series of sometimes hair-raising test flights over Northeast Land and endless stretches of ice pack, that the *Norge* finally cast off from her moorings, bound for the Pole.

For those unused to flight in an airship, the inside of the cabin was cold, cramped, and uncomfortable. The noise of the engines, the howling of the wind, and the constant creaking of the framework assaulted their ears. Not infrequently, ice that had formed on the propellers was suddenly thrown backward against the underside of the ship, making a frightening din. To make the discomfort more intense, they had forgotten to bring any drinking water, and so had to drink tepid coffee instead. There were only two seats in the pilot cabin, one of which Amundsen persisted in occupying, although his large feet, clad in grass-stuffed reindeer-skin boots left no room for stretching. Amundsen tended to be out of sorts and grumpy whenever he was in an unfamiliar environment; he would much rather have been on a sailing ship in a stiff wind or behind sledge dogs struggling over treacherous ice.

When the polar flight was in the planning stage, Nobile had described it to the press as follows: "Our undertaking is twofold: an expedition of exploration, for which the credit will go to Amundsen, and an aeronautical feat, planned by us Italians, for which I assume all responsibility." But during the entire flight, Amundsen hardly ever moved from his seat, uncomfortable though it may have been, seemed indifferent toward his supposed part of the work, and evidenced no plan at all to undertake meteorological research or any kind of study of the polar wastes while flying over the ice pack. He was to all effects, as Nobile complained later, merely a "passenger."

A further complaint was that Amundsen did not even fulfill his planned duties as a navigator, and that Riiser-Larsen actually played the part, taking compass and sextant readings and mapping the airship's position, speed, altitude, and general progress from hour to hour. It was he, not Amundsen, who assumed the responsibility of calculating exactly when they flew directly over the North Pole—a fact that was crucial in claiming the record as the first aircraft to do so.

The flight northward was relatively without incident, and, after a monotonous passage over the fractured and hummocked ice of the arctic wilderness, they reached the Pole on May 12. Although there was much excitement when it was announced that the *Norge* was hovering over "absolute zero degrees north," some of the men, such as the mechanics, who had never been anywhere near the polar regions were disappointed. Perhaps they had expected to view a tall mountain peak rising from the icy wastes, instead of the crusty white ice pack extending as far as the eye could see.

But they had not long to contemplate the sight. Shortly after the crew held a brief ceremony and dropped various national flags at the Pole, Nobile ordered the engines up to cruising speed and they continued over the rim of the ice cap toward their destination in Alaska. This destination was initially to have been Cape Barrow, at the northern tip of the territory, but the weather conditions there were too hostile.

The end of the flight proved to be the most critical and dangerous of the entire trip, at a time when most of the crew, including Nobile, had been on duty seventy hours without sleep. The worst enemy was sleet. As Nobile recounted it:

> The ice forming on the propellers as we went through fogs, and hurled against the underside of the bag, had pretty well scarred up the fabric covering the keel, though it had not opened up the gas bags or caused any hydrogen loss. We had used up all our cement in repairing the fabric.
>
> So I determined to fly on down the coast to where we could get a ship out and land there. We wired ahead to Nome, but as we passed over Teller—which we first mistook for Nome—a severe storm was raging ahead and I decided to land there.
>
> We had no landing party, of course, so we piled a lot of loose equipment in a bag and lowered it as an anchor or drag, and began valving gas. Presently, a dozen Eskimos came out of their igloos and with the two or three white men there, steadied the ship, and we made a perfect landing. Within an hour, the great bag of hydrogen was deflated and the ship was ready to take down.
>
> And we were ready to go to sleep.

The flight of the *Norge* turned out to be, tactically, an aeronautical success, the first of its kind by a dirigible. Amundsen and Nobile would not, however, be remembered as first to fly over the North Pole. On May 9, three days before the *Norge*'s crossing, Richard E. Byrd and Floyd Bennett claimed that honor in a plane carrying the colors of the United States, a feat that gave rise to ongoing debate over whether they had truly flown over the Pole or missed it by more than 100 miles.

Though under power all the way, the airship had acted, in effect, much like a controlled balloon, caught in the steady current of the prevailing wind. Except for the Alaska touchdown, the most difficult leg of the trip had actually been that from Rome northward over the mountains to northern Europe, and thence to Spitsbergen. In all, the ship had traveled 7,800 miles in 171 hours of flight.

But if the flight itself was without great disruptions, the clash of personalities and nationalities made up for it.

The British edition of Amundsen's book *My Life as an Explorer*, published a year after the flight and written jointly with Lincoln Ellsworth, Hjalmar Riiser-Larsen, and others on the expedition, contained this passage: "We never heard an angry word or saw an unpleasant expression during the entire flight."

This picture of idyllic coexistence was hardly borne out by the Norwegian versions of Amundsen's remarks. One book, by a prominent arctic explorer, contains fifty-six varieties of epithets that Amundsen hurled against Nobile. The hard-headed Norwegian, cantankerous and ill at ease inside the cramped quarters of a dirigible, took issue with just about everything the Italians said or did and even went so far as to claim that Nobile had nearly wrecked the airship during an episode over the Arctic Sea in which the *Norge* was rising dangerously fast. Contrary to Amundsen's charges, Nobile had actually averted disaster; he ordered two crewmen into the ship's nose to act as human ballast, which allowed him to bring the ship down to a safer altitude. Amundsen's lack of knowledge about airships, and the language barriers on board (various men were conversing in Italian, English, and Norwegian), allowed him to fill in the gaps of what he did not know with the worst thoughts about Nobile. And after they'd landed, he had the temerity to try to seize all the honors of the polar flight for himself.

Most of Amundsen's bickering was petty, such as his complaint that Nobile and two other Italian fliers appeared in "gorgeous uniforms" that were entirely unnecessary to an arctic expedition, and that Nobile insisted on adding weight to the ship by bringing his small fox terrier, Titina, along for the ride. Amundsen did not acknowledge Nobile's painstaking attention to the issue of weight and safety. Nobile had stripped everything possible from the *Norge's* interior to make the ship lighter and allow the addition of extra fuel supplies and hydrogen tanks necessary for such a long journey.

Amundsen did have one genuine grievance, however—one that was entirely out of Nobile's hands: After the landing in

Alaska, Benito Mussolini had immediately tried to grab as much credit as he could for the Italian airship and the participation of the Italians in the flight. He sent orders to Nobile to tour the United States, speaking before groups of Italians, to publicize this great and historic venture in the name of Italy.

Naturally, the Norwegians were infuriated, and even though Nobile had no taste for the assignment, much of Amundsen's bitterness was directed at him as the nearest target. Amundsen could not forget that Mussolini had insisted that the Italian government sell, rather than lend, the airship to Norway, and that during preparations for the flight several Fascist leaders had tried futilely to squash the expedition and form one of their own in a larger dirigible to be constructed by General Crocco and piloted by Giuseppe Valle.

The feud was so real that it erupted into many articles over the next few years, with each side defending its own position and damning the actions of the other. In late 1927, two articles were published in *World's Work*, then a leading international magazine, in which Nobile and Amundsen each presented his side of the argument. Those articles pretty much put the issue to rest, at least as far as the public was concerned.

All in all, it was a messy and unfortunate way to end a flight that has been repeatedly recorded as a highlight in aviation history. Both Amundsen and Nobile would have been better served had the press drawn more attention to their joint accomplishments than to their faults.

4

THE NEXT BIG STEP

Through the Machiavellian interplay of jealousies and politics following the *Norge* flight, Nobile managed to maintain friendly relations with at least two of his Scandinavian colleagues. One was Dr. Finn Malmgren, the meteorologist of the expedition; the other was Hjalmar Riiser-Larsen, Amundsen's Norwegian aide.

At Teller, Alaska, in May 1926, just after the *Norge* landed, Nobile and Riiser-Larsen, greatly elated by the success of the flight, talked long and enthusiastically about the prospects for a second expedition. Nobile had blueprints for an improved version of the N-1 and was convinced not only that he could fly over the Pole, but also that he could make a number of landings on the ice over a period of weeks and return with priceless scientific data. Riiser-Larsen shared his enthusiasm for a while but quickly lost all desire to participate when the bitter feuding began.

The late 1920s and early 1930s marked a period of international rivalries in aviation and exploration, with a number of nations engaged in a series of races to be first. Following Byrd and Bennett's history-making flight, Sir Hubert Wilkins was soon to claim flying honors for Australia. Nungesser and Coli were to give their lives for the honor of France in an unsuccessful attempt to fly the Atlantic. The Norwegians and Germans had enviable records of success in exploration. The Russians had been plodding relentlessly into the Arctic for years. But Italy, despite the rabid nationalistic fervor whipped up by Il Duce, had accomplished little to impress the world. So it was inevitable that the publicity-hungry Mussolini would try to claim credit for much of the *Norge* expedition's success.

After the American tour, Umberto Nobile returned wearily to Italy, where he was unwillingly subjected to a round of receptions, awarded the Military Order of Savoy, and otherwise publicized in a manner calculated to stamp his successful venture with the Fascist trademark. His position—as the shy, reluctant recipient of public acclaim—was similar to that of Charles Lindbergh when he returned to New York from his historic flight across the Atlantic. But there was an ironic twist. While Nobile squirmed uncomfortably in the limelight, another flier—the most publicity-minded of them all—was forced to sit on the sidelines, equally uncomfortable. Italo Balbo was still waiting for his big opportunity, which was to come within a few months when the affable General Bonzani would be squeezed out of his post as air minister to let this brash young Fascist with the familiar goatee step in. Balbo had ambitious and dramatic plans for leading Italian armadas of planes across Europe and eventually across the ocean. Not only would that impress other countries with Italy's prowess in the air, but it would show off Balbo's undisputed abilities as a pilot and flight leader.

Nobile was receiving public attention that he did not want; Balbo was seeking attention he could not get; and Mussolini was caught in a pincers movement, trying desperately to glamorize Italy's name on the one hand and to avoid party fractures on the other.

Fortunately, the situation was neatly resolved when Nobile decided to go to Japan, toward the end of 1926, to fulfill a commitment he had made to the Japanese navy regarding air-ship construction. A few weeks after his departure his friend Bonzani was replaced by Balbo as air minister.

The Italy to which Nobile returned after the *Norge* flight was even more in the grip of considerable political tension when he began making plans for his new dirigible expedition to the Pole. All during 1927, underground forces were at work to discourage him. Key workers at his airship plant were sum-marily hauled off, accused of being Reds, and transferred to jobs where they would be under the more direct supervision of the government. Nobile found himself repeatedly tied up in red tape for vague and inexplicable reasons.

The unassuming engineer, however, had one quality Balbo had not counted on: a determination that amounted almost to fanaticism. He thought nothing of working eighteen or twenty hours a day. It was rare that he saw his wife and daughter more than one day out of every two weeks. As fast as the red tape began to entangle him, he went to work to get free of it. He had one big advantage over his enemies: because of his popular standing with the public, he could not be attacked openly by even the highest-ranking Fascist leaders.

Thus it was that plans for the ambitious *Italia* expedition proceeded steadily though slowly, checked in part by the difficulty of finding private backers in a situation where it was obvious that the government was going to lend no financial support. Nobile was not a man to pursue matters on a limited scale. He scoffed at the idea that a single flight to the North Pole and back to the starting point would be sufficient to achieve a glorious scientific victory for Italy. He was not out for publicity. To accomplish what he had in mind, the airship would have to navigate many uncharted areas from a home base—probably Spitsbergen—before venturing to the Pole. Balbo felt a great measure of relief when he saw the magnitude of Nobile's plans. "Let him go," said Balbo, "for he cannot possibly come back to bother us any more."

While the airship was under construction, Nobile began selecting a crew from among the hundreds of applications that poured in. As a nucleus, he asked five of the mechanics who had been with him on the *Norge*—Alessandrini, Arduino,

Caratti, Cecioni, and Pomella—if they would risk another expedition, more dangerous than the first. All accepted at once. To round out the group of mechanics, he selected Calisto Ciocca, a slender, wiry man who had been in his employ for many years and had accompanied the *Norge* as an alternate but only as far as Kings Bay. As chief technician, Nobile settled on Natale Cecioni because, in addition to his mechanical abilities, he was experienced in helping to maneuver the dirigible at the controls in the cabin.

At a time when there was no radar, no radio beaconing, few other navigational aids, and almost no meteorological ground stations, it was vital that the officers and men in the pilot cabin have enough accumulated experience to keep the airship on a steady course, at the most beneficial altitude from the standpoint of winds, and at the most favorable airspeed to make good forward progress yet conserve fuel. Hence, good navigation skills were crucial.

To find the position of an airship over the surface of the earth, one estimated distances and directions in relation to ground features at known locations. But in the arctic wastes, there was nothing but ice and sea for hundreds of miles—no distinguishable features could be seen on the surface below. Celestial navigation was all important: using the sun, moon, and other heavenly bodies by sighting with a sextant to determine the airship's altitude, position, and ground speed. But the sextant was of limited use when visibility was blocked by fog or impenetrable curtains of clouds—as it often was in northern latitudes in the spring. In such instances, the navigator could rely only on a compass and an estimate of the direction and velocity of the wind to determine ground speed and the probable distance and direction from the last sextant-oriented bearing.

Nobile anticipated that, if they were socked in by clouds and fog, he might have to descend almost to the pack, lower the ice anchor, and hover, almost stationary, until the weather cleared, rather than risk heading in the wrong direction and consuming precious fuel.

For navigation, two experienced navy officers were needed, so Nobile applied to the admiralty, rather than trust his own judgment in an area in which he had little experience. Two commanders were immediately recommended: Adalberto Mariano, thirty, and Filippo Zappi, thirty-one. Mariano was a big man, heavily built and with broad shoulders, inclined somewhat to be sedentary rather than athletic. Slightly senior to Zappi in rank, he was an excellent navigator, had a keen mind, and had an imagination that turned to inventiveness. Zappi was not as brilliant, but he was agile and rugged and had a quick wit, a good sense of humor, and an engaging personality. In appearance and manner, he seemed more a diplomat than a naval officer. Most importantly, he had served as second in command of Italian navy airships and was qualified as an instructor in lighter-than-air craft.

A third officer came, by chance, into the picture at this time: Lieutenant (later Lieutenant-Commander) Alfredo

Viglieri of the Royal Navy. Viglieri, twenty-eight years old and over six feet, was perhaps the huskiest of the lot. He harbored romantic dreams of exploration, which had been given further impetus by Lindbergh's dramatic flight in 1927. When the navy began making plans for a part-time base ship to accompany the expedition and perform hydrographic tests, Viglieri was qualified by the admiralty as a navigation officer. Then, when Nobile decided that the airship should have a third navy officer who might actually be lowered onto the ice pack with a three-man team, Viglieri was reassigned. When Nobile informed him of the danger involved, Viglieri's enthusiasm rose still more. He accepted the assignment at once.

To complement the naval officers, Nobile then chose Felice Trojani, thirty-one, to take spells at the elevator wheel and assist with technical matters. Trojani, a fine engineer, was a slight, scholarly man who had been an employee at Nobile's plant for twelve years. Although he was, physically, on the delicate side and inclined to be quiet and shy, Trojani had a sound technical mind. He had accompanied Nobile to Japan to help fly and demonstrate the Italian-built dirigible that was being sold to the Imperial Japanese Navy.

Radio navigation was still in its infancy, and although Nobile knew that the *Italia*'s radio set would be useful in the initial stages of the flight when the airship was close to ground stations, it would be more and more ineffectual as they proceeded toward the Pole. But unlike many of his contemporaries, he had unswerving faith in radio. With painstaking care, he went about the task of selecting the type of sending and receiving equipment that would meet his specifications of extremely light weight plus enough power to maintain contact with the base ship during all flights of exploration. To operate this equipment he selected two well-qualified men: Ettore Pedretti and Giuseppe Biagi. Though equally experienced, the two men could hardly have been more unlike in physical appearance. Pedretti was fair, blue-eyed, and almost Nordic. Biagi was short, dark and robust, and could have been mistaken for nothing but an Italian.

Selecting the scientists who would accompany the expedition was probably the most exacting job of all. Nobile had fairly well settled on the first of these, Finn Malmgren, because of his association on the *Norge* expedition and because he was unrelenting in his efforts to make sure he was accepted. He was Swedish, a professor at the University of Uppsala, and well known as a meteorologist. Short, fair-haired, and intense and enthusiastic at his work, he was, at thirty-three, physically fit and well versed in arctic exploration and methods of living in the far north. He was high-spirited but could be moody and introspective. However, Nobile accepted this as not surprising for a Swede, judging it more important that the man had fine qualifications, including the fact that he had also completed significant work in oceanography, a scientific area that Nobile wanted to explore in every way possible during the expedition.

Malmgren was, therefore, chosen as director of all meteorological services of the expedition. A second area Nobile had planned to cover was that of radioactivity and electricity in the atmosphere north of the Arctic Circle. This interest tied in directly with his philosophies on the importance of radio in navigation, which he thought should be improved radically over its existing state, and also, of course, with the many problems of flying lighter-than-air craft through storms and under extreme weather conditions. One scientist came more and more to mind for this assignment. In 1926, while at Kings Bay prior to the *Norge* flight, Nobile had met a young Czechoslovakian professor, at the time only twenty-nine, from the University of Prague. He was Dr. Francis Behounek, who had gone to Spitsbergen to undertake a series of studies in atmospheric electricity, and who requested that Nobile let him install an apparatus in the pilot cabin of the *Norge* for measuring conductivity. This had been approved, but little research had actually been accomplished.

Now, as director of the Prague Wireless Institute, with an enviable reputation in his field, Behounek seemed like an excellent choice. His scientific experience outbalanced the fact that, physically, he was not suited to either the rigors of an expedition or the weight limitations of the airship. He was an enormous man, completely round faced and stout, and although he was extremely good natured and enthusiastic about his work, physical exertion often left him red faced and panting.

The third scientist was an Italian, Dr. Aldo Pontremoli, thirty-one, professor of physics at the University of Milan. Nobile had not met Pontremoli until they were introduced by a group of Italian scientists who felt that the professor would be invaluable in several ways. He spoke four languages fluently, had a great talent for conducting experiments under difficult conditions, and unlike the Czech was lithe and athletic, physically strong, and adept at performing almost any demanding task that might be assigned. From the moment Nobile accepted him, he worked day and night, never taking time off, to complete his scientific plans, accumulate and check out instruments, and develop better methods for conducting research in the air.

The roster for the expedition was rounded out by the addition of two journalists who were to be based at Kings Bay and would alternate in covering each of the proposed flights of the *Italia* from the base. The first was Francesco Tomaselli, thirty-four, of Venice, who not only was professionally qualified as a writer and doctor of letters, but also was a captain in the Alpini, the Italian mountaineering troops. The other was Ugo Lago, twenty-eight, of Syracuse, who was also a doctor of letters and physically well qualified for arduous, long-term exertion.

After many months of careful selection, the crew was thus assigned and ready. Of the eighteen members of the expedition, Nobile, at forty-three, was the oldest. With the rest mainly in their early thirties, and two men at twenty-eight, it was a youthful expedition.

Thus, well staffed and well equipped, the expedition's largest question mark would be the dirigible itself. The *Italia* was a sister ship of the *Norge* but with some significant modifica-

tions in design, such as stronger rudders and elevators, a device for lowering a crew to the ice during clement weather to
make scientific observations, and alterations that permitted
the airship to hover in one position with very little fuel consumption. Nobile and his officers devised many improvements in equipment, striving to find ways, for example, to
make operating machinery lighter but more efficient.

The *Italia* was a relatively small dirigible, designated at
18,500 cubic meters, with a total weight of 25,000 pounds.
She was of the semirigid type—that is, with framework at bow
and stern and along the keel but relying on the gas inside her
to keep the bag's shape. In the upper part of the cigar-shaped
bag were the lifting cells, filled with hydrogen gas. Beneath
them were air cells, which had no lifting capacity but were inflated with variable amounts of air to keep the bag taut at all
times. As hydrogen was valved off during flight, air was fed
into the lower cells through a vent in the nose to keep the interior pressure at the proper level.

The control cabin, barely 20 feet long by 8 feet wide and 7
feet in height, was a structure of steel tubing, walled with canvas and floored with lightweight wood. It was affixed directly
to the bag, so crew members could climb a ladder from the
center of the cabin right up into the keel. Once inside the bag
(and, in effect, standing on the roof of the cabin), a crew
member would have a view down the whole length of the
keel—325 feet of V-shaped steel tubes that formed the airship's vertebrae. The keel was, like the cabin, walled with

three layers of canvas, glued to each other (weft to web, or crosswise, for strength) and varnished outside with aluminum paint. The same paint was applied to the bag itself, giving the ship a silvery appearance in the sky.

The *Italia's* keel was partially compartmented to provide sleeping space for the crew and storage space for equipment. Looking down it, one could see sledges, rubber boats, provisions, arms, spare parts for the engines, extra propellers, and—hanging like odd Chinese lanterns—small cans of fuel. Hammocks were stretched crosswise along the keel, swaying over the catwalk that provided a footing. Going from one end of the ship to another was a process of ducking and dodging, to keep from waking off-duty crewmen or to avoid getting knocked on the head. In flight, it was a noisy place, where those trying to sleep often wore arctic earmuffs to muffle the roar of the three engines, the creaking of aluminum ribs and supports, and the pounding of wind, rain, or hail on the skin of the airship—often described as being on the inside of a drum.

For propulsion, the airship had three Maybach engines, each providing 250 horsepower. The three, operating together, were capable of driving the ship at an airspeed of 75 miles per hour. The two forward engines were attached, one each, to the port and starboard sides of the airship by steel tubing and were housed in small gondolas, just large enough for a mechanic to crawl into for maintenance and refueling. The gondolas were reached by horizontal gangplanks, with handrails that projected out on either side. The stern engine hung aft of the control cabin, affixed by steel tubing, its gondola reachable from the keel above it by a short ladder.

One of the hazards that was most noticeable during the *Norge* flight was the impact of ice pellets flung at the bag from the propellers when proceeding through clouds. So special layers of strong, rubberized fabric were added in the vulnerable areas. Icing up was a problem in other ways, too. Incrustations on the gas valves could cause serious trouble, either wedging the valves so they leaked or freezing them shut so no gas could be let out in an emergency. Nobile devised protective hoods that would keep the valves dry. The formation of ice on the top of the bag was another hazard. Under certain conditions, the accumulation could become heavy enough to weight the airship and force her down. So the fabric at the top was rubberized as a deterrent to ice formation.

When the expedition was almost ready to set out, its equipment was as complete and efficient as any that could be found in 1927 and 1928. In planning, Nobile relied on the advice and experience of such seasoned arctic explorers as professors Hoel of Oslo and De Geer of Stockholm, Captain Otto Sverdrup and Fridtjof Nansen. From them, he obtained recommendations on the best types of sledges, fur suits, skis, snowshoes, and rations for traversing the polar wastes. He had in mind planned landings on the ice pack, so that parties could traverse the ice and complete the kinds of scientific studies that were not possible from the air. Also, of course, he had to bear in mind that if the *Italia* were to be forced down on the ice and damaged beyond repair, they would have to establish a camp for an indeterminate amount of time and send scouting teams to seek assistance, which might take many days or even weeks. With these experts, Nobile also discussed his unique plan for lowering teams to the ice in the elevator–hoist rig he had invented, or to the sea in a collapsible boat, to make special studies of the ocean and to take samplings and temperature readings at various depths. At one time, he even had an ambitious plan—later scrapped because of the logistics problems of carrying enough supplies for such a venture—of establishing a camp with a team of scientists who would remain on the pack for as long as a year, taking meteorological readings and making observations of the drift and change of the arctic ice pack.

To determine the best kinds of rations to carry, he consulted with Nansen, then went to Copenhagen, to the firm the explorer had recommended, to order a special type of pemmican, the dried, powdered, highly nutritious mixture of meat, fat, and vegetables that kept well under trying conditions.

In addition to the flight to the Pole, and the lowering of men onto the ice for scientific study, Nobile also planned to explore the Siberian Coast, Nicholas II Land, Greenland, small, isolated islands in the midst of the ever moving ice packs, and the approaches to the geographical North Pole. Some of these were areas where few mortals—if any—had ever trod.

THE NEXT BIG STEP

In every detail, Nobile labored painstakingly day and night to take into account all contingencies and rule out as many elements of chance as possible. He could have asked for no better crew members, no finer equipment, and no more thorough planning in the late 1920s. Still, a high element of risk was inevitable. Like a man climbing a tall mountain who can see only the blue skies above him and not the black storm approaching beyond the slope, Nobile knew he was headed for many unknown perils.

5

PREMONITIONS OF TROUBLE

A t a quarter past one in the morning of April 15, 1928, from the dimly lit field in Milan, Italy, the ghostly *Italia* rose slowly into the air for her long journey to Spitsbergen, base for the polar flights. The weather report was unnerving, but Nobile had little choice, for he had a tight schedule if he wanted to accomplish his mission before the summer fogs closed in to obscure navigation.

"We shall have some excitement," reported meteorologist Malmgren, almost with enthusiasm at the challenge. "After studying the weather reports, I can predict nothing better for the next few days." In the Arctic, the "good season," if you can call it that, is early spring, when the round-

the-clock darkness of winter is starting to break up and before the problems of summer set in. In warm weather, the
pack starts to decay, making over-ice operations difficult;
and the mists settle in like blankets, rendering air operations just as hopeless. Only in the spring is there a brief
respite when there are many hours of daylight and relatively
few hours of fog.

The flight of the *Italia* had been scheduled for this time of
year—in between the extreme cold of winter and its icy winds
and the rising temperatures of summer. Another reason for
avoiding higher temperatures is that they would cause the gas
in the airship to expand and necessitate valving, which de-
pleted the hydrogen supply and would cut short the time the
ship could remain in flight.

When the airship headed for the mountains of Germany,
there were on board twenty people (plus Nobile's little terrier,
Titina), 3,000 pounds of equipment, 4,000 pounds of ballast,
700 pounds of oil, and 8,600 pounds of petrol—a staggering
load for a dirigible the size of the *Italia*.

Even the thirty-hour trip from the Valley of the Po to a
stopover at the airfield at Stolp, Germany, on the Baltic Sea,
was one of the most rigorous ever successfully undertaken by
an airship. Almost from the moment she was airborne, the
Italia was under trial, and during the 1,250-mile run she was to
encounter rain, hail, snow, fog, heavy winds, ice, and lightning, each one of which had proved fatal to lighter-than-air
craft at one time or another.

PREMONITIONS OF TROUBLE

The first test came as the *Italia* crossed the karst between Trieste and Sadobrava. The men at the controls were startled to hear a shout from mechanic Pomella, who was running forward along the catwalk in the keel. "I think we have suffered some damage to the left horizontal fin!"

"Have Alessandrini take a look," said Nobile. A cross fire of icy winds had blasted the dirigible, warping the frame this way and that as conflicting gusts of up to forty miles an hour tore at the envelope. As it turned out, the damage was serious, not only because it decreased maneuverability but because one weakened member placed an additional strain on the other control surfaces of the ship. Nobile reduced speed and tried to keep the nose pointing into the wind.

At eight that morning, the *Italia* was observed over Kormend and Sopron, two towns on the Hungarian border, out of the mountain storm but proceeding through gray skies. By the middle of the afternoon she was passing over Bruun in Czechoslovakia and headed for trouble in the Sudetes.

When Nobile asked for a weather report from Prague, Malmgren reported that it was "dismal," and that the Meteorological Bureau warned that over Moravia and Silesia they could expect lightning and winds of at least thirty-five miles an hour, with gusts rising much higher.

"Shall we change course, General?" asked First Officer Mariano.

Nobile opted to keep going until they could see more positively what lay ahead.

DISASTER AT THE POLE

As the *Italia* approached the Sudetes, the sky appeared to be completely barred by thick walls of menacing black clouds. Only in one direction, toward a narrow valley, could any daylight be seen. Nobile and Malmgren held a quick consultation. Under any other circumstances they would both have decided to turn back. But to retreat might mean the loss of so many days that the polar flight itself would be jeopardized. Their decision was to head for the valley and take their chance on finding an avenue of less hazardous air right through to the other side of the mountain range.

For an hour, the *Italia* had no difficulty. Then, without warning, masses of clouds closed in from all sides, effectively cutting off escape in any direction. A murderous hailstorm lashed out at the fabric of the ship, pelting the thin skin with such fury the officers and crew felt as though they were on the inside of a bass drum. Above them brilliant flashes of lightning indicated the intensity of an electrical storm higher up in the mountains. In this black aerial tunnel between the mountains, Nobile had to feel his way along, letting Malmgren navigate by instinct. On the one hand, there was the constant danger of crashing head-on into a mass of sheer rock wall. On the other hand, to rise above the mountains was suicide, for there lay the dangers of lightning. Nobile, vividly aware of what could happen to 18,500 cubic meters of highly inflammable hydrogen if touched off by static electricity, chose to risk striking the cliffs.

At times, the *Italia* cruised within three hundred feet of the ground, low enough that the terrain could occasionally be made out when lightning flashed through rifts in the clouds. One of the closest calls came when Viglieri was at the steering wheel. Trying to peer through a break in the clouds, he suddenly saw dead ahead a huge cross topping a mountain peak. Yanking the wheel hard over, he managed to avoid disaster by a matter of barely a few yards. For an hour, the ship played tag with the mountains before emerging on the other side of the pass, where the thunderstorm was less violent. The last few hours of the trip to Stolp, Germany, were calm, and at 7:15 in the morning of April 16, the storm-beaten *Italia* nosed gingerly down to the airfield at Jesseritz.

An inspection of the airship, including a study of her gauges, was discouraging. Almost two-thirds of the fuel had been consumed battling the winds, and every last pound of ballast had gone overboard to keep the ship in proper trim. The upper tail-fin had been ruptured, as well as the horizontal fin, and the wooden propellers had been seriously nicked by hailstones.

And this was only a preliminary flight. The venture over the Arctic Ocean would involve storms of greater force, combined with icing and mist conditions that would make navigation extremely perilous. Undaunted, Nobile ordered the crew to rest well, wired Rome for emergency technicians and spare parts, and reconciled himself to a week's delay in order to effect repairs before proceeding to Spitsbergen.

As it turned out, the repairs took ten days, to the great delight of Italo Balbo, Valle, and the other enemies of Nobile who had gone to great lengths to forecast that the expedition would end in a dismal failure. In an official report to Mussolini, who had asked that he be kept apprised of the *Italia*'s progress, Balbo stated, "I think our predictions were right that the expedition will fail, for the airship is already having difficulties just getting to its takeoff base."

In the meantime, Umberto Nobile's brother, Amedeo, radioed from Kings Bay, where he had gone to supervise the establishment of the base camp, that the mooring mast and temporary hangar were in order. The hangar, a flimsy, roofless structure, was the minimum protection the airship would need from the ground winds while engines were overhauled and supplies carefully loaded and balanced in their storage positions. The great canvas-and-frame doors had been seriously damaged by a storm, but Amedeo had completed repairs.

There was only one serious obstacle: the base supply ship, *Citta di Milano*, was still at Tromsö, Norway, an island whaling and supply port. The captain, Giuseppe Romagna, had hesitated—with an alarming display of timidity—to set out because he had received a report that Kings Bay was becoming locked in ice. Though the *Citta di Milano*, an antiquated, poorly equipped vessel, had been loaned out by the Italian government as the minimum assistance it could get away with giving to the expedition, she was to fall far short of her purpose. The delay in heading for Kings Bay was merely the start of the ship's exasperating maneuvers at crucial times during the expedition's progress. In this instance, however, her commander had no excuse for hesitation. The small Norwegian steamship *Hobby* had successfully navigated to Kings Bay, to land Amedeo Nobile and initial supplies for repairing and expanding the hangar.

"Proceed at once to Kings Bay," wired Umberto Nobile from Stolp. Romagna finally ordered his ship under way but only after checking with Rome, whence his orders had to be verified. It was a frustrating and, as it later proved, highly precarious arrangement, which jeopardized the lives of the officers and men of the expedition.

Nobile had been so dubious about the dependability of the *Citta di Milano* that he had previously made arrangements with Norwegian authorities to have one hundred miners from the coal mines at Kings Bay put at his disposal to assist with landing operations on the arrival of the *Italia*, in the event of any emergency. The Norwegian government had agreed without reservation.

On April 30, the Geophysical Institute in Tromsö reported good weather along the Scandinavian Peninsula, though there were winds of 25 miles an hour over the Barents Sea. "Such a situation is as good as one can hope for this time of year," said the report. "There are uncertainties and risks, but these are inevitable."

Nobile resolutely decided to take off. But a violent wind had sprung up at Stolp, so strong that ground crews could not even get the *Italia* out of the hangar without endangering her.

Finally, on the evening of May 2, the wind subsided. Nobile consulted with Finn Malmgren. They would be certain of head winds all the way across the Baltic Sea, but these were forecast as abating along the coast of Sweden. Rain and snow-storms were also forecast en route. The two men decided to proceed. Further delay was impossible. So the airship nosed out into the gusty dawn at 3:28 A.M. on May 3, with a strong north wind blowing directly at her at a speed of almost 30 miles an hour and a gray overcast ahead.

Despite head winds, the *Italia* made good speed, for Nobile had ordered the engines at full power, partly to cut down on the air time and partly to check their performance. On the final trip to the Pole there would most certainly be strong head winds on at least one leg of the flight out and back. The 410 miles to Stockholm were covered in less than eight hours. Sailing serenely over the lovely Swedish capital, the *Italia* was given an escort of several seaplanes that had taken off to greet the explorers.

"There—there is the house!" shouted Finn Malmgren excitedly. Every one in the pilot cabin knew what he meant, for the Swedish scientist's mother lived in Stockholm and was awaiting word of her son. Slowly Nobile circled, dropping low enough so that Malmgren was able to wave and drop a weighted letter of greeting to his mother. Then the ship rose, headed north, and disappeared over the Gulf of Bothnia.

"We will have to ease our course more to the eastward," advised Malmgren an hour later. Though Nobile had intended to head directly north over the gulf, the wind, combined with a heavy fog that had swirled down from the direction of the Arctic, made this course too hazardous. The *Italia* swung to the east, crossed over Finland by night, and at 1:49 A.M. on May 4 passed over the town of Rovaniemi in northern Finland. Two hours later Nobile and Malmgren had cause for great concern. Radio operator Biagi had handed them the most recent weather report from the Tromsö Geophysical Institute:

> Depression between Bear Island and Spitsbergen moving eastward. Pressure falling in front of the center. In the rear, over ocean between Spitsbergen, Jan Meyen and Greenland there is north to northwest Beaufort 5 [winds of about 25 miles an hour]. The north wind system will spread eastward. . . . We consider it advisable to increase the speed of the ship in order to utilize present favorable landing conditions.

Nobile had cut out one engine and reduced the speed of the other two after clearing Stockholm. He immediately gave orders to start the third engine and maintain full power on all three. It would be a critical race against time and the elements.

By six that morning, the visibility had become so bad that the *Italia*'s position could no longer be determined. Because of traces of ice forming on the bag, the general hesitated to ascend into colder air. But after an hour of tension, straining to sight dangerous peaks in their path, Nobile decided that ice was the lesser evil and ordered Commander Zappi to tilt the bow skyward. As the elevator controls turned, moving the large horizontal fins at the stem, the ship planed gently upward. Two hours later, Malmgren decided they had proceeded far enough so that there must be sea below.

Down through the darkness, the airship slid, as the altimeter needle spun around. Suddenly the ship broke through the mists, only a few hundred feet above the ocean, and there, on the coast not far away, they could make out the welcome sight of Vadsö, their next stopping point. Within fifteen minutes the ship was attached to the mooring mast, but not before a gust had dashed her prow against the framework, causing slight damage to the envelope.

Nobile had intended staying at Vadsö only three or four hours, long enough to refuel, replenish the gas cells with hydrogen, and take in fresh stocks of provisions and water. But once again a storm rose from the north. All that day the *Italia* clung to her exposed mooring mast, whipped by blizzards that occasionally swung the ship 360 degrees around the revolving masthead. The situation was so dangerous that Nobile boarded the *Italia*, tried to catch catnaps lying down in a collapsible boat in the keel girders, and left orders for all motormen to have their propellers ready to spin at a moment's notice. As the gusts increased, the engines were started so that the nose, still attached to the mast, could be kept pointed into the wind. This eased the strain, but even so those inside the ship could hear her internal framework creaking. The wind velocity rose to 40 miles an hour, accompanied by heavy snowfall. At any moment violent gusts could wrench the dirigible loose and throw her to the mercy of the storm.

Suddenly from the far end of the stern came a sudden crack, a sound like a pistol shot that penetrated the whine of the wind. One of the steel tubes in the framework had broken under the strain. Nobile sent riggers to repair it at once.

Around noon of the next day, the wind subsided and the snow turned into a heavy rain that ran down the vast sides of the ship and slammed against the canvas-walled pilot cabin with the force of a waterfall. Everything became drenched, but it was an inconvenience the officers and men had to face, since the ship could finally take off. The weather report for the Barents Sea was satisfactory except for strong contrary winds up to 30 miles an hour between Bear Island and Spitsbergen. Along the landing field at Kings Bay, a wind of 25 miles an hour was reported. Nobile delayed the takeoff a few hours to let the wind settle; then at 8:34 P.M. on May 5 the Italia rose slowly from Vadsö and headed north to Spitsbergen.

The weather improved slowly. By 5:30 the next morning it was clear enough over Bear Island in the middle of the Barents Sea for the Italia to circle over the lonely observatory hut below, a gesture of thanks for the indispensable help of the two meteorologists stationed there.

Between Bear Island and Spitsbergen the weather showed its true colors, and the sky darkened rapidly. According to the Tromsö forecast, the crew members should have met a strong head wind from the north. Instead, they suddenly found themselves in the center of a violent front advancing from Iceland with gusts of about 50 miles an hour. As the airship approached Spitsbergen's bleak, jagged coastline and snow-caked peaks, she was suddenly smothered in a thick blizzard. Claws of wind-driven sleet clutched at the shivering bag.

Radio operator Biagi called out a report from Kings Bay, where the *Citta di Milano*, which had left Spezia with a crew of 166, had finally arrived after her bumbling start. Kings Bay reported a rapidly falling barometer and an increasing wind at ground level.

At the same instant, Sub-Lieutenant Ettore Arduino, the chief motor engineer, relayed bad news to the general: one of his engines had just gone out of commission and could not be repaired in the air. It was now touch and go whether the *Italia* could even reach Kings Bay or would have to drift with the wind until the storm abated and then try to make safe haven elsewhere. Such a course would be a bitter blow to the explorers and a setback that might put them more than a week behind schedule.

By noon on May 6, however, the battle was all but won when Mariano, at the controls, sighted Kings Bay and the base ship, *Citta*, in the harbor.

Nobile smiled grimly. Despite the reluctance of her captain, the *Citta di Milano* had made the trip in the nick of time. But if it had not been for the two delays caused by storms and the need for repairs, the *Italia's* crew would have achieved an ironical record: the first polar expedition to have arrived at its base camp before the base camp party appeared on the scene. Now at least, they could count on having plenty of hands from the *Citta* to assist in the delicate and hazardous maneuver of landing in a gale.

Slowly the airship circled the base field. Then General Nobile received a shock. Upon radioing Captain Romagna for fifty men to complement the small ground crew landed by the *Hobby*, he was told that they "could not be spared from their duties." Duties?! What was more important to the entire expedition than to see that the *Italia* did not come to an inglorious end right then and there?

"My men are not duty-bound to act as a ground crew," said Romagna. It was true. Seamen and technicians they may have been, but there was no written contract that they would handle standing lines for an airship. When Nobile protested, he was told that orders would have to come through the office of the admiralty in Rome. And he might easily circle for several days before Rome would radio a reply. Furthermore, he learned with great shock that the assistance he could expect from the base ship at any time during the expedition had been greatly weakened by an odd arrangement: the *Citta* had been assigned to making weather observations and charting meteorological data for several weeks. And indeed Captain Romagna seemed to consider that his primary duty and giving assistance to the *Italia* merely a side assignment that he would carry on when in the mood to do so.

"Get me the miners!" shouted Nobile, calling down through a landing megaphone, from about 150 feet altitude, to his brother. Within a matter of minutes, the Norwegians had dispatched a large crew—men who knew nothing whatsoever about the problems of landing a dirigible but who were strong and willing, something Nobile could not say for his countrymen aboard the base ship.

After almost two hours of tense maneuvering, the airship was housed in her flimsy hangar. Once again, she had smashed against the landing mast with some damage to her prow. But it was easily repairable and could wait until the next day. Nobile collapsed with relief. It was eighty-two hours since he had been able to take anything more than fitful catnaps.

The next day, rested and ready to prepare for the great unknown that lay ahead, Nobile wrote in his log in a somewhat melodramatic way that was the style of the time:

> *Now that we are in the fighting line we can even afford to fail, as men die in battle; but it would have been better to fail during the march we were forced to make, before reaching our post in the vanguard. . . . Two years ago I navigated here a ship with a foreign name; and so at all costs I must now bring to her destination the ship which bears the banner and the name of Italy. There can be no failure!*

After repairing the damaged engine and the prow and structural members weakened during the arduous trip north, Umberto Nobile launched the first of his planned assaults on the Arctic. This was to be an exploratory trip far to the east toward Nicholas II Land. He had outlined five major flights of exploration to be taken in May and early June from Spitsbergen. In addition to the flight over the North Pole, the *Italia* was to explore the north coast of Greenland, Nicholas II Land, Siberia, and Franz Josef Land.

The first attempt lasted only eight hours. A blizzard closed in from the north shortly after the *Italia* took off on May 11 for her first flight into the Arctic. In addition, the wire cable running to the rudder was found to be so badly frayed in one spot from constant strain that it had to be strengthened with an emergency splice that might not stand up under heavy weather. It was when ice began forming on the envelope and snow began sticking to it, that Malmgren expressed his blunt opinion that they should turn back, and Nobile agreed.

On that same day, at Kings Bay, after a reasonably fair morning, the sky had darkened until it appeared almost like night. The effect was unusually disturbing at this season, for Kings Bay enjoys twenty-four hours of daylight during the late spring and early summer. The blizzard descended on the hangar shortly after the *Italia* returned and was once more housed within it shortly after four that afternoon.

By early morning, May 12, the storm had reached a peak. At first the swirling winds swept the snow from the top of the *Italia's* envelope in the roofless hangar. But later, as the snowfall increased and the wind died, Nobile watched with growing concern while the blanket of white grew deeper and deeper. Soon the weight had caused the airship to settle so much that the pilot cabin and stern engine boat were actually touching the floor of the hangar.

First Officer Mariano ran forward along the keel after one inspection of the interior. "The lateral fins are so heavily loaded with snow that the metal plating shows signs of buckling," he said. Nobile reinforced parts of the fabric with a special rubberized patching material, and by the time the storm had abated, the dirigible was ready for her next assault on the arctic wastes.

This second flight was also in the direction of Nicholas II Land. From the time of leaving, at 1:20 P.M. on May 15, the flight lasted sixty-nine hours. It was blessed with excellent visibility a good part of the way and gave the scientists a chance to explore visually, as well as by instrument, some 25,000 square miles of unknown Arctic Ocean, ice packs, and land masses. Dr. Malmgren recorded valuable meteorological data, along with significant observations on the nature of the ice, and Dr. Pontremoli concentrated on studying his specialty: magnetic fields and atmospheric radioactivity.

By mid morning three days later, the *Italia* was once again moored at her hangar at Kings Bay, this time under a clear blue sky, with a backdrop of magnificent Spitsbergen mountains gleaming like jewelry from their encrustations of snow and ice. In all, the airship had flown 2,500 miles on the trip to Nicholas II Land. Nobile and his officers were in a jovial mood that day as they lay down on their bunks for a well-earned rest. With any luck at all, the exploratory flight over the North Pole should be a momentous and historical venture.

6

DESTINATION ZERO

Five days later, before dawn on May 23, the polar flight began. Since the return from Nicholas II Land, Umberto Nobile had tirelessly checked each item of equipment personally and rehearsed the officers and men on the minutest details of the flight to come. One maneuver, tricky and dangerous, had yet to be put to the test, though it had been practiced successfully before the expedition left Italy. Nobile described it in his journals as follows:

> The new and interesting part was to have been the descent on the ice, which I proposed to make near the Pole, or wherever else it might be possible. The object was to carry out some oceanographical observations in which Malmgren and I were more particularly inter-

ested: above all, to sound the sea and take samples of water at various depths, down to 2,000 meters, at the same time measuring its temperature. . . . To take these measurements we should have to anchor on the ice, or preferably in the water. The second was the more proba-ble, since it would always be possible to find a pool of water or a channel; so I had prepared most carefully for it, studying every detail of the maneuver and testing it in practice. . . . I intended to move from a height of about 100 meters. Once this was done we would bring ourselves down to within 50 meters of sea level, and from this height let down the men and instruments in the pneumatic basket (with an inflated raft which would float and could be paddled to the nearest ice mass). I myself would go down first, not only to get an idea of any possible difficulties or risks, but also to plant our flag on the ice. Once back on board I should send down Pontremoli, Malmgren and Mariano. While they were carrying out their observations, Behounek would make measurements with his instruments on board . . .

This same plan was considered to be feasible for a descent to the ice pack if open water proved to be too far away from "absolute geographical zero" (the North Pole), but that would be more hazardous and would be impossible unless the air were completely calm. Either way, the plan meant that once the men were landed, they would be temporarily stranded if a wind should arise and force the dirigible to ascend to wait out the blow. Such a stranding could last for days, even weeks if the wind continued in force and the *Italia* had to return to Kings Bay for refueling. So Nobile prepared large canvas sacks containing a tent, sleeping bags, wind-tight suits, reindeer-skin gauntlets, firearms, colored powder for marking a location in the snow, smoke signals, a Nansen stove, matches, fuel, and concentrated food supplies.

Each member of the expedition departed from Kings Bay wearing, or having on hand, woolen underwear, a mountaineer's cap, long woolen hose, heavy gloves and outer gauntlets of leather, solid leather shoes, and a thick woolen sports suit, topped with a lambskin suit of trousers, tunic, and hood. This clothing was sufficient for explorers to withstand arctic temperatures as low as 21 degrees below zero and continue to march along the ice, making reasonably good progress without undue fatigue.

As the *Italia* left Kings Bay in the sunlight of the arctic dawn on that fateful flight, she was described in one press report as "a shimmering silver shape, glinting far above the ice hummocks and dimly seen from below. How different from those labored tours of old, when sledge parties left their floe-hemmed craft to toil among the ridges in the white glare of the Arctic . . ."

The weather report from Tromsö had been as favorable as could be expected. The northward journey toward the Pole was deceptively without incident. The sky was clear, visibility

50 miles, as the ship headed west for Greenland, then north on the twenty-seventh meridian. For the first eight hours the pointed prow and sharp-edged keel cut through drifting patches of mist like some gargantuan knife. She rode easily and quietly, but then the mists built up slowly until they were exasperating for the men on watch at the wheel and those trying to plot a difficult course over a terrain where each square of white below looked just like the next.

Behounek and his two fellow scientists groused about the frustration of not being able to use their instruments when there was nothing on which they could be sighted. It was of little consolation that Malmgren philosophically promised "better visibility soon."

Visibility was not the only problem. By late afternoon, Nobile was becoming increasingly concerned with something other than the mist: a wind that was growing in strength. Though it came from the south, helping rather than hindering the *Italia* on its headstrong dash to the Pole, it presaged two disquieting developments: first, Nobile would have to abandon plans for landing three of the expedition members on the ice pack at the Pole because the gusts were too strong to permit use of either the land anchor or the sea anchor and the pneumatic basket; second, and more ominous, the return trip would be greatly slowed down if the wind continued at its present rate. As he estimated it, the flight to the Pole could be accomplished in less than twenty hours, but the return trip might take almost double that if the wind conditions persisted.

For several hours, Nobile tried to analyze the advantages and disadvantages of an alternate plan, which was simply to continue cruising beyond the Pole, bearing east and ending up at Mackenzie Bay in northwestern Canada, a route somewhat similar to that taken by the *Norge* in 1926.

When he discussed this option with Malmgren, the scientist advised him that it would be better to make the return trip to Kings Bay, since the south wind would eventually die, making the return trip easier than bucking head winds to Canada. That would then make it possible to carry out the important plans for scientific research en route. And so the *Italia* flew onward, into slightly clearing skies, reaching the North Pole at 12:24 A.M. on May 24. "We are here!" shouted First Officer Mariano, who, in relatively clear weather, had been shooting the midnight sun with his sextant to determine the airship's exact position.

"All engines, half speed," Nobile ordered chief engineer Ettore Arduino. "Helm full circle. Elevators down."

Slowly, the airship eased through the gusts lower and lower until the ice pack loomed sharp and clear. Exact geographical zero lay directly below, an uninspiring wasteland of tortured ice, fractured and jumbled by the pressures of the heaving Arctic Ocean below the surface.

Reaching the Pole was, like climbing an almost unconquerable mountain peak, a moment of great emotional experience. Nobile, with the light of accomplishment shining in his eyes, was deeply moved. He now had a silent rite to perform. After circling for long enough to make doubly sure of the position, he leaned out of the cabin at exactly 1:20 A.M. and let fall the Italian flag. This was followed by the gonfalon of the city of Milan, which had helped to sponsor the expedition, then a little medal of the Virgin of Fire, which some citizens of Forli had entrusted to him to drop on the summit of the world. Then, from a height of about 450 feet, Nobile dropped a large oaken cross entrusted to him personally by Pope Pius XI and tied with a cloth bearing the tricolor of Italy.

Nobile and the others watching were overcome with emotion. The officers saluted the objects as they were dropped with stiff formality. And radio operator Biagi transmitted a message to Rome to the pope, the king, and Mussolini, announcing this act of reverence to their nation. There was pride in everyone's heart as the engines were stilled and a tiny gramophone competed with the whistling arctic wind to play the faraway, wistful notes of a sentimental Italian favorite, "The Bells of St. Giusto." Commander Zappi, second officer, turned to his leader with tears in his eyes and cried: "Viva Nobile!" Finn Malmgren approached to shake him warmly by the hand, followed closely by Behounek, the Czechoslovakian—these two foreigners thought of Nobile first as a scientist and explorer, and only second as a representative of Italy. The general opened bottles of an eggnog specially prepared in Rome and preserved for the occasion, a rich blend of eggs, milk and well-aged wine.

Then, after almost two hours of circling at the Pole, the *Italia* headed southward again, into the swirling mists and increasing wind—and into trouble.

It was 2:20 A.M. on May 24 when the airship left the Pole, on a course southward along the twenty-fifth meridian east of Greenwich at an altitude of three thousand feet. It had taken nineteen hours to reach the Pole from Kings Bay, cruising along the Greenland coast. The route home was more direct. But twenty-four hours after leaving the Pole, lunging and warping into the wind all the while, the storm-beaten airship was barely halfway to its destination. When the mists cleared on infrequent occasions, the shadow of the ship could be sighted veering drunkenly over the white mirror of the ice pack, wiith its snowfields, rough hummocks, and dark crevasses.

Inside the canvas-walled pilot cabin, the wind whistled bitterly, piercing its way through the tiniest cracks. "If only this head wind would let up, General," complained Arduino at one point, "we could make fine progress. The engines are bearing up, but the strain on them is heavy." Nobile nodded silently. He had been without sleep for two days. He could not close his eyes for even five minutes, tortured into wakefulness by the realization that the fuel supply was diminishing at an alarming rate.

"Soon we will cut the speed," he promised.

From time to time, foreman rigger Renato Alessandrini climbed down the companionway to the pilot cabin from the catwalk inside the huge bag to give reports on the gas cells and the ever creaking framework. "So far, no damage, General," he commented at one point. "But is there no way we can ease off? I'm afraid one of the main braces may buckle if we lunge the way we have been."

"The wind is bound to die," Nobile assured him. "Malmgren reports we are almost finished with the struggle." It did not require the warning of Alessandrini to alert him to the strain on the ship. Even in the pilot cabin, he could feel the entire framework quiver and sense the change of pressure in his eardrums as the great bag rose and fell in the gale, twisting and warping with each gust.

What startled Nobile, though, was the sudden crack, like a rifle shot, that unexpectedly sounded above the whine of the wind and the labored drone of the engines. "Ice!" exclaimed Mariano, looking up apprehensively from the chart table, where he and Alfredo Viglieri were plotting the airship's course. There came a second sharp crack, then another.

"It's being whipped from the propeller blades," said Viglieri. "If this keeps up, the envelope will soon look like cheese-cloth."

Nobile quickly ordered three crew members to find and patch all holes they could spot in the fabric made by the flying shrapnel of ice. And, having temporarily cut the engine speed, he now ordered Ettore Arduino to increase the engines from 1,200 to 1,300 revolutions per minute. To his dismay, this action did not produce any noticeable increase in airspeed. Furthermore, when engineer Felice Trojani made a check of petrol consumption, he found that the additional burden on the engines had increased the forward speed of the ship barely 7 miles an hour but was consuming almost double the amount of petrol. This situation had continued from seven in the evening until three in the morning of May 25. Nobile was finally forced to reduce the engine power once more.

He had no sooner done that than Malmgren appeared by his side to warn him that they had to push the engines to the limit and get out of the region, since the weather was deteriorating at a disturbing rate.

If Nobile had any doubts, he soon realized that he had little choice. Within an hour he found that, with erratic winds blowing the ship from one side to another and squalls striking the bag from several directions at once, nothing short of full speed could keep the ship maneuverable.

Dr. Francis Behounek, who had been making compass readings, reported that the *Italia* was frequently off course by as much as 30 degrees, no matter how hard the helmsmen wrestled to keep her straight. Every time the wheel was turned, those in the after part of the keel could hear the wrenching of the giant vertical fin as the rudder strained against the wind.

At the elevator wheel, Natale Cecioni, chief technician, was having an equally impossible time trying to control the upward and downward bucking of the ship. She handled like a seesaw, he later explained, giving him the impression of riding in a high-speed elevator that kept changing direction unexpectedly.

By 7:30 that morning, Nobile knew his airship was in real trouble. He said nothing, but the dark lines on his face revealed his feelings to Giuseppe Biagi, the wireless operator, who, though only a second-class officer, was a man who had, in his working relationship, been close to Nobile for many years. He knew the sensitive Nobile better perhaps than any of the other expedition members—better even than the officers closer to Nobile in rank: Commanders Mariano and Zappi.

At that hour, Biagi radioed the base ship at Kings Bay, which had been transmitting compass directions at infrequent intervals and without much accuracy: "If I don't answer, I have good reason."

Nobile, understanding only too well that the *Citta di Milano*'s radio bearings could be way off (as yet radio directional systems were only crudely developed), realized that the *Italia* might be as much as 100 miles from the compass points transmitted. At that time he estimated his position as 250 miles northeast of Moffin Island, the bearing point just north of Kings Bay. In actuality, as it later turned out, he was almost 350 miles from that goal. The position was dead reckoned from the last sextant sight Mariano had been able to take several hours earlier, before the ship plunged into the heavy storm clouds. Though the airspeed had been maintained—even increased—the forward motion over the ice pack had been diminished beyond all of Nobile's fears by the force of the wind.

It was at 9:25 A.M. that the first critical accident occurred. Nobile was standing by the door of the wireless room awaiting a radio report from Kings Bay when he heard a cry: "The elevator wheel has jammed!" He ran forward and found Trojani trying vainly to release the wheel, which had frozen in place, with the horizontal elevator fins forcing the *Italia* in a downward direction. The wheel would not give so much as a single degree. The situation was all the more serious because at that moment the airship was battling her way at an altitude of less than 1,000 feet, where the head winds seemed slightly less severe than above. In a few minutes the cabin would strike the ice pack.

"All engines, emergency stop!" Nobile's shrill voice resounded above the roar of the wind and the flapping of canvas, as he shouted the order and the engine controls were switched. With no forward motion the dirigible would be at the mercy of the wind but would rise upward like a free balloon. Gradually, the descent slackened as the speed decreased. When Nobile looked out of one of the ports, he could see the ice pack a bare 300 feet below. As soon as forward motion stopped, the airship began to ascend. Nobile knew the wind would be pushing the ship backward—away from any safe landing place.

DISASTER AT THE POLE

At 3,000 feet, the ship suddenly rose through a misty stratum of luminescence and popped into brilliant sunlight. The rays of the sun streamed into the cabin, a deceptively welcome sight. Nobile knew it was extremely dangerous to remain there longer than just time enough for a sun sight with the sextant and to repair the elevator controls. Temperature was a tricky factor in dirigible control and flight. The change from continual overcast to bright summer sun could rapidly expand the gases in the bag, causing new dangers—which was exactly what was happening. They could not afford to valve off too much precious hydrogen to lower the pressure, because the ship would become heavier once it descended again below the clouds. Then there would not be enough lift left in the gas cells to prevent the ship from crashing to the ice or into the ocean. And the reverse problem was that they had little ballast to throw overboard to prevent such a crash—other than the petrol, which was their lifeblood if they wanted to survive to reach civilization.

7

THE DOWNFALL

By 9:55 A.M., Cecioni had managed to repair the elevator control by chipping away the ice that had jammed it and realigning the cables. Nobile ordered two of the three engines started, and when the *Italia* had picked up enough speed for maneuverability, he eased her down again into the mists. At 1,000 feet he could sight the ice pack intermittently once more through the snow and wind-driven clouds. After several minutes of calculation, he noted with some relief that they were able to maintain 30 miles an hour over the pack using only two engines. The head wind must have diminished a little in intensity, just as Malmgren had predicted it would. There was a chance the expedition would make Kings Bay after all.

DISASTER AT THE POLE

For half an hour the ship cruised without difficulty, and, though she was still taking a severe pummeling from the wind, the strain was less than before. Malmgren remained calmly and confidently at the helm, with Commander Zappi standing by and giving occasional instructions. Cecioni remained at the elevator wheel. Beside him, near the engine telegraph signal, stood Trojani, maintaining contact with the enginemen. In the rear of the pilot cabin, at the navigation table, Nobile sat with Commander Mariano and Lieutenant Commander Viglieri, continuing to plot speed calculations and distance estimates on the chart. Biagi was, as usual, in the radio shack (next to the chart table, but compartmented from it). Dr. Behounek held his normal post near the compass, toward the rear of the cabin.

Outside the pilot cabin, the three enginemen were at their respective positions: Attilio Caratti in the left engine gondola, Calisto Ciocca in the right, and Vincenzo Pomella in the stern boat. Above, in the wedge-shaped keel section of the long bag, Ettore Arduino walked back and forth along the catwalk, regularly glancing down through observation ports at the three engines to see whether they were icing up. Near him, Renato Alessandrini, the foreman rigger, moved along the "balloon deck" from gas cell to gas cell, inspecting valves, checking framework, and looking for any evidence of escaping hydrogen. In a crude bunk space toward the stern of the bag and next to the keel, Professor Pontremoli and the journalist Ugo Lago had been asleep for some hours, unaware of the accident to the elevator control and the ascent above the clouds.

It was precisely at 10:25 A.M. that General Nobile detected the first alarming list toward the stern of the ship and at 10:26 that chief technician Cecioni at the elevator wheel sensed something amiss and shouted, "We are heavy!"

The general turned with alarm toward the instruments. The ship was cruising now at approximately 900 feet yet inexplicably falling at the startling rate of 2 feet per second. By all principles of flight navigation, she should have been rising, for her hydrogen gas cells were adequately full to compensate for the ship's gross weight. Moreover, the inclinometer indicated the bow pointing skyward 8 degrees.

Under the circumstances, there was only one order an airship commander could give. "All engines. Emergency. Ahead at full!"

Eyes glued to the instruments, and noting that the increase in speed had absolutely no effect, Nobile added a second order, "Up elevators." This was a normal procedure for gaining altitude fast. The bow tilted skyward still more, wavering finally between 16 and 19 degrees of inclination. But the ship continued to drop with frightening rapidity.

"She's still heavy, General," reported Commander Zappi, who was standing near the elevator wheel at his usual post and could see that all controls were fighting the descent.

"Alessandrini!" Nobile shouted above the wind at the foreman rigger, who had poked his head down the ladderway hatch to see what the trouble was. "Run aloft and check the stern valves." One cause of the stubborn action of the ship could be that hydrogen was escaping astern, possibly where condensed moisture had frozen on an escape valve and jimmied it partway open. The rigger, his face deathly white, scrambled up the ladder leading through a hatch in the roof of the cabin and disappeared sternward along the gangway in the airship's keel.

"Look! There is the ice pack!" Dr. Malmgren, in the very nose of the cabin, where he was handling the ship's directional steering wheel, was the first to see the treacherous rubble of ice below. He clutched the wheel spokes so tightly that his knuckles went white, vainly attempting to ease the *Italia* away from what he hoped was nothing worse than a localized downdraft of air currents, caused by vacuum pockets or temperature changes.

The others tried to peer below through the ice-encrusted glass of the ports. It was almost impossible because of the increasing slant of the cabin floor. When Nobile leaped to one of the side windows, he was horrified to see how close the ice pack was. Yet, rather than having the sensation of falling, he seemed to feel that the ice was rising toward him, as though lifted by a gigantic tidal surge in the cold sea beneath it. Now he had to accept the fact that the airship, even with full power and nose tilted skyward as much as 21 degrees, could not counteract the unknown force pressing her downward. She was about to crash.

•

"Stop all engines! Close all ignitions!" There was nothing humanly possible to do except prepare for the crash and minimize the danger of fire and explosion from the highly volatile hydrogen gas in the long, cigar-shaped envelope of the ship overhead.

"The elevators have lost all response!" shouted Zappi the moment power was diminished. "This wheel is dead." He had rushed to the starboard side to take over the elevator controls.

"Ballast! Cecioni, heave the ballast chain!" ordered Nobile. This was a heavy chain, weighted at intervals with what looked like small cannon balls, usually lowered like a rope ladder during landing operations. As each metal ball touched ground during the final 100 feet or so of descent, the airship was lightened by a few pounds and thus brought more gently to earth. But Cecioni was having difficulty untying the line that secured the chain to its bracket because of the unnatural angle of the cabin and the difficulty he had hanging on.

"Hurry up! Hurry up!" The ice pack was less than 100 yards below them.

Then, abruptly, Nobile realized that, although the starboard and stern engines had sputtered to a stop as ordered, the port propeller was still rotating at full speed and sucking the airship into a sharp bank. He leaned out an open porthole in the flimsy canvas walls of the pilot cabin and shouted across to engineman Caratti, who for some reason had not gotten his signal. At the same instant he glanced back and saw that the third—or stern—engine, which hung by guy wires from the weight-heavy tail of the *Italia*, was about to strike the ice.

Inside he caught an unforgettable glimpse of motor foreman Vincenzo Pomella throwing up his hands to protect his face from the impact. Nobile ducked his own head inside again, and through the forward pilot window, to which he rushed instinctively to help Malmgren hold the wrenching wheel, he could see the ice rushing up at him. There was not even a layer of snow to pad the blow, just sharp-toothed blocks of jagged white that looked as hard and unresisting as granite.

"God save us!" With the words on his lips, Nobile felt the breath jarred from him as there came a bone-crushing impact. A spar of framework butted him brutally across the head; then he was twisted and thrust downward by fabric and cables above. Clearly, and almost as though it were not really happening to him, he heard his leg snap. He shut his eyes, and the thought burned caustically across his brain as he blacked out, "It's all over now."

When the dirigible crashed on the ice pack in the Arctic Ocean northeast of Spitsbergen at approximately 810°14′ of latitude north, 280 14′ longitude east, on the morning of May 25, 1928, the disaster marked the beginning of what was to become an epic struggle for survival. It also initiated one of the most extensive series of arctic searches in the annals of polar expeditions.

Chief technician Natale Cecioni remembered little about the actual crash. At one point he cried out, "We don't have time to waste!" This was when Commander Zappi lunged over to try to spin the elevator wheel so the bow would point skyward. It was only moments later that Cecioni was ordered to the center of the cabin to lower the heavy ballast chain to help break the fall. He was still wrestling with this on his hands and knees when there came a smashing impact and he was spun forward in a somersault and hurled through a tearing wall of canvas and struts feet first onto a mound of fractured ice, where he lay with a splintering pain in his legs.

Engineer Felice Trojani, at the engine signals, was in the process of giving orders to the three enginemen when the crash came. He felt the cabin slant sharply toward the right side. There was a shrill scraping sound as the rear engine boat slammed against chunks of ice. Then he too was projected violently out of the cabin, through torn and tearing canvas, and onto soft snow. He rolled over several times and instantly got to his feet, automatically taking off his glasses, which had not even gotten cracked, to wipe the snow powder from them. For an instant he thought he was alone; then he saw other human figures moving in the snowy glare. It was a strange and almost unreal sight. Part of the cabin seemed to be loose on the ice pack, yet above him the dark mass of the *Italia*'s bag rose in slow motion, its massive prow tilted slightly skyward, two of its engines dangling motionless as though they might spin to life at someone's command. The left wall of the canvas-and-frame cabin remained attached, with torn strips of fabric fluttering below it like banners. A few ropes trailed, along with three or four ragged ends of metal framework. On the side of the bag, just above the wedge-shaped keel, he could clearly read the huge black letters **I T A L I A**.

The envelope itself was creased like a dried-up hot dog. Then the whole airship drifted lazily northward, gathering speed in the wind, as though some unseen power plant within had started operating.

Before the crash Alfredo Viglieri was still standing at the chart table with Commander Mariano, noting that the distance from Kings Bay appeared to be about 175 miles, when he realized the airship was doomed. Looking out one of the starboard portholes near the chart table, he could see the ice growing closer. He was already bracing himself with his hands against the table in order to offset the slant of the cabin floor, so he simply poised there, knees slightly bent to absorb the shock, and waited for the crash.

Beside him, Mariano was doing the same thing.

Viglieri glanced aft for a brief moment, feeling that perhaps the rear end of the cabin would absorb the shock and the airship would merely skid along the ice and stop, in a kind of crash landing. Then he saw that the stern engine gondola was barely twenty yards above the ice and that it was going to strike hard. He had time to think of nothing else. Even as he turned his head forward again, there came a great shudder, followed immediately by shattering sound. Uneven masses of ice loomed outside the porthole, and Viglieri found himself lying in a tangle of canvas and bent framework, waiting for other debris to collapse on top of him.

Suddenly, it was much brighter than it had been, as though the sun had briefly appeared through the clouds. Then he realized that the roof of the cabin had been torn loose, the way you would rip off a box top. And the bag itself was rising instead of collapsing on top of him. As he rose awkwardly to his feet, miraculously unhurt, he saw far above him the vision of one man, gripping the bent handrails of the gangway to the starboard engine. The man stared down with a look of utter horror. Was it horror at the sight below him or terror at realizing he was being carried back into the sky?

Cecioni, lying on the ice with his face up, saw the great bag above him too, so close that for a few moments he thought it was descending on top of him. His first thought was that the hydrogen might catch fire, and he could not get up and run because both legs were injured. Then the bag seemed to move upward again, away from him. And he could make out Ugo Lago and Dr. Aldo Pontremoli, awakened from their sleep by the last-minute shouts and orders and about to descend to the pilot cabin to see what was the matter. They stared down through the torn gap where the companionway should have been, looks of astonishment frozen on their faces and their mouths open but not uttering a sound. Near them Alessandrini clutched a broken girder, his eyes wide with horror as he saw the men tumbled out on the ice and the mass of wreckage below.

Of the six men still aloft, only chief engineer Ettore Arduino, with his quick reflexes and instinctive alertness, made a move. The sub-lieutenant, apparently sensing immediately what had happened and realizing that the crippled ship could never hope to return to the scene, was tossing overboard fuel, provisions, equipment—anything he could lay his hands on. This courageous gesture provided the group on the ice pack with supplies that became their only hope of survival.

For Petty Officer Second Class Giuseppe Biagi, the crash was a tragedy that he had been expecting silently and stoically for the two hours that preceded it. He alone, of all those in the pilot cabin, had no final-minute activity to occupy his mind as the *Italia* plummeted onto the ice pack. He had no elevator wheel to struggle with, no ballast chain to untangle. And it was too late, in those days of spotty radio communication, to make contact and click out any kind of wireless message. He hunched there, immobile and numb, as, looking out on the right side of the cabin, which was heavily down, he saw the ice rising toward him at frightening speed. He closed his eyes and for some reason instinctively wrapped his arms around the small emergency radio set as though it would in some way protect him from the impact. The right side of the cabin struck first, though Biagi did not later recall hearing any great noise—just a kind of crunching of brittle framework against brittle ice. The radio slammed painfully into his stomach. Then all was quiet.

For several minutes Biagi lay beside the radio and the wreckage of the cabin that had been his home for so many hours in the air. The wind had been knocked from his lungs, and he felt as though he were under clear water where he could see everything around him but could not breathe. After the dark confines of the radio cubicle, the white glare of the arctic ice seemed to swallow everything else up in it.

Off to one side he heard Mariano's voice intoning, almost in annoyance, "*Va bene, va bene* . . . all right, all right, we are here." It seemed like a strange, laconic remark to make in the face of such disaster. Then the voice continued peevishly, "Where is the general?"

Slowly, Biagi rose to his feet, gasping for air and testing each limb in order to see which ones were broken and in pain. Except for the ache where the radio had jarred his ribs, he seemed to be intact. Close by, he heard a moan, curiously drawn out by the whistling wind. It was Natale Cecioni, badly injured. Near him lay Nobile, Malmgren, and Zappi. Nobile, always slight and fragile in appearance, had blood on his head and seemed to be dead. Four others were standing up: Mariano, Behounek, Trojani, and Viglieri.

Then Nobile stirred and, without getting up, began talking in a ghostly, hollow voice. His words were indistinguishable to Biagi but were apparently part of a prayer, for the radio operator made out what sounded like "Lift your hearts to God." Then the general started to shake with emotion and in a vibrant, unearthly voice cried out. His words echoed against sounding blocks of ice: "*Viva l'Italia! Viva l'Italia!*" Others took up the chant, and Biagi heard the words slip from his own throat, though he did not know why he said them.

After a few more minutes, Mariano turned to the injured and began trying to determine the extent of their wounds. Nobile and Cecioni were the most badly hurt. Both had broken legs. Nobile also had a broken right arm and seemed to have fractured a rib. Malmgren had an injured shoulder, and Zappi was complaining about a severe pain in his chest. Biagi assisted as best he could, though he had no knowledge of first aid. Then he noticed the radio transmitter near him and cried out, "The radio! Our field radio is intact!" Every man turned toward him, the ones lying on the ice as well as those who were standing. It was a moment of great hope.

General Nobile partially rose on his uninjured left arm at this and spoke softly to Mariano. "I feel myself dying. I think I have only a few hours to live and cannot do anything for you. Do all you can yourself to save our men." He motioned toward Biagi and the radio set, as though indicating that this was the key to survival.

"Yes, General," replied Mariano. "Set your mind at rest. Now there is hope. Soon we shall be in communication with the *Citta di Milano*."

Nobile started to sink back, but suddenly he sat up again. His eye had caught sight of a dark object in the snow beyond the pitiful group of survivors and half hidden by hummocks of ice. It was one of the large canvas emergency sacks. He called to Mariano to get to it as quickly as possible, for it contained essential items they would need for survival, including a silk tent, provisions, and at least one sleeping bag. Mariano gave a sharp order, and Trojani quickly retrieved the sack and untied the cord at the neck. In addition to the items mentioned, it also contained a fur bag, boxes of pemmican and chocolate, a Colt revolver with one hundred cartridges, a Very signal pistol, and matches.

In the meantime, Biagi, having determined that the radio set was in fair shape, immediately began searching for other pieces of equipment with which to erect an aerial and get the transmitter in operation. There was so much debris on all sides that he thought there must be among the rubble some valuable items of equipment that should be salvaged at once. In his search, he wandered away from the group. It was then that he found Pomella.

Vincenzo Pomella, thirty, the foreman motor mechanic, had been in the rear engine gondola at the time of the crash. His gondola had been wrenched loose, and there were bits of wreckage scattered in evidence of the force of the impact. He was seated on a block of ice. He had one shoe off and was bent forward in a position to put it on and retie it.

To Biagi, the motionless Pomella looked dazed. He walked over to his comrade and shook him by the shoulder. "Are you all right, Vincenzo?" Pomella did not answer. Biagi shook him slightly again. This time Pomella merely toppled forward and rolled over on the ice. One side of his face was blackened as though from a crushing bruise, and there was a dark blotch of blood oozing from his blue-lipped mouth. He was dead.

After Biagi had reported the tragedy to Commander Mariano, he set about methodically erecting an antenna from several lengths of steel tubing that had broken loose from the dirigible. This framework he attached to a solid section that had once served as a compass binnacle in the pilot cabin, securing the whole contraption firmly with guy wires fashioned from some snapped control cables. The antenna was quite presentable when finished, and Biagi, in a mood of great optimism, even attached a small strip of cloth at the top, bearing the colors of Italy.

Within a few hours, Biagi had the set in operation, with the transmitter properly tuned, and was ready to send out his call. "SOS *Italia* . . . SOS *Italia* . . ." Life on the floe had begun.

Of all the survivors on the ice pack, only one was happy: Nobile's little terrier, Titina. When the ship crashed, she had been thrown clear without so much as a bruise. Accustomed to life aboard an airship, she had reacted as if this were merely a routine, though bumpy, landing, and had scampered out across the ice pack to sniff at odd pieces of wreckage and lick patches of salty ice. She returned to the scene of the crash as the men were picking themselves up and attempting to determine the extent of their injuries. She was an odd sight amidst the pain and confusion, and several of the survivors gazed at her in mute disbelief. They had almost forgotten Titina was aboard, so quietly and unobtrusively had she conducted herself on the trip.

For Nobile, the first day on the ice pack was a tortured nightmare. He lay immobile, unable to help himself because

of the fractures and pain in his left leg and arm and the tight-
ness in his chest that prevented him from breathing without a
searing pain. After several hours on the ice, he realized
through a kind of delirium that he was becoming numb with
the cold. "The sleeping bag," he mumbled. "Please bring it
here and get me into it, if you can. Then I shall be able to die
here in peace."

Though the others were clothed in heavy coats lined with
lamb's wool at the time of the crash, Nobile, as was his habit,
was wearing only a woolen jersey, a catskin waistcoat and
lightweight army officer's trousers. "Bring the bag here at
once," ordered Mariano, who, as second in command and uninjured, was trying to supervise the welfare of the wretched
little group. Little by little, he eased Nobile into the sleeping
bag, a task made difficult because the general's broken limbs
gave him excruciating pain at the slightest movement. Once
inside, he passed out from pain and exhaustion and lay motionless for almost an hour.

When he came to again, he saw Mariano, Viglieri, Trojani,
and Behounek wandering across the icy wastes searching for
materials that might have fallen into crevasses. Commander
Zappi, the only survivor with formal training in first aid, was
attending to the broken legs of Cecioni, who sat on an ice
hummock gruffly cursing his luck. But Zappi himself was in
poor condition, with an intense pain in his chest and several
ribs badly bruised if not broken. He clenched his teeth every

time he bent over to wrap strips of cloth around the impro-
vised splints on the mechanic's legs.

"Now it is your turn, general," he said, seeing that Nobile
had revived somewhat. With great difficulty, Nobile was
pulled out of the sleeping bag. After his arm and leg were ban-
daged in crude fashion, the bag was slit at one side and both
Nobile and Cecioni were placed in it, since they were the
only two men who could not move about to keep warm.

Through the haze of pain and shock, accentuated by the
constant strain of the flight and the many hours without sleep,
Nobile vacillated between agonized consciousness and a kind
of semi-coma. In the latter, he could not control his thoughts
and saw faces constantly revolving around him as though he
were in some kind of seance. He saw the faces of his wife and
daughter, his younger brother, and others who were close to
him. But, more clearly and persistently, he kept seeing the haggard faces of his colleagues on the ill-fated expedition.

Vincenzo Pomella—with the boyish face and blue eyes—
who had been on the *Norge* expedition, and who used to work
two, or even three days on end without sleep, was now asleep
forever. He was the only one yet known to be dead. And his
parents—they were in southern Italy somewhere, perhaps
even now wondering how this fair-haired son who loved adventure was making out, whether he was eating well and staying warm enough, and performing his duties in the same com-
mendable way he had on the *Norge*.

THE DOWNFALL

By this time, counting noses, the survivors had realized which of their companions were missing. Where were the other motormen? Drifting north still? Or had the bag of the *Italia* been successfully brought down on the ice, perhaps not far away? There was Arduino, the one who had been seen throwing supplies out of the huge, flopping bag as it rose. It was just like him, always calm and serene and cool in emergencies. Never grumbling or criticizing or complaining, despite hardships. How valuable it would have been to have him here on the ice as a companion—dependable, a genius when it came to putting broken parts together and making them work. Well, Arduino would have a good companion—if they still lived: Caratti, handsome and gregarious. And then there was that other old hand from the *Norge*, Renato Alessandrini. Memories. "You are growing a little fat, Renato. . . ." Nobile's lips parted in an unconscious laugh. Yes, the jolly Alessandrini had put on a great deal of weight since the last flight two years ago. But how like a monkey he was, even so! Scrambling up and down the ladderways, racing along the catwalk with never a finger laid on the grab rails, balancing along the rubberized fabric at the very top of the *Italia*'s envelope, checking the hydrogen escape valves. "You must not eat too much, Renato. You will never get through the hole in the prow . . ."

More faces of those who had vanished in the bag. Not quite so clear now. Ciocca. Slender and lean, always cheerful. An old associate, who, despite youth, had worked on dirigibles as a mechanic for years. What was there he could not fix? Great endurance.

Then there was Ugo Lago, the journalist. An impetuous Sicilian with expressive dark eyes and a volatile personality. Lago, who, as an alternate for Tomaselli (the second journalist back at the base), had been selected for the Pole flight by a flip of a coin. How like a schoolboy he had been in his excitement as the coin had flipped into the air and Fate had selected him—not Tomaselli—for the final flight.

And last, of the six men who had vanished aloft in the bag of the *Italia*, there was Aldo Pontremoli, formerly professor of physics at the University of Milan, who even now might have been quietly at home conducting experiments to add to his already extensive scientific knowledge. If the remains of the *Italia* should be brought safely to the ice, Pontremoli would be invaluable to the survivors in planning methods of existing until rescue came. Mentally alert, physically strong, he had such a zest for the expedition he had been frequently found pumping fuel, helping to repair torn fabric, reinforcing braces, and doing any of a dozen other chores that were not his responsibility at all. Nobile moved slightly in the bulky sleeping bag, and suddenly the sharp needles of pain that seemed to pierce his leg to the bone roused him from his dreamlike thoughts. For a few minutes he himself had been up there, floating in the broken bag with the six lost men, seeing each one as he reacted to the tragic emergency. He moaned and shook himself, and his eyes began to focus on the desolate scene around him. This was the reality, this little patch of crumpled ice, the scattered supplies, the broken parts of the airship, the pain-seared bulk of Natale Cecioni lying beside him.

Although dazed at first, Nobile found his head clearing to the extent that he could evaluate what had happened and begin trying to determine their chances of survival. He was certain that his own chances were slim, given the extent of his injuries and no hope of medical attention. It was fortunate at least, he ratonalized, that the three naval officers were alive and in good condition. Mariano, though far from the athletic type, was strong and capable. Zappi was energetic and resilient, and not likely to lose his head in any emergency. And Viglieri, the youngest at twenty-eight, was physically strong, completely dependable, and loyal to the point of a high degree of personal sacrifice when necessary.

Nobile was worried, however, about his engineer, Felice Trojani. He was a Roman, used to city life, a slight man, who might easily be the first to break down physically under the rigors of the forced imprisonment on the ice. Still, he was a clever technician, had always been calm and reflective during the twelve years the general had known him, and might be of great use to Biagi in repairing and maintaining the emergency radio set.

Of all the survivors, it was Finn Malmgren who caused the general the most concern. He was a brilliant man yet often a moody one. Nobile held tremendous respect for Malmgren's scientific ability. Had he not felt this way, he would never have taken the advice of the meteorologist to return westward to Kings Bay rather than head eastward, with the wind, toward Mackenzie Bay in northern Canada. Now, more than ever, they might need Finn's expertise and experience in predicting sea and weather conditions.

Shortly after the crash, Malmgren had approached Nobile and, stooping grotesquely because he had injured his shoulder, said, "General, I thank you for the trip. I go now under the water!" With that, he turned and headed for an open channel of water, intent on drowning himself and ending his misery at once.

"No, no, Finn," Nobile had gasped. "You do not have the right to do this. We will all die when God has decided, not us."

Malmgren had then turned back, with a look of surprise. He had not expected the general to give such an order. After all, he was injured, perhaps critically, he said. So he would be a hindrance to the others and lessen their chance of survival. He slumped down on the ice in a sitting position and put his head in his hands—the picture of total dejection.

Nobile thought this was the end of his morbid thoughts, but he was mistaken. Later in the day, the Norwegian attempted to slip away with the revolver, intent on putting a bullet to his head. This time, it was Commander Mariano who spotted his purpose and prevented the suicide attempt. He was adamant in ordering Malmgren to remove such thoughts from his mind, emphasizing that they needed his skills badly if they were to survive and determine how to exist on the ice pack and know what weather to expect and how and when the ice might break up and present new dangers to them.

Although Malmgren yielded, it was obvious that he was despondent and blamed himself for having given inaccurate meteorological advice and thus placing the airship in an untenable situation that made the crash inevitable. No amount of consolation on the part of Mariano and the others seemed to convince him that he was not to blame.

Unlike the depressed Malmgren, who seemed unable—at least for the time being—to play an active role in establishing the camp, the other non-Italian on the expedition, Dr. Francis Behounek of Prague, set about his duties as though the disaster were just a routine affair. He knew far less about arctic conditions than his fellow scientist, but he did have an intense stamina and will to survive. He was the calm, thoughtful personality whose composure could be no more disturbed by unexpected calamity than his massive frame could be ruffled by a summer breeze. He held great respect for Commander Mariano. "That man directs everything with complete calmness and composure," he remarked to Nobile, "as if he were aboard his little naval craft in calm Chinese waters."

When Mariano, Viglieri, Trojani, and Behounek had collected what provisions they could, they surveyed the ice pack to determine where there were cracks that might widen as the sea below heaved and swelled, and then carefully erected the small, eight-by-eight-foot tent on what seemed like the safest site, a sheet of relatively smooth ice about fifty yards square. Under its protection they stored the food rations, and around its perimeter they stacked other supplies found.

By the end of the day, the emergency camp was presentable enough to give the survivors hope that they could hold out for rescue—provided, of course, that Biagi could make contact with their supply ship without delay. The tent, designed for only four occupants, was cramped and uncomfortable with ten men and little Titina crowded into it as they settled down to try to sleep and build up their strength for the hardships to come.

In every man's mind was the picture of the makeshift radio tower, and in every man's ear the imaginary echo of the brief messages Biagi had sent out at hourly intervals, until he was too exhausted to keep on: **SOS Italia . . . SOS Italia**.

To Nobile it seemed as though he could almost see the sound waves piercing southward through the mists to Kings Bay, where at any moment a startled radio operator would be electrified by the message and shout for Giuseppe Romagna, captain of the *Citta di Milano*. Biagi had been certain the set was transmitting properly and on its assigned wavelength. Yes, from here on, it was just a matter of time before the message was intercepted.

How much time, how much excruciatingly slow time it was to take, the struggling survivors were going to find out before their ordeal was over.

8

PICKING UP THE PIECES

Sleep the night of May 25 was almost impossible, not only because there was little distinction between night and day, but also because there was almost no way to lie down in any kind of comfortable position. Except for the injured Nobile and Cecioni in the sleeping bag, most of the others catnapped in sitting positions, huddled inside the tent.

Early the next day, they searched the area for any equipment and supplies not already collected. Among those found scattered over the ice were two sextants, a mercury artificial horizon, calculating tables, and chronometers. By great good fortune, these articles had been on the cabin wall that remained on the ice, along with two navigational charts of the area. Commander Mariano assembled these in one location, and on the 26th there were enough breaks in the clouds so he could take sun sights and calculate their position as 81°14′ of latitude north and 28°14′ of longitude east.

"It is not too accurate," he apologized, "but it will do for now, especially since we cannot give out our position to any living soul anyway."

Because the intervals of breaks in the clouds were short, it was impossible to get accurate sightings. But in any event, Mariano knew they were somewhat to the northeast of several small islands, notably Charles XII, Foyn, and Broch. The drift of the current was southeast, which might sweep the ice pack close to one or more of the islands within a matter of days. General Nobile was heartened by this news. With any luck, they might even drift to the top of Northeast Land.

With all remaining supplies located, they estimated that they had enough emergency rations for twenty-five days with each man getting a daily portion of three hundred grams of solid nourishment, mostly in the form of pemmican and chocolate. The men hoped to supplement these provisions by catching fish near the edge of the floe on which they were situated.

The tent had been erected on a high stretch of flat ice, not only for dryness, but also for visibility. To make it more conspicuous to search planes, the survivors daubed the walls with red dye from several unbroken altitude bombs. These were glass balls filled with red liquid, designed to be dropped from high altitudes. By timing the period from the moment of release until the bombs splattered on impact, a navigator could determine an airship's altitude over any given point of land or ice. And thus it was that the pitiful little shelter, more muddy and drab than bright, acquired the name by which it would be known throughout the world: The Red Tent.

What with food supplies and surplus items of clothing brought in for protection against dampness, the cramped little tent became even more choked. Part of the radio equipment had to be brought in, for instance, for protection from the elements, along with the batteries, which might have been weakened by exposure to the cold and damp salt air.

The tent had a fabric floor, designed so that it could be pitched directly on ice. And the interior had been purposely designed with a soft blue tone, as relief from the white glare of the ice outside. This tiny world, barely high enough to stand up in, was to be a virtual prison for Nobile, and even more so for Cecioni, in the weeks to come. It was also to be the scene of a great deal of debate and argument as taut nerves became frayed and the officers had conflicting opinions on various courses of action.

One of the first clashes came when the dog, Titina, had the misfortune to bang against Cecioni's injured, and highly sensitive, leg. The mechanic swore, in great pain, swatting the animal with his large hand.

Nobile protested, then ordered Cecioni moved to another part of the tent. The mechanic had already complained several times, that located close to the radio equipment, he was always being accidentally knocked by Biagi. But he did not relish the new position either, since it was darker and colder than where he had been.

"Do you want me to die, General," he muttered peevishly, "putting me over here?"

"Don't complain," responded the general, irritated at the clout Cecioni had given the dog. "Even that place is too good for you."

Much of the tension came from frustration over the problems of radio communication and extreme exasperation at the apparent stupidity of the personnel aboard the *Citta di Milano*. Every two hours Biagi would hear the same meaningless transmission. "We have not heard your radio again. We are listening for you on the 900-meter band and on short wave. We imagine you are near the north coast of Spitsbergen, between the fifteenth and twentieth meridians [far, far from their actual position]. Trust in us. We are organizing help."

Over and over this message would be repeated, yet it was evident that the *Citta* was sending it only as a routine, and that the ship's radio was doing little, if any, monitoring in an attempt to raise a signal from the missing survivors. In fact, most of the messages Biagi picked up continued to be personal messages from those aboard the base ship to families back home. "Do not worry about us," was the context of most of these. "We are safe and in good health!"

In a more favorable light, though the *Citta*'s messages were irritating in the extreme, Biagi did intercept several hopeful news bulletins from the broadcasting station at San Paolo in Rome. He learned that all of Europe had expressed anxiety over the *Italia*, and that rescue expeditions were to be formed.

Life began to settle into a routine about two days after the crash. Each man was assigned a certain time and place within the tiny tent. Watches were set up, so there was always one man scanning the skies and the horizon (when it was visible) for signs of search planes or a ship. Or, as Malmgren advised, to raise sight of land, since he estimated that the current in this part of the Arctic Ocean would carry the ice pack steadily southward. Routine duties were also assigned by Nobile and by Mariano, the second in command, not because there was much housekeeping to take care of, but to keep minds and hands occupied.

The biggest problem of the moment was cold. None of the men were adequately clothed for existence on the pack. Biagi, for example, was the only one wearing leather boots at the time of the crash. The others had what was referred to as "Eskimo footwear," heavy enough and warm enough but not solid on the bottom for walking around on sharp ice.

Sleep continued to be difficult, no matter what steps were taken to provide a buffer between their bodies and the floor of the tent, which was as hard as cement, uneven, and bumpy and of course just as cold as the ice underneath it. There was only one blanket, which five or six men might be trying to use at the same time, stretching it over them and huddling close together for warmth. The man who slept next to Behounek

was always envied, for the big Czech was by far the most cor-
pulent member of the group and radiated the most warmth
over the largest area.

Shelter itself became a symbol of hope. The Red Tent was
not only the beacon that they hoped would eventually guide
searchers to them, but it was also a symbol of protection—on
the outside against the weather, and on the inside, with its
soft color, against the relentless, blinding glare of the Arctic.

This compulsion with the idea of shelter was evidenced by
one petty incident that occurred several days after the crash.
In searching for supplies that might have been scattered over
a wide area, the survivors constantly had to pass by the body
of their unfortunate comrade, Pomella. He had been turned so
his face was down and partially covered by snow and ice in an
attempt to form a makeshift grave. Yet no one could rest content until a crude roof had been raised over the body, fabri-
cated from some pieces of canvas and metal tubing from the
wreckage.

Two large tins of dry matches had been found among the
scattered supplies, so there was never any question about
lighting a fire. Fuel, however, was something else. There was a
little petrol; some odds and ends of useless material that was
inflammable, such as splintered framework from the cabin
and strips of canvas from the fabric skin; and a little paper. A
cooking pot was made from an old petrol tin, cut off at the top
and scoured repeatedly with snow until the inside was relatively free of the original contents. In this, pemmican was

cooked in the form of soup. It had an unappetizing taste at first, and in appearance was even less attractive. It always looked dirty, and when dipped out of the tin pot with a metal cup, sticky drops would cling to the sides like beads of sweat or grease.

The pemmican was complemented with some scraps of chocolate doled out as dessert. The biggest problem, however, was water. Malmgren was appointed to take over this problem, since he was more familiar than any of the others with methods of obtaining water. Locating freshwater ice was extremely difficult, to the astonishment of most of the men, who had felt that they simply had to melt a little snow or some of the higher chunks of ice to get potable water. It was from Malmgren's explorations that enough water was collected in another petrol tin to prepare the first meal of pemmican soup. The mixture had a distinctive flavor of peas, though a little salty, and was relished more for its warmth than its taste.

By this time, all of the rations had been gathered from various parts of the ice. At final count, these consisted of 160 pounds of pemmican, 90 pounds of chocolate, 20 pounds of malted milk, 7 pounds of butter, and 7 pounds of sugar. There was also a small chunk of provolone cheese left over from luncheon supplies put aboard at Kings Bay, and a box of Liebig's meat extract, a delicacy that had been found in the dead Pomella's knapsack. The 284 pounds of rations made the situation much brighter, increasing the original estimate of a twenty-five-day food supply to forty-five days.

Another good sign—more spiritual—was the discovery, intact in the snow, of a small image of the Madonna of Loreto, which had accompanied Nobile on the *Norge* flight, as well as on the *Italia*. This was immediately, and reverently, affixed to the lone pole in the center of the Red Tent. It was kept company by two more items discovered shortly thereafter: photographs of the Queen and of Mussolini.

After the distraction of gathering supplies, the morale of the survivors went quickly into a decline. Two factors were largely responsible for this. The first was the weather. Though the wind finally shifted, in a well-delayed response to Malmgren's prediction when he recommended the course of the return flight, the weather continued to be oppressive. Clouds pressed down from overhead, and the damp mists churned around on all sides, giving the impression of meteorological imprisonment as well as physical isolation.

The second was the radio reception. With each passing hour, the chances of making contact with the *Citta* seemed more and more remote. The clear reception of San Paolo and other stations on the receiver indicated that there was nothing wrong atmospherically to interrupt radio transmission, and that therefore it must be some undetected flaw in Biagi's transmitter that was preventing contact with the outside world. So the factor that had raised their spirits the most in those first gloomy hours was now proving to be insubstantial. Only two people continued, with grim determination, to have faith in the radio: Biagi and Nobile.

PICKING UP THE PIECES

The men began to drift into a kind of morbid complacency, safe for the time being, with enough food, and with little idea of what to do next other than to sit tight and wait. But this security was due for a rude shock. On the night of May 27, when all but a single lookout remained in the tent to sleep, there came a sudden, unexpected report like the sound of an artillery piece in action. It was followed by the ear-splitting noise of ice in movement.

"The pack is breaking up!" shouted Malmgren, who recognized the sound for what it was, the sudden splitting of ice. "All outside at once!"

Those nearest the entrance threw open the flap, while the others seized Nobile and Cecioni and began half carrying, half dragging them outside. Underfoot they could feel an immense heaving and shuddering as the rotten, decaying ice was fractured somewhere beyond the nearby hummocks.

"How serious is the movement?" asked Nobile.

"I don't know," replied Malmgren soberly, "but if a break occurs near the tent, we should move immediately to another location on the pack—perhaps one hundred yards to the east."

Biagi edged over to the tent's entrance, ready to dash inside and snatch up his radio if the peril increased. Then, as abruptly as it had begun, the noise subsided, leaving only a kind of faraway echo in the distance. The danger was over. But this was a natural alarm they were to hear time and time again, and always with the same painful shock to their nerves.

During periods of despondency, some of the crew even expressed the opinion that it would be better to be hurled into the water and drown in a matter of minutes than to continue this increasingly hopeless and excruciating existence on the ice.

This dreary existence on the floe was in sharp contrast to the earlier functions of the explorers as members of a well-coordinated crew. Whereas each man had previously been energetically engaged in the duties of flying the airship, and pursuing responsibilities for which he had been specifically trained, he was now without familiar duties, with few clear-cut responsibilities, and with almost no training for meeting the unpredictable situation. What had in flight been a unifying force—teamwork—started to disintegrate, sometimes leading to clashes of opinion and authority that would never have occurred in flight.

Mariano and Zappi, as naval officers of equal rank, tended to draw together, unconsciously forming a solid unit of their own to stand up against conflicting units. Cecioni lay alone in his physical anguish, paralleled by Trojani, who, somewhat of an introvert to begin with, stood apart from the rest in his own mental misery. Malmgren and Behounek were drawn together by their scientific interests. Viglieri was perhaps the least affected by this new life, since he had borne less responsibility in the air than his two superior officers and was more or less accustomed to being occupied with a variety of assignments.

Biagi, by contrast, began to emerge as an unobtrusively heroic type. Quiet and hard-working on board the airship, he had been overlooked, one way or another, by his companions because radio was little regarded in those days. Now, however, he had emerged as the only man familiar with that mysterious device developed by another Italian, Marconi, which might help in the end to save the survivors. In this new role, Biagi assumed his responsibility with determination. He alone was too absorbed in his job to become involved with many of the petty bickerings to which the others fell prey. If there was one man who could be singled out as generally liked and respected by all the survivors without question, it was Giuseppe Biagi.

The case of General Umberto Nobile was another matter. By his own admission, he had never considered himself as a military superior but rather a civilian commander of the expedition. He preferred not to give orders when he could make suggestions or recommendations. He wished to be considered as a kind of "head of family" rather than an officer, and as a scientist and engineer rather than a tactical leader. This role was an untenable one from the moment the dirigible crashed.

While in the air, and even more when organizing and planning the expedition, Nobile's engineering skill and aeronautical background had been more than adequate to weld the members of the expedition together in a common purpose. Now, however, in the unfamiliar surroundings of the pack, he did not grasp the necessity of having one man as an absolute leader. Nor did he perceive the demand for rigid, military-style discipline. He felt, too, that his physical disability required him to relinquish some of his authority and in its place substitute group discussion, whereas his decision should have been just the opposite: to hold all members of the group strictly accountable to him as the commander, to weigh differences of opinion, and to make final decisions in such a manner that no misunderstandings lingered after he had issued his directions.

At the moment, however, the question of leadership seemed of little consequence to any of the survivors. Food, shelter, and the other physical requirements of just plain existing were the only things that mattered. Later, they would also be greatly concerned by another disturbing factor: the speed and direction in which the ice pack was moving relentlessly and beyond all human control.

Three days after the crash, on May 28, an island was sighted. It was nothing more than a dark speck far beyond the white hummocks of ice, yet it loomed in each man's sight as large in importance as though it had been an entire continent. Land!

"That is Charles XII Island, I am sure," said Mariano, after taking sights and studying the damp, badly creased chart salvaged from the wreckage. "Yet, if my first observations were anywhere near correct three days ago, we have drifted a substantial distance in a very short time . . . as much as twenty-eight miles."

The weather shift that Finn Malmgren had predicted just before the crash had brought an increase in the movement of the ice pack.

PICKING UP THE PIECES

Was this a good sign or a bad one? No one knew. On the one hand, the rapid drift of the ice could carry them quickly to a large body of land such as Cape Leigh Smith, or it could, on the other hand, sweep them far to the southeast, toward the great unknown territory the *Italia* had partially explored several weeks before.

Nobile and Mariano concluded that the drift would eventually carry them toward Franz Josef Land. This was dismal news, for Franz Josef Land was a desolate wasteland where they might never be found, even if they succeeded in leaving the pack and setting up camp ashore. Nobile asked for the soggy copy of *Arctic Pilot*, the only book they had found and, fortunately, most valuable under the circumstances. On page 264, the general read: "The principal direction of the ice stream in Northeast Land is towards the east. . . ." It was just what Malmgren had feared.

That information, combined with the sighting of Charles XII Island, set Mariano and Zappi to thinking: Would it not be possible for the survivors to march across the ice so they could go farther south when the ice pack touched Foyn Island?

"There is the problem of the injured," said Zappi aside to Mariano.

"We could construct sleds."

"Perhaps," said Zappi, "that wireless tower would make a good sled frame." He laughed bitterly. "I do not think it will ever be good for anything else, despite Biagi's confidence in his set."

Shortly after they had all received their meager ration of pemmican soup and a bit of chocolate, Nobile overheard Mariano in conversation with Malmgren. They were discussing the possibility of a march. A little while later Mariano, this time with Zappi, came to Nobile, and for the first time openly brought up the question of a march across the ice. The general immediately objected, saying the group must take no action until radio contact had been established with the *Citta di Milano*.

But he could not convince the two men that the radio offered any hope. They left him with the proposal that four men should set out immediately to march across the ice: Malmgren and the three navy officers, Mariano, Zappi, and Viglieri.

"They mustn't be allowed to go," pleaded Cecioni at once. "They ought not to abandon two helpless men just like that! We should all set out together." Cecioni had become feverish and slightly delirious from his severe injuries. Somehow he imagined he would be well in a few days. Then he would not only be fit to march, but would actually help carry the general on his strong back.

That evening, a discussion was held. Malmgren expressed the thoughts of those advocating the march, saying that all hope of the radio working was unrealistic and that the only possibility of salvation lay in sending a patrol toward Cape North in hopes of meeting potential rescue expeditions.

"Who would go?" asked Nobile.

Mariano stepped forward immediately, expressing his willingness. Zappi also volunteered, suggesting that Malmgren and the three navy officers should be the ones in the party. But Behounek, the Czech, interrupted. He and Trojani had been rejected by the others as not physically fit to endure the hardships of a forced march. "For my part, I willingly remain with the general. But I do insist that one of the naval officers stay with us. We must have someone who can take our bearings. Otherwise, what's the use of the radio operator?"

Nobile agreed but added that there was no need to rush such a serious decision and that it was better to wait a few days to see exactly how the drift was carrying the ice pack. There was another reason for his opinion: he was certain that Biagi's transmitter would soon make contact. What was more, Biagi had that very evening, before the discussion, intercepted a message saying that the *Hobby* in search of the *Italia* crew, was about to proceed to Hinlopen Bay, a point much closer to the survivors. The closer it came, the greater the chance that the SOS from Biagi would be picked up. The meeting ended with Malmgren, Mariano, and Zappi disappointed that they had not pushed their plan across immediately.

On the morning of May 29, Charles XII Island was no longer in sight. In its place they could make out two small islands, which they identified as Broch and Foyn, some ten miles away to the south and west. Cecioni, convinced he would ultimately be left behind to die, was furiously trying to

fashion a sledge from pieces of metal tubing, wire, and framework. He had plenty of tools, from one of the mechanics' bags
found in the wreckage. It was a pitiful sight to see this husky,
broad-shouldered man dragging himself painfully over the ice
and refusing all offers of help.

Because of the change in position caused by the drifting ice
pack, Biagi found that he was receiving news broadcasts better from the San Paolo radio station than from the *Citta di Milano*. Hence, in his persistent SOS calls every other hour at
the appointed time, he transmitted an additional message requesting that San Paolo transmit on a different wavelength. It
was a problem of skip distance, explained Biagi. Radio waves
frequently bounced right over close stations but could be
heard by others farther away. And so it must have been with
the pitifully small set on which Biagi and Nobile placed so
much hope.

The discussion of a possible march toward land had
brought into the conversation some deliberation on a curious
phenomenon several of the survivors had seen on the morning of May 25. About half an hour after the crash, and after
the great gas bag of the *Italia* had drifted off over the floes, a
thin column of smoke had been seen rising some miles to the
north. Then it had been obliterated by the mists.

Had this been from the dirigible? Did it mean that the *Italia*
had exploded in the air or crashed and burned on the ground?
Or was it some kind of smoke signal sent by the six men still
aboard?

PICKING UP THE PIECES

The men on the ice speculated back and forth as to whether the bag, losing gas rapidly, might also have crashed on the ice and that the survivors had lit a fire for a smoke signal. Malmgren suggested that he might take a scouting party northward. But in the end, they all realized that their first priority was to contact civilization and let a competent, well-equipped search party look for other possible survivors.

By the evening of the 29th, Commanders Mariano and Zappi could hold themselves in check no longer. They were convinced that Biagi's radio was a failure and that the expedition was doomed unless it moved to a new location where it would be sighted by rescuers. To Nobile's statements that the march should be put off a few days to see whether the *Hobby* might pick up their radio signals as she headed north, others reminded him that their provisions were limited and they had to act quickly or face starvation.

Finally, after much discussion with Malmgren, Zappi, and Mariano, the general was convinced not so much that the march would achieve the desired results, but that to forbid it would only breed dissension in the camp. Nobile wanted two men to try: Mariano and Zappi. Malmgren felt that he should be included, for a total of three. And Zappi kept insisting that the number should be four, with Viglieri added. On this point, Nobile refused to give in, and the trio was thus decided.

Malmgren estimated that they could cover about eight miles a day over the ice, but nearer land where the ice would be smoother, as much as twelve. He traced his expected route on the chart as proceeding across the ice to Foyn Island, then Cape Bruun, Cape Platen, Scoresby Island, and finally Cape North, asserting that they could cover this distance in no more than sixteen days.

The long discussion had tired the survivors, and when it had been settled that the three men should be Mariano, Zappi, and Malmgren, a feeling of relief came over the camp. Nobile tried to sleep, but the thoughts racing through his mind kept him awake in the midnight light filtering through the tent for many hours. From time to time, the bulky Cecioni lying beside him moved convulsively in his sleep and clutched at the general's arm as though to make sure he would not awaken in the morning and find himself deserted.

The sky was overcast that night, but Nobile had need for sun sights to check their position, so when the tent grew lighter around midnight and the sun started to shine through the clouds, he awakened Zappi and Mariano, and they went out to use the sextant.

In a few moments Zappi reappeared and spoke in undertones. "I saw a large bear out there on the ice!" After the rest of the sleeping men were awakened, Malmgren took the Colt pistol and crept outside. When he spotted the animal some thirty yards away from the tent, he judged it to weigh at least five hundred pounds. Behind him, Mariano and Zappi followed with a knife and an ax, to protect the scientist if the pistol, exposed to dampness, misfired. Inside the tent, Nobile grabbed his small terrier and held her mouth so she would not bark.

Closer and closer Malmgren approached. The bear looked up from its foraging but did not move. Malmgren took careful aim. His pistol seemed pitifully small in relation to this huge beast. He fired once, twice, a third time. The bear turned, ran a few paces, then collapsed and was dead.

"We should cut the animal up immediately while the flesh is still warm," advised Malmgren after he had approached cautiously to make certain no life was left. "There ought to be about four hundred pounds of meat, and the skin will be useful."

All the men except Nobile and Cecioni circled the animal to assist in the challenging operation. Bear meat! It would taste like a delicacy after the skimpy rations of the past five days.

After the meat had been partially cut up and the others had lain down again, Nobile fell asleep with great relief. This added food supply would make a great difference in their plans. Zappi, Nobile thought, would not be so eager to leave now that they were assured of ample provisions, and they could give the radio a fair test before deciding the perilous march across the ice had to be undertaken.

9

FRUSTRATION

During the uncertain period of the first few days on the ice, one name was constantly in the minds, and on the lips, of the survivors: *Citta di Milano* . . . *Citta di Milano*. On her rested their main hopes for communication and eventual rescue.

Where was this base ship now, as May drew to a close? Was she heading northward out of Kings Bay, as the news reports picked up from the San Paolo station indicated? Were the troops of the Alpini being outfitted and rationed for a forced march across the arctic wastes to look for signs of the *Italia*? Surely the officers aboard the base ship would realize that the lives of the crew members could depend on the speed of the rescue teams. While after-the-fact opinions vary, it became evident at the time that few experts in arctic exploration had any faith in the antiquated ship's ability to cope with polar storms and floating ice.

What is evident is that, back at Kings Bay, the *Citta* lay placidly at anchor day after day off the little town of Ny Aalesund, her rigging decked in colorful pennants, in direct contrast to the rusty drabness of her warped and battered old hull. On her bridge, the captain and mates paced the worn deck, uncertain what to do and convinced that the safest course was to stay put. To be fair to captain and crew, this do-nothing attitude was probably nurtured by the fact that there was no reliable information about the crash or the possible whereabouts of any survivors.

Lolling on deck in the still, cold air, the seamen could sense the atmosphere of indecision, as rumors floated around that the *Italia* was down on the ice . . . that she was floating without power, like a balloon to Alaska . . . that she had exploded in midair—or that she had slammed into an iceberg. Inside the radio shack, the steady crackling of transmitter and receiver could be heard as message after message went out over that remarkable, and somewhat mysterious, device known as the wireless. To the ordinary seaman, hearing the sound and watching the steady traffic of officers and others to the radio shack, it appeared that events of great significance were taking place, what with the number of messages being pressed upon the wireless operator.

Messages were indeed flooding the airwaves, but few could be classified as significant. First there were the news reports to various newspapers from correspondents at Kings Bay. These were little more than journalistic rehashes of the rumors and though each newsman was careful to report to his editors that nothing had yet been verified, he did not hesitate to express an imaginative opinion as to what *might* have happened. And those opinions were often received at the other end as pure statements of fact, whether because of faulty radio reception, because of the elimination of cautionary phrases when messages were condensed, or because the editors simply wanted to break a good story without cluttering it with hedges.

Then there were the personal messages, their priority and length running in direct proportion to the rank and standing of the sender. The situation brought out the ham in many a man aboard the base ship, who could not resist this splendid opportunity of having his name flung out over the ether, even though the most important thing he had to say was to "Give my love to little Antonio for me," or "Don't forget that Father Dominic's birthday is on the sixth of June."

Finally, after some of the personal messages had simmered down, there were the long "official" communiqués from Captain Romagna to Rome. What should he do under the circumstances? Would the navy please give him orders? Was this a problem of the Air Ministry? Did the government plan on sending a search expedition? He did not want to tread on any official toes by taking the wrong step. Since the *Citta* was the expedition's base ship, the captain would naturally expect it to remain at its base until ordered to embark elsewhere.

The radio messages underwent a process in executive channels similar to erosion. After due time had elapsed and they had worn their way into official mentalities, answers would flow back through the same channels, and eventually to the *Citta*. Sometimes the process took two or three days. And the answer was usually in the form of a question: "What further information do you have on the *Italia*? We can give no orders without further information on the airship's whereabouts."

Why didn't the *Citta di Milano* proceed farther north under her own initiative at this point, when it became evident that no one in Rome was going out of his way to accept responsibility? The most popular excuse seemed to be that she was "not equipped and suited" to the task. But then neither were several small vessels of other nations that, voluntarily or under orders, were to steam at great risk into unknown seas on their own searches.

The *Citta* was, admittedly, an old hulk assigned to the Spitsbergen area to undertake hydrographic research as well as to serve as the *Italia's* base ship. She was not outfitted as an icebreaker, and her engines were too old for this type of service. Nevertheless, she could have moved freely at that time of year somewhat farther north and east than Kings Bay. The situation was in part traceable to Romagna. Although he was not personally hostile to Nobile and his officers and crew, he lacked the initiative of some of the other ship commanders who did decide to venture northward. He was further hampered by his lack of knowledge of radio and how it might be used to make and retain contact with the survivors. The *Citta* had received regular reports from Biagi during the flight to the Pole and at the start of the return trip. At seven in the morning of May 25, some three and a half hours before the crash, the *Citta* had clearly received the message from Biagi that the *Italia* was fighting head winds and needed full power to make any headway at all. Romagna had interpreted this to mean only that the airship would be late reaching the base, not that she was in dire trouble. So neither he nor his officers tried to continue communications or track the airship's course during that critical period.

It is interesting to note that, at the time of the crash and for many days thereafter, Guglielmo Marconi, the noted inventor in the field of radio, was himself aboard the *Elettra*, a ship he used for many radio experiments, in the Tyrrhenian Sea. Monitoring the airwaves to try to pick up information on the disaster, he was astounded at the messages being sent from the *Citta*, practically every one concerned with private matters. "No wonder," he said later, "that on the *Citta di Milano* the SOS of the survivors could not be picked up by radio operators. They simply were not paying attention to her signals."

Aboard the *Citta* were two people, however, who were greatly concerned over the apparent silence. The first of these was Ettore Pedretti, the member of the *Italia* expedition who had been on the memorable flight eastward over Nicholas II Land but had been left behind on the polar flight because it had been Biagi's turn for duty. Pedretti, assigned to the radio shack on the base ship, did not hesitate to criticize Romagna for his policies. But he had no authority to take any action whatsoever. And it is probable that he believed what Romagna stated so convincingly, that the survivors could not possibly have any radio operable enough to use anyway.

The second man was Amedeo Nobile, Umberto's brother, who was quartered aboard the *Citta* at the time but had no more authority than did Pedretti. His duties related to meteorological observations at the base, which were reported regularly for use in analyzing flying conditions. It had been on his reports, for example, that judgments had been made about previous takeoffs and landings of the airship. This work involved reading instruments that measured temperature, atmospheric pressure, wind and cloud speeds, humidity, and magnetism. It was not part of the research work carried on in flight by Malmgren, Pontremoli, and Behounek.

Hence, when Amedeo tried to intercede on behalf of his brother, he was told to go fly another weather kite and stop meddling in affairs in which he had no experience. So the best Amedeo had been able to do was to pay a visit to the *Hobby*, which had transported him to Kings Bay in the first place, and try to push rescue attempts from this small Norwegian steamship.

It was fortunate that the survivors on the ice pack did not realize how little was being done on their behalf by their Italian compatriots at Kings Bay.

FRUSTRATION

However, they were hardly being ignored by others. At Oslo, Norway, on the evening of May 26, a testimonial dinner was being held in honor of two daring flyers who had just flown in an aeroplane from Alaska 2,200 miles across the Arctic Ocean to Spitsbergen. The men were Sir Hubert Wilkins, an Australian hero of World War I, who was later to try to take a submarine to the North Pole, and Captain Carl Ben Eielson, of Norway, one of the outstanding polar pilots of his time. During the dinner, word began circulating that the *Italia* was missing and presumed to have crashed or been forced down on the ice, though she had accomplished her basic mission of reaching the North Pole.

At the banquet table sat one of the greatest explorers of them all, the grizzled Roald Amundsen, taciturn by nature and for two years not even on speaking terms with Umberto Nobile. He was still extremely bitter over the *Norge* experience. His statements about Nobile had been blunt and uncomplimentary ever since the day Mussolini had ordered Nobile on a speaking tour of the United States, after the *Norge* flight, in an attempt to grab biased credit for Italy for the expedition's success.

Looking at Amundsen, reported the newspapers, "there was not one of those present who did not remember the bitter quarrel between the two men." Yet, when Amundsen heard that Nobile was lost, he turned to his old arctic companion, Oscar Wisting, and said: "Tell them at once that I am ready to start on a search for the *Italia.*"

The New York Evening Sun later reported: "It is to Amundsen's credit that he forgot any and every grievance he ever had against Nobile, and made a gallant effort to aid his former shipmate." *The New York Herald Tribune* added that he had volunteered, "forgetting the bitter quarrel between himself and Nobile over the division of the glory of the *Norge* expedition." The feud between the two men was, at the time, almost as well known as the feats they had accomplished.

Immediately upon hearing of the *Italia* disaster, the prime minister of Norway cabled Premier Mussolini. Norway, he said in the message, was much closer to the scene and hence an ideal nation to undertake rescue operations. Furthermore, Norway had many experienced explorers and arctic guides who could contribute their personal talents to the search, along with equipment of all kinds. It was further hinted that the great Amundsen would be a natural leader for such an expedition. The Italians side-stepped this last by pointing out that, as a matter of protocol, the Norwegian military would be supporting the search effort and that Amundsen, as a civilian, could not be chosen as the leader. The issue was resolved by appointing Lieutenant Hjalmar Riiser-Larsen, who had accompanied Nobile and Amundsen on the *Norge* flight, as an appropriate choice as expedition commander.

The search quickly became a national undertaking among the Norwegians. The Swedes, Danes, and Finns began to follow suit, while private as well as public groups of explorers made plans and gathered equipment. Mayors of all small towns across the northern coast, and eastward into Lapland, were notified to establish lookout points to watch for signs of survivors and to aid rescuers. All whalers then navigating arctic waters were sent urgent messages to join in the search and submit reports of anything they might sight. And a chain of coastal observers was established throughout every inhabited part of Spitsbergen and the surrounding islands.

Almost every arctic explorer of note had a hand in the preparations, either personally or, if too old to be active, by sending money or advice. Nansen, Hoel, Sverdrup, Ellsworth, and others all had opinions as to what had happened and where the survivors were most likely to be found. In short, the size and extent of the activity were such that the rescue operations became the greatest ever seen in the history of polar disaster. Dozens of ships and planes and hundreds of people became involved. In large cities like Oslo, public focus on these operations was so intense that hotels actually mimeographed daily news bulletins for patrons informing them of any known developments.

Several names began appearing in the headlines that, though unknown beforehand, were to become household words throughout Europe. The *Hobby* whaling vessel began a series of search cruises north of Spitsbergen, after transporting personnel and equipment to the scene. The 350-ton Norwegian vessel *Braganza* followed suit, along with a Russian icebreaker, the *Malygin*. In the air, a slight, delicate-looking Russian aviator named Boris Chuckhnovsky was soon to

•

break into the news, as was an Italian named Umberto Maddalena and a Swedish soldier of fortune, Lieutenant Einar Paul Lundborg. Lundborg had served in several wars, first as a captain in the German army, later as an aviator for Finland in the struggle against Russia.

Roald Amundsen, rebuffed in attempts to organize an expedition from his own country, both because of the official Italian attitude and because of his financial plight, focused his efforts on France. The French were eager to get into the act, but, while there were many daring aviators who might volunteer for such an assignment, there was a lack of qualified arctic talent and experience for the undertaking. Into this gap stepped Amundsen, "The White Eagle" of Norway, to offer his name and fading reputation to a country that still looked upon him with a certain awe. And, because Amundsen was both colorful and controversial, France was now assured of getting her share of the newspaper headlines.

In the United States, despite the distance from the scene of the struggle, interest was strong and sustained. There were many Italian groups that were always interested in affairs concerning the country of their birth. Nobile's name had become known to them through the *Norge* expedition, which was well written up in *National Geographic* magazine, and through his lecture tour. Around the Detroit area and other parts of the Midwest, he was well known personally from the months he had spent working with Goodyear on lighter-than-air projects.

Official photo of General Umberto Nobile (circa 1927).

Nobile in 1928, with his daughter, Maria, and dog, Titina.

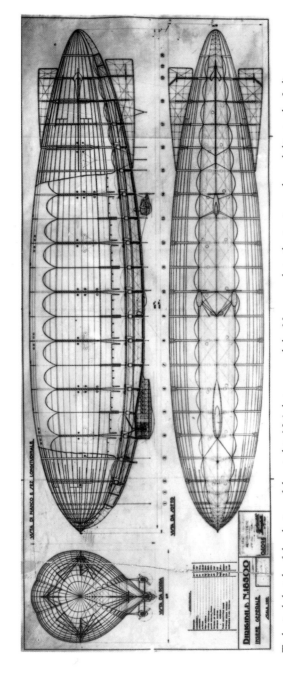

Technical sketch of the design of the airship N-1, later named the *Norge*, and similar in size and capability to the *Italia*.

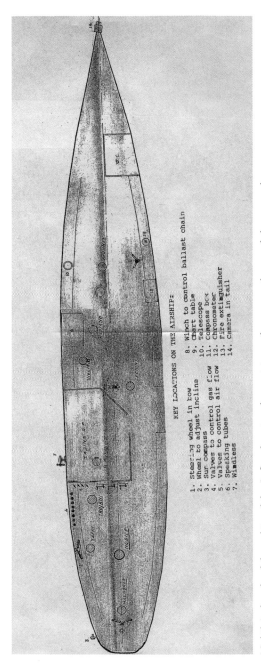

KEY LOCATIONS ON THE AIRSHIP:

1. Steering wheel in bow
2. Wheel to adjust incline
3. Sun compass
4. Valves to control gas flow
5. Valves to control air flow
6. Speaking tubes
7. Windless

8. Winch to control ballast chain
9. Chart table
10. Telescope
11. Compass box
12. Chronometer
13. Fire extinguisher
14. Camera in tail

Nobile's sketch of the cabin of the *Italia*, showing the positions of crew members and the controls.

German air corps soldiers assisting the landing of the *Italia* at Stolp, Germany, during the airship's journey from Rome to the Spitsbergen polar base. (National Archives)

Nobile with Titina in the doorway of the pilot cabin, at Stolp. (National Archives)

At Vadsö. Malmgrem (second from left) with Nobile (far right) and Norwegian officers.

The *Italia* at her mooring mast at Kings Bay. The temporary hangar can be seen at right in the background.

The *Italia* in her roofless hangar. The chain hanging down was a system of ballast using very heavy iron balls that could be lowered to the ice and therefore keep the airship stable during low-level studies of the pack.

The interior of the *Italia*'s cabin, showing the control panel for communicating orders to the enginemen in the motor gondolas.

Left to right: Unidentified crewman, Vincenzo Pomella, Attilio Caratti, Calisto Ciocca, and Giuseppe Biagi, with snowshoes and skis, about to be loaded on the airship at Kings Bay.

Aerial view of ice pack, photographed from the *Italia* on the first polar test flight.

Motormen Ettore Arduino and Calisto Ciocca on the rail connecting the two forward engines of the *Italia*. They would later be among the men carried off by the dirigible's air bag after the crash.

 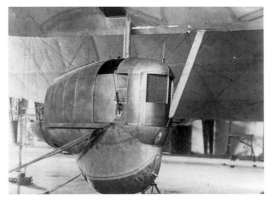

Motorman Vincenzo Pomella and the engine gondola in which he was killed during the crash.

Signed portrait of Queen Elaina of Italy, given to the airmen on the launching of the *Italia*. This was in the destroyed cabin, but was saved and hung in the Red Tent as a symbol of hope.

Official military portrait of Italian Navy Commander Adalberto Mariano, who, along with Finn Malmgren and Filippo Zappi, set out on foot from the Red Tent in an attempt to find help.

Captain Gennaro Sora with Varming and van Dongen, prior to setting out with dog sleds on their ill-fated search for the *Italia* survivors.

Major Umberto Maddalena of the Italian air force (in helmet) getting ready to leave in his Savoia hydroplane to look for the survivors. (National Archives)

Captain Riiser-Larsen, leader of the Norwegian rescue team, readying his plane for takeoff on one of this search flights.

Nobile, immediately after his rescue by the Swedish aviator, Einar-Paul Lundborg.

Lt. Einar Christell, who accompanied Lundborg, aboard the ship *Quest*, and checking his seaplane for departure.

Cartoon from a Swedish newspaper depicting lieutenants Schyberg and Christell trying to find a safe spot to land as they reach the ice floe on which the survivors are stranded.

Lundborg's overturned Fokker at the Red Tent site. An inflatable boat is in the foreground.

Another view of the Fokker, here being used by the men as a temporary shelter and clothesline. Biagi's radio aerial can be seen in the background. (National Archives)

The steamer *Braganza* at Kings Bay. (National Archives)

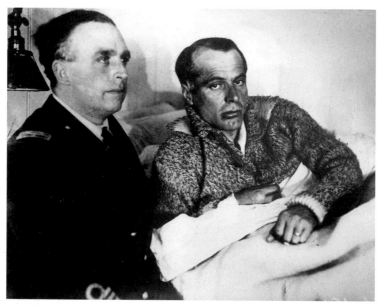

Nobile (right) with Captain Romagna aboard the *Citta di Milano* after his rescue.

Nobile (with cane) on his way to the Italian Consulate in Copenhagen during the return of the survivors to Italy.

Nobile in his apartment in Rome in 1958, at the time he was interviewed by the author. He is displaying the revolver he and the other survivors had at the Red Tent. Photo: Thecla Haldane

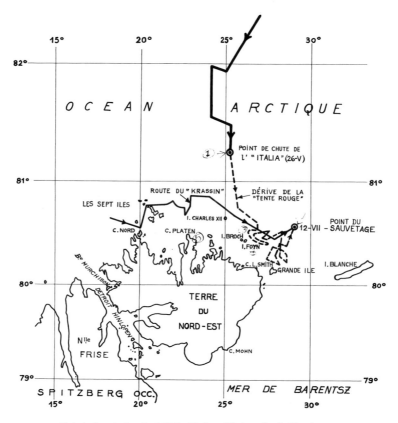

Point de chute de l'"Italia" – Dérive de la "tente
rouge" – Route du "Krassin" – Point du sauvetage.

French map given to the author by survivor Alfredo Viglieri, who penned in
the crash point (1), rescue point (2), and meaningful geographical locations
(3, 4, and 5).

FRUSTRATION

A number of Americans offered assistance, including well-known explorers like Lincoln Ellsworth, who knew Nobile from his association with him in the *Norge* expedition. Ellsworth had been cabled by Amundsen shortly after the latter announced his intention to participate in the search.

Of all the major countries directly concerned with the *Italia* or its crew, or which lay within the general area of the disaster, only one displayed a reluctance to take action. That one, ironically, was the homeland for all but two members of the expedition: Italy. The *Citta* continued to remain safely in the harbor at Kings Bay; the Italian leaders concocted all kinds of excuses for a wait-and-see attitude; and many of the Fascists seemed to be deliberately trying to create other news-worthy events in a puerile attempt to seize back the publicity that had been taken from them. It was as though they felt the *Italia* to be part of an underhanded scheme to steal the show just as the party was beginning to make an impression on the newspapers of Europe.

An example of this deplorable state of affairs is provided by the case of Arturo Mercanti, a well-known business man of Milan, who had been chief of the air force in 1923, during the first months of the Fascist regime. An aviator himself, and a long-standing friend of Nobile, he had personally requested that the Italian air force dispatch planes to Kings Bay to assist in the rescue operations. In early June, after repeatedly being turned down, shunted elsewhere, or confronted with bureau-cratic red tape, he finally blew the case wide open by threatening to send assistance out of his own pocket and at the same time to make it known to the press that the Italian government was not solvent enough to risk a few lire of its own money to help save Italian lives.

This threat resulted in definite action, and a pilot and crew were reluctantly assigned to the task. Fortunately, the pilot was an air force major, Umberto Maddalena, who did not give a damn about political implications or criticism in Rome. He was certain he could locate the *Italia* survivors, if there were any, an attitude that many Fascists did not interpret to be in their best interests. Fortified with these personal convictions, if not the blessings of his government, Maddalena took off for Kings Bay in one of the outstanding Italian air machines of his day, a Savoia hydroplane with a powerful engine geared for both a forward propeller and a pusher type in the rear.

Arturo Mercanti himself later went to Kings Bay, where he was able to observe firsthand the incredible incompetence of the rescue organization. The Italian government, instead of trying to coordinate activities, seemed actually to be leaning over backward to avoid an official connection with any plan to locate the survivors.

This, then, was the situation in early June, a time of the year that could not have proved more difficult for arctic operations. The ice pack was beginning to disintegrate; travel afoot was frustrated by accumulations of slush and water on the surface of the ice; ships were endangered by tremendous blocks of razor-sharp ice that broke off from the pack and drifted with furious currents; and travel in the air was often rendered impossible by heavy fog banks that cut visibility to zero.

To add to this state of confusion, nobody had even an educated guess as to where the *Italia* survivors were or what had befallen them. More than "too little, too late," this was a classic comedy of errors, in which the stage was so overflowing with actors that each one was unable to move for the congestion.

It was a situation tailor-made for newspaper copy. There was always—every day and at any hour—someone taking off on, returning from, or about to depart for, a rescue mission. And each one was so uncertain and so hazardous that editors were habitually holding front-page space for expected accounts of would-be rescuers who had themselves met with disaster or been rescued in the nick of time.

10

SPLIT DECISION

I n the morning following the killing of the bear, Commander Zappi reentered the tent after going out to take a visual check of their position, and announced that the scouting party should leave at once. The drift, he reported, had carried them within seven miles of Foyn Island. Mariano came in to confirm this news and to add his own opinion that they should set out at once. Though Nobile was still against it, he saw that nothing could be accomplished by delaying the march, and that ordering the navy officers to remain in camp longer would only cause friction and a dangerous disintegration of morale.

After breakfast, a tasteless broth made from the bear meat, flecked with tough, gristly chunks of flesh, Nobile gathered the entire group inside the cramped, smelly tent to determine how the clothing and food supplies should be split. The rations were divided proportionately, and the three men were provided with 73 pounds of pemmican, 42 pounds of chocolate, 7 pounds of malted milk, and 2 pounds of butter.

It was agreed that to take any bear meat was impractical. And after the greasy, unpalatable breakfast, none of the three men had any desire to lug chunks of it anyway. They were to take the woolen blanket salvaged from the wreckage, wind-tight arctic suits, several pairs of *finskos* (reindeer-skin shoes), a pair of waterproof boots apiece, extra pairs of thick wool socks and gloves, two bottles of petrol, a small container of alcohol from the compasses, a length of rope, a roll of varnished cloth from the lining of the pilot cabin, and a pair of snow spectacles. For weapons they would be given the axe and the knife, leaving the pistol for the men at the base camp. This latter point did not worry Malmgren, who commented that bears were extremely rare at this season and latitude, despite the night's encounter.

Each man was to wear a combination of thick wool suit, Iceland wool jersey, and complete lambskin suit overall, covered with solid cotton to keep out the wind and dampness. On their feet they would set out wearing three pairs of thick socks, cat-skin slipoffs, and finskos on the outside. Their heads would be covered by fur caps under woolen mountaineering headgear, and their hands by fur gloves made with special flaps to permit finger movement but provide additional protection.

SPLIT DECISION

Later in the day, Finn Malmgren walked into the tent alone to talk with the general. Now that he and the others had received permission to make the march, he seemed greatly relieved and no longer showed signs of the depression that had almost driven him to suicide. He was sorry to leave Nobile on the one hand, yet on the other was inspired by the knowledge that he could take action instead of sitting and waiting day after day. His injured shoulder pained him—how much Nobile was not to learn until later, or he would never have permitted the Norwegian to leave the camp.

Earlier, Malmgren had predicted that they were all doomed men, but now he seemed optimistic about their chances. He outlined his plans. "We shall march as fast as possible. In about a fortnight I hope to reach Cape North. Thence we will push on to Kings Bay. The moment we arrive I will get in touch with the Tromsö Geophysical Institute in Spitsbergen. I'll be able to get information about the winds that have been blowing each day in this region, as well as data about the drifts and currents north of Northeast Land. So I shall discover, more or less, where to find you."

He further explained that his plan was then to fly back with a pilot in a Swedish plane to locate the camp's exact position and land on a smooth part of the ice. It was also possible that a seaplane could land nearby, what with the melting conditions and the increasing formations of canals across the ice pack.

As Malmgren talked, Nobile grew less pessimistic about the venture, though he was acutely aware of the dangers the three men faced. But losing Malmgren was to be a great sacrifice for him and the party remaining at the camp, for the Norwegian was the only member of the expedition who had a good knowledge of the weather and how to select a safe position in the event the ice pack started to break up. Nobile questioned him at some length on the latter subject.

"It would be better for you to find a safer spot," came the reply, "but keep your eye on the canal to the open sea. If it continues to eat into the ice and gets within 50 yards of the tent, then move everything as quickly as you can. If a crack, no matter how small, should appear under the tent area, move camp at once or you will lose valuable stores, possibly lives."

The canal Malmgren was talking about was a gigantic rift in the ice that stretched from a point 100 yards or so from the camp as far as the eye could see. As the weather grew warmer in June, these canals would form all over the ice pack, extending themselves deeper and deeper until several joined and the pack was thus broken into segments.

"We will make straight for Foyn Island first," explained Malmgren, "following the direction of the canal. If we find that it extends all the way, we will turn back and fetch you. Cecioni can make a raft from the gasoline drums for us to carry both of you on." Now, even Nobile thought this plan to be realistic. If the group could once get to Foyn Island together, the survivors could hold out for a matter of months, with no concern about drifting or disintegrating ice.

SPLIT DECISION

Malmgren's reassurances were so positive that the other members of the group began scribbling notes to their wives and other relatives, to be delivered by the three men setting out. Behounek, usually so calm and self-contained, now wept openly as he wrote what might be his last message to the outside world, to his fiancée and his sister. Viglíeri wrote to his mother, Biagi and Cecioni to their wives, but the latter was so overcome with emotion that he finally had to stop and could not continue until Nobile wrote the words for him to copy tearfully and almost illegibly. Then Nobile wrote seven pages to his own wife, including many paragraphs of instruction on the education and welfare of his beloved daughter, Maria, and ending with a note of comfort to his family: "Perhaps God wills that we shall embrace each other again one day; that will be like a miracle. If not, do not mourn my death, but be proud of it. Be certain that I shall have done my duty quietly to the very last. If it be God's will that I die out here, you must not imagine it a terrible end. All will take place with serenity and Christian resignation."

The preparations for leaving took up most of the day. Then came a big shock. A journalist aboard the *Citta* had broadcast the theory that the *Italia* had "probably" struck a mountain in the fog, with the inference that all hands had perished in the resultant explosion. This theory was so solidly accepted as fact that, on that evening, the men in the Red Tent heard a broadcast reporting a speech of the president of the Italian Senate.

In it, in very moving words, he expressed sympathy for the crew of the *Italia*, which had "sacrificed itself" for science. It was quite evident that, in the eyes of Italy, the survivors had been given up for dead.

The news strengthened the three men's desire to depart. The small group gathered sadly in the tent while the general solemnly rationed out the last meal they would share. It consisted of three tablets of malted milk apiece and several lumps of sugar. As the men bunched in the cramped quarters, slowly and silently munching the rations, each wondered how many days away lay rescue—or death. Was it a mistake to split up the group? Perhaps it made no difference. Perhaps they were all doomed, no matter what desperate course of action they tried.

"Well, we should be off." Mariano broke the silence and rose awkwardly. He moved toward the general and embraced him, followed by Zappi and Malmgren. There were tears in their eyes, and the husky Cecioni, the rough-talking, nonsentimental mechanic, appeared to be the most strongly moved of all.

The three men walked outside, picked up their heavy packs, each weighing almost sixty pounds, and stood there while the rest of the survivors adjusted the straps. Then they were off, crunching purposefully across the ice pack to the west, where they knew Foyn Island lay.

"Good luck!" called Nobile from the doorway, where he had dragged himself. "And God go with you!"

SPLIT DECISION

Viglieri, Trojani, Behounek, and Biagi followed the trio's progress with their eyes as they stood there, until the marchers had vanished behind high hummocks and were swallowed up by the mists. Then they turned away. Biagi walked over to his radio set, and the call went out once again. The others hardly paid attention anymore to this ordeal the radio operator had set for himself every other hour, as though he were doing penance for a sin.

"SOS Italia . . . SOS Italia." There was no answer. Only the rising and falling chatter of static, and the metallic clatter of the flimsy aerial pole as it whipped steadily in the soft, damp wind that seemed to pull the mists closer around the numb survivors at the ragged little red tent.

11

THE SHORTWAVE DILEMMA

The departure of Mariano, Zappi, and Malmgren left the rest of the survivors at the Red Tent with a strange feeling of relief. The arguments and discussions about the feasibility of reaching land by an over-ice march had eroded nerves to a raw edge and completely disrupted the feeling of solidation attained after the survivors had settled into a routine. For Nobile it was more than relief; it was a release from certain problems of authority and discipline. Mariano and Zappi were symbolic. They represented the navy and with it the long-established customs of command and obedience. Although approval to make the march had been obtained after joint discussion, Nobile could not help feeling that he had been talked into the project against his will and against his judgment.

"The departure of the three," he wrote later, "seemed to have freed us from an incubus."

The departure represented more, however, than freedom from dissension over whether the march should be made at all and who should go. It marked a distinct change in Nobile's attitude and position among his men. "From that day on," he told me, "I became more than a leader; I was a father to them. They all clung to me. We clung together, forming a little family."

This is a significant clue to Nobile's complex, and often misunderstood, personality. He had, on the one hand, some of the qualities of greatness that inspired one friend to liken him to Albert Schweitzer. He possessed a real humility and a deeply ingrained sense of duty. Yet, on the other hand, his very real human flaws were greatly accentuated by the circumstances, his title, and his position. His very conscientiousness, his desire to make sure that every man had his say in all matters, tended to weaken rather than strengthen the unity of the group. He had a personal conviction that every man was equal when facing nature in its rawness; that every man had a right to make decisions; and that on the ice there was, as he later said, "nobody to command but God."

Nobile, in profile, presented many contradictions. He was an intellectual, yet he had advanced rapidly in a harsh, non-intellectual, society. He was a man of peace, disqualified even for acceptance as an enlisted man during World War I, yet he was commissioned as one of his country's top-ranking officers. He was a man lacking in the popular concepts of leadership, yet leading one of the most important arctic expeditions in history. He was a man openly accused of cowardice, yet he was courageous enough to dare what many of the bravest of his countrymen could not: blunt opposition to the Fascist regime. He was a man often accused by his opponents of stupidity, yet he had more technical knowledge and skill than many of the top engineers in Europe. And now, in perhaps the greatest paradox of all, he was in undisputed command—as both expedition head and ranking officer—of a group smaller in size than an army squad, yet he chose not to exert his prerogative of command. Was this a display of weakness? Or was it a unique application of his personal conviction that nobody but God had the right to command in this extreme situation?

Following the departure of the three men, Alfredo Viglieri assumed two basic assignments. The first was the continual charting of position on every occasion when the weather was clear enough to take sights. The second was the preservation and distribution of food. The bear that Malmgren had shot was cut into large chunks and hung up. Viglieri made a list of all supplies of food on hand and after each meal noted the quantities that had been consumed. He divided the food into a number of shares, wrapping them in waterproof canvas from the wreck of the cabin, and tied the packets at intervals along a rope. In the event of a sudden break in the ice, any packet that slipped into a crevasse or canal would be saved, like a mountain climber roped to his companions.

By June 3, Viglieri had noted a marked change in the drift of the ice pack. After taking observations that day, he came into the Red Tent quite excited. "The current is taking us closer to land than we had hoped for," he said. "My latest calculations show that we are four miles north-northeast of Foyn Island and about five and a half miles northeast of Broch."

Although the drift would carry them closer to land, explained Viglieri, the current would sweep them right back to the southeast again. Unfortunately he was right, for on June 4, they were farther away from the islands than ever. Foyn and Broch were like maddening hallucinations that strike a thirst-crazed man lost in the desert. They were to come and go many times—now luring the men to try an attempt at a march, now dashing their hopes with cruel persistence as they vanished into the mists. Often, it seemed to the survivors as though the ice pack itself was not moving, and that these islands were visions of torture, which came and went like a pair of demons to taunt and harass them.

"Well, we must rely on the radio," said Nobile resignedly. "We can never hope to make it across the ice." But there was not the slightest indication that any of the SOS signals had been heard. He decided finally that the *Citta's* operator must be listening for calls at the wrong time, since Biagi had been transmitting regularly at fifty-five minutes past every other hour, according to the original plan. These calls had been of short duration, to avoid exhausting the batteries. When he left on the march, in fact, Finn Malmgren had advised Nobile not to use the radio at all for three weeks, figuring that at the end of this period he would have made contact with rescuers and the radio would then be needed to send out the new position.

Although the transmitter could be used only sparingly because of the great drain it made on the batteries, the receiver used relatively little current and could be turned on at low volume for several hours each day. Mostly it was used in the early evening, at which time news broadcasts were picked up. On the evening of June 4, Biagi sat mute and expressionless, tuning in routinely to what the others thought was a news broadcast, but suddenly he clapped his hands together and looked up in delight.

"Victory!" he cried exultantly.

"What is it?" asked Nobile. "Have our signals been heard?"

Cecioni raised himself from his sleeping bag; Behounek and Viglieri scrambled to their feet expectantly; and even Trojani, usually silent and morose, showed signs of surprise on his face.

"No, no, it's not that." Biagi's exultant expression changed to one of sheepish mortification. "It was just the soccer game. The Italians beat the Spanish team by seven goals to one."

The others slumped back into their positions, with expressions ranging from exasperation to resignation. "I knew it," grumbled Trojani. "It was too good to expect that your crazy chatter-box could ever pick up anything important."

Biagi's quiet optimism remained unswayed by that remark and the other taunts thrown his way. Cecioni, always in the tent and always uncomfortable, could not refrain from constantly needling his companion. Any criticism of Biagi or the radio set disturbed Nobile greatly, but it did not discourage Biagi in the slightest. Biagi was given to uninhibited bursts of song on occasion, sometimes inspired by what he heard on the radio between news reports. One morning he sang an old Italian favorite, "Gina, My Lovely Gina," with such wholehearted exuberance that the others could not help joining in. As those in the tent picked up the tune one by one, the others on the outside came to the tent flap to poke their heads in and add to the strange chorus.

"Just listen," said Viglieri in some surprise in the midst of all this, "our silent friend, Trojani, is singing too. He has a fine voice." Never had the arctic wastes echoed with such music as resounded from the little Red Tent that morning during the first week of June.

Such moments were rare, however. Usually, the men were silent, each working on whatever tasks he had been assigned or selected on his own. Cecioni turned out to be a remarkably good hand at sewing. Using a sailmaker's needle and thread from the emergency kit for repairing rips in the airship canvas, and cutting sections from the waterproof bags that held the mechanic's tools, he fashioned a much needed pair of shoes for Viglieri. The navy officer had been caught in the crash with a badly worn pair, and his feet were too large for any of the extra Eskimo boots found in the supplies.

The plump, unathletic Behounek, though amiable and sociable, found talking in a foreign tongue too much of a chore, except when necessary. He preferred to sit with a pencil and the scientific notebooks that had providentially been spewed out onto the ice with him and jot down data that might prove important. This included a record of their changing latitude and longitude each day, estimates of the speed of the drift one way and another, temperature recordings, and descriptions of the weather and condition of the ice. In between jottings, he meditated on the significance of the data his consorts, Malmgren and Pontremoli, had gathered with him on the *Italia's* earlier flights out of Kings Bay.

Engineer Felice Trojani assisted Viglieri in organizing and distributing rations and other supplies. Since he had not been injured in the crash, he was in good enough physical condition to accomplish many of the tasks that involved heavy work, such as moving equipment or protecting it with blocks of ice. Gaunt, with heavy-rimmed glasses and virtually silent for days on end, he presented a picture of almost humorous gloom as he shuffled around the camp. Despite this brooding morbidity, he fulfilled his chores punctually and with absolute discipline.

During that first week of June, Nobile began to feel that the routine of their existence was perhaps in itself so monotonous as to cause depression among the men. "What would you think about shifting our assignments and hours around, just for a change?" he asked Viglieri.

"It might help," said the navy officer, "although, since there is so little difference between night and day, we may not find it much of a change at all."

When they tried a shift, reversing the schedule so that what had been the midday meal now was eaten at midnight, with other activities varied accordingly, the plan did not work. What no one had realized was that even the slight variation in the position of the sun from night to day was enough to make an inverted schedule uncomfortable and unnatural. So they returned to the old pattern.

Meals were the milestones in the ordeal. Around 8:00 A.M., shortly after awaking, the survivors ate breakfast, which consisted of twenty grams of chocolate apiece and three malted milk tablets (one gram each). Lunch, the chief meal of the day, was served around 2:00 P.M. The entree was bear meat, which they tried for a time boiled. It was tough, unsavory, and on the greasy side, and when cooked it had a pallid color like that of mildewed leather. Later, they tried roasting it, a process that was easier on fuel but resulted in uneven cooking that often made them nauseated. Each man had approximately a half pound of the meat, followed by five grams of cube sugar.

In the evening, around seven, more bear meat was served, this time a quarter of a pound per portion, followed by desert—either twenty grams of chocolate or ten grams of malted milk. The pemmican, which would keep indefinitely, was not touched as long as the bear meat lasted—a period of slightly more than two weeks after the departure of Malmgren, Mariano, and Zappi.

Though other bears were sighted, none ever came close enough to shoot at—except one. Biagi was sitting at his transmitter one day when he heard a short section of the radio aerial come crashing down just above the tent. He peered out, to find himself face to face with a tremendous brute, which could have laid him out cold with a single paw slap. Biagi, startled, leaped up to look for the pistol, but the action frightened the animal, which hastily loped up and over a hummock and disappeared long before anyone could get a shot at it.

Other forms of game supposedly abundant in the arctic eluded their efforts at capture. On several occasions, when canals opened up in the ice not far from the tent, seals were sighted coming out of the water to enjoy the sun. But they always slid back into the water and vanished, possibly frightened by the barking of Titina.

The appearance of the seals suggested to Biagi, however, that the canals might be possible places to fish. So Cecioni immediately went to work to devise some fishhooks from spare parts of metal. These were attached to thin lines and small chunks of bear meat impaled upon them. For hours Biagi, Behounek, and Trojani dangled these in the dark waters of one canal, their fishing poles fashioned from lengths of tubing. Nothing happened. Not a nibble, not a shadow under the water, not a ripple to show any sign of fish.

"I guess they don't like bear meat any more than we do," said Biagi with a shrug. "Who could blame them?" So the idea of a fresh fish dinner was reluctantly abandoned.

Considerable numbers of sea birds also settled on the snow hummocks around the camp. These were tame enough to have been captured with makeshift bolos or some other crude weapon, and would have provided a certain amount of fresh food. But somehow the men never seemed quite desperate enough to attack them. The sounds of the birds and their gracefulness as they soared through the air provided a lift to the men's morale. And to kill them would have seemed, as in the fable of *The Ancient Mariner*, like an ill omen.

Food was not only nourishment to the body but played an important part in the men's recreation. Cecioni, for example, invented a game to be played when it was his turn to distribute the chocolate ration. He would break the chocolate into various sizes and place them on a makeshift table in the tent. Then they would all play *mora*. At a given signal, each man would hold up any number of fingers he desired. The total number of fingers would then be used to count around the group from a designated starting point and wherever the counting ended determined the winner of the largest piece of chocolate.

Food was a form of reward, too. Any man who sang a song or otherwise helped to entertain his comrades would be given a lump of sugar by the general. The same was true for some outstanding accomplishment or invention that added to the comfort or well-being of the survivors.

By the end of the first week in June, the weather began to turn gloomy, so that even these slight boosts to morale had little effect. Then the southward drift continued with such an increase of speed that they could see the two islands disappearing rapidly. A wind had sprung up, too, and the tent stays and canvas flapped so noisily that the men had the constant impression they were aboard a sailing ship. For a long time, Viglieri was unable to take any sights at all. His estimate of the drift was very pessimistic.

"Soon we will not only be far beyond Foyn and Broch islands," he informed Nobile, "but we will have moved on past Cape Leigh Smith." (The cape had, on clear days, been visible occasionally to the south.) This was depressing news, for once their ice pack drifted beyond the cape, it would be out in uncharted waters where there was no hope of reaching land.

Now it was Nobile who began devising a plan to make a march across the ice. Would it not, he wondered, be best to send the four able-bodied men—Viglieri, Biagi, Trojani, and Behounek—on a westward march, so they would have some chance of saving themselves when the pack ice brushed the cape—if indeed it ever reached that far? There was little chance that he and Cecioni could ever be saved if this plan were followed, but it was quite obvious that neither of them could walk any distance on foot.

The idea scared Cecioni. "We could make a sled," he suggested, "and then we could all go over the ice together." But Nobile turned the idea down immediately, saying that dragging a sled would so hinder the move that all of them would be lost.

Other plans were discussed and discarded. Then out of the blue came a new kind of hope. On the evening of June 6, Biagi had been sending his usual brief SOS and then turned off the transmitter to listen to his receiver, which was tuned in on the San Paolo news broadcasts. For a while he sat there placidly listening. Then suddenly he shouted, "They have heard us!"

Everyone in the tent froze in silence. Biagi clamped the headphones tighter and began writing furiously in his radio notebook. Viglieri looked over his shoulder and watched the words being formed:

> *The Soviet Embassy . . . has informed the Italian government that . . . an SOS from the Italia . . . has been picked up by a young Soviet farmer, Nicholas Schmidt, at Archangel . . . on the evening of June third. . . .*

When Biagi paused, turned, and handed the message to General Nobile, every man in the tent had a look of astonishment on his face. It seemed impossible, and just when their hopes were at the lowest ebb. Each one read and re-read the message dazedly as it was passed around.

So wonderful was the news that they broke out three extra tablets of malted milk per man, fifteen grams of sugar, and a few thimblefuls apiece of pure alcohol from the compasses, which Nobile had been carefully preserving for medicinal purposes.

Now Biagi sat down and sent out his messages with renewed fervor. Archangel had been too far away to pick up the SOS clearly and had been unable to read the position report at all. The radio operator had not been able, either, to make out the name of the island, Foyn. But these seemed like minor details. All that mattered now was that they had been heard.

During the morning of the next day, June 7, Biagi continued to send intermittently, and at one time for a period of about an hour and a half. Judging from the news reports, there had been some confusion about the location of the survivors. The words "Foyn" and "circa," Italian for *around* (which had been added to indicate that the position to follow was approximate and not exact) had become jumbled and were read as "Francesco." It was this mysterious location, Francesco, that the rescuers were trying unsuccessfully to pinpoint.

That evening, when the San Paolo news reports were due to come in over the receiver, all the survivors except Trojani, who was on guard duty outside, gathered by the radio set in high excitement. Biagi started copying the important bulletins in his log book, as was his custom. Then he looked up in great dismay.

"What is wrong?" asked Nobile, after Biagi had abruptly stopped writing.

"Everything," said Biagi bitterly. "A radio ham in the United States reported he picked up our message."

"Well, that is good news," said Nobile, puzzled.

"No, this is some damned crank. He has not picked up our message at all. He just wants to grab publicity, so he has told the world we are near the eighty-fourth parallel—right out in the middle of the ocean!"

The hours wore on and on, and into the next day. The morning of June 8 seemed like the many fruitless mornings that had preceded it. Biagi continued transmitting and listening. Now, to avoid the confusion over the word "Foyn," he described their position as "about 20 miles from the northeast coast of Spitsbergen." Viglieri had just taken an accurate solar observation during a period of sunshine, and this, too, went out over the air.

That evening the men again crowded around the radio set to hear the San Paolo broadcasts. Right after the press reports, Biagi suddenly looked at Nobile, more excited than he had ever been before.

"They are calling us! They are calling us!"

It was San Paolo, calling directly to the Red Tent to say that the *Citta di Milano* had picked up Biagi's message in the morning.

"It can't be, it can't be," said Nobile, trembling with the fear that this, too, would prove to be false. Or that another crank had contacted the *Citta* with a fraudulent message and fictitious location.

Everyone was tense with emotion as they stood there, fingers clutched tightly and perspiration running down their faces into their dirty, matted beards.

"The *Citta di Milano* heard you well this morning," read Biagi from the notation he had jotted down. His fingers trembled so he could barely read, "And has received your coordinates."

Biagi paused and looked at Nobile again: "And listen to this, General. They do think it is our message, but this time they want to make sure: "Give Biagi's registration number. We must send it at once." He handed the paper to Viglieri.

Later that day another confirmation came, this time to the effect that Biagi's number had been received and confirmed. And that the coordinates showing their position had been clearly read. Nobile was jubilant. And, remembering a promise he had made to give Biagi an entire bar of chocolate on the day he made undisputed contact with the base ship, he asked Viglieri to award the prize. It was a strange honor, out there on the ice pack in the bizarre setting of the Red Tent. While the others laughed and cried in their joy and danced around the tent pole, Biagi solemnly accepted his prize, almost half a pound of confection. Then with equal solemnity, Biagi broke the chocolate in two unequal pieces and handed the larger one back to Viglieri, to be divided among his companions.

Nobile then ordered a special feast with more sugar and malted milk tablets passed around to all hands. It was a moment of great jubilation and hope. But for those who expected a rescue ship to appear over the horizon at any moment, severe discouragement and depression were to follow the days and days to come. For Mariano, Zappi, and Malmgren were still out there on the ice, far from any contact, and the *Citta di Milano* was still anchored at Kings Bay with only enough coal burning in her boilers to provide steam for her needs at rest.

12

AGAINST THE ODDS

O f all the structures on the bleak island of Spitsbergen, none was more lacking facilities, comforts,
or livability than the little shack with the crude let-
tering "Grand Hotel Foyn." This stood near the flimsy dirigible hangar at Ny Aalesund, a wooden shed originally erected
by the Italian expedition to house supplies. Now it was occupied by eight soldiers of the Sixth Alpine Regiment:
Sergeant-Major Sandrini, Sergeant-Major Gualdi, Corporal
Bich, and Privates Casari, Deriard, Guidoz, Pedrotti, and
Pelissier. All were expert mountaineers, skiers, and regular
members of the Italian army, brought along by General Nobile to help with the movement and disposition of supplies
and to serve as a rescue team whenever needed.

There was little for these men to do once the *Italia* had disappeared into the polar sky on May 24, and they huddled in uncomfortable hammocks inside the chilly Grand Hotel, bored, restless, and little comforted by the banner each had affixed near his billet: "Remember that you are an Alpine soldier." Tragic though the news of the airship's misfortune was, it at least meant action for these men and a fulfilment of the purpose for which they had been brought there. Disaster had certainly not been unexpected. Polar explorers as far back as anyone could remember had always set forth with the odds stacked against them. It was part of the price man paid for daring to venture against the elements.

In command of the Alpine squad was a man who had been recommended to Nobile as one of the three best skiing instructors in the Italian army, Captain Gennaro Sora. Sora was a handsome young officer, frank, independent, and extremely self-confident. He lived for only two things: the snowbound mountains and the troops under his command. He and his men had proved themselves well during the days before the *Italia*'s final flight by moving equipment out to the hangar and the airship from the base ship, which was anchored offshore and difficult to reach when the snow was deep and treacherous.

By the time four days had elapsed after the dirigible should have returned from the Pole—no later than May 26—Captain Sora was convinced that the *Italia* had crashed. If it had gone down in open water, that was tragic, but if it had crashed somewhere on the ice pack, then it could be reached on foot.

Sora looked over the charts that he had discussed long before-hand with the general. Since it was known that the airship had reached the Pole safely, and since there was then no reason to suspect disaster, the captain reasoned that the airship had come a good way south before running into trouble. Logically, the course for men on foot would be eastward along the north coast of Spitsbergen, as far as Northeast Land. After questioning fur hunters en route, they would then venture out on to the slowly moving ice pack and scout in the vicinity of the islands off Cape Brunn: Schubler, Broch, and Foyn.

Captain Sora proposed his plan to the commanding officer of the *Citta*, since the Alpine troops were under the jurisdiction of the base ship. "I would like to set out at once with my men," he said, "since delay might be fatal to any who still survive."

Romagna shook his head: "You cannot go on a wild goose chase. We do not even know for sure that the *Italia* has crashed. And if she has, we do not know where."

Captain Sora explained why he believed the airship must be down and why the best area to search would be northeast of the Spitsbergen islands. But Romagna stubbornly refused to listen. He had little confidence that ski troops could survive on the pack ice, and if they were lost, the responsibility would be all on his own neck.

The days went by. Sora's men were beginning to have a hard time living up to the mottoes on their banners, since all they did was sit and wait. When the radio message came through to the waiting world from Biagi, Sora and his men danced in the snow with delight. Now they would receive orders to make the march and at least begin to justify their existence.

But their enthusiasm was quickly squelched. Romagna had no intention of letting them risk their necks. They would have to wait for orders from Rome. What orders? When? Nobody seemed to know.

On the afternoon of June 13, Sora could stand it no longer. He went to Captain Romagna and requested that he be permitted to take his men on a search party across the ice.

"I cannot authorize you to go," replied Romagna. "It is too dangerous for your men, and you may accomplish nothing."

"Too *dangerous*?! My men have been trained to face and accept danger."

Sora, then informed again that he would have to get orders from Rome, knew full well they would never be given. So he spoke out bluntly and said that, with or without orders, he would set out on his own.

"If you go, I will have you court-martialed," warned the commander of the *Citta*.

"Do as you like," said Sora, "but I am going to look for Nobile." With that, he turned and walked out, leaving Romagna red-faced with anger.

With the situation what it was, Sora reluctantly decided not to involve any of his men in a deliberate act of insubordination, although all of them wanted to go along regardless of the consequences. Sora left orders that they should continue to press requests to Romagna for permission to make a search. If such a request was ever approved, they were to set out toward the same group of islands Sora was headed for. He then made his way to the small whaler *Braganza*, whose captain had agreed to transport him as far as his ship would go, to the vicinity of Cape North. On board were two other men who were to accompany him in the hazardous search: a Danish engineer named Varming and a Dutch explorer, Van Dongen.

As soon as Sora had left the *Citta di Milano*, Captain Romagna transmitted a high-priority message to the Air Ministry in Rome about the serious insubordination of the Alpine officer. Now he was on record as having tried, at least, to prevent risking any Italian lives in the search for Nobile.

On the night of June 18, in the perpetual daylight of summer, Captain Sora, Van Dongen, and Varming disembarked from the *Braganza* at Beverly Sound and set out across Cape North with nine huskies and a Nansen sled that had been specially built in Norway to the design of the explorer Otto Sverdrup. The men had ample provisions, medical supplies, and a collapsible boat, in the event they should have to cross open water. Sora's daring plan was to cross the wide bay between Cape North and Cape Platen—pack ice all the way except for Scoresby Island in the middle—then across Dove Bay to Cape Brunn in an eastward trek, and finally northeast to Broch and Foyn and Schubler islands.

Sora had organized his three-man rescue team as a kind of personal rebuke to the do-nothing attitude of the Italians at the base. In the meantime, the Russians had seized the opportunity to announce and put into effect a feasible rescue plan. On June 10, the quickly formed Russian Relief Committee appointed Professor Samoilovitch head of the *Krassin* search expedition, and five days later that ship, the most powerful ice-breaker then in Europe, was ready to leave the port of Leningrad.

The *Krassin's* departure was part of a political design. For, with all due respect to the integrity of Professor Rudolf Samoilovitch, a friend of Nobile, and to others who contributed to the Relief Committee, the Russian government saw an excellent opportunity to gain publicity—and particularly to show communist initiative in a favorable light in comparison with the fascist lack of same. However, the actions of the officers and men aboard the *Krassin* indicate that they were unaware of any political implications and were simply risking innumerable dangers to aid fellow arctic venturers.

The element of competition was also evident in the moves made by some of the other countries that began sending out rescue teams: Norway, Sweden, Finland, and, in a small way, France. Newspaper accounts of the day tended to be melodramatic in their treatment of rescue operations, and reporters thrived on the emotional speeches the leaders of some expeditions made before setting out.

The most emotional, most melodramatic, and most tragic of all was the case of Roald Amundsen. After his dramatic statement at the explorers' banquet ("I am ready to start instantly!"), he found to his embarrassment that he had neither the means nor the sanction of his government to start at all. "The White Eagle of Norway" had once been a great national hero. But in his later years he had come to rest on his laurels and, even in the celebrated *Norge* flight, had actually gone along as a passenger, with Riiser-Larsen taking over many of the details of organization. His controversy with Nobile later, and his reputation for being constantly in debt, made the Norwegian government uninterested in selecting him as the leader of the rescue expedition. For Norway it would have meant an unwanted international dispute with Mussolini, so Amundsen was tactfully bypassed.

This left the White Eagle stranded in his nest, valiantly lauded by the press for wanting to rush to the aid of a man he disliked, but with nothing to show except empty words. In one histrionic scene he had remarked: "Ah, if you only knew how splendid it is up there [in the arctic]! That's where I want to die. I wish only that death will come to me chivalrously, will overtake me in the fulfillment of a high mission."

Having made such statements to the press, Amundsen was more determined than ever to participate in the rescue operations. And so, with a fellow explorer, Lief Dietrichsen, he convinced the French to supply a biplane flying boat, and a crew piloted by Commandant René Guilbaud. He also wanted to take along Captain Oscar Wisting, a long-time colleague on polar expeditions and one of the finest arctic experts alive, but the French insisted that the plane would be overweight, even with just Amundsen and Dietrichsen added, and it was only after considerable pressure that they gave in to including Wisting.

Now Amundsen was faced with a lack of what he had long referred to as "a necessary evil with no independent value": money. So he cabled his old friend, Lincoln Ellsworth, who had contributed generously to the *Norge* flight. Ellsworth replied promptly but through a misunderstanding sent a relatively small amount, which the disgruntled and indignant Amundsen immediately labeled pocket money. When Ellsworth learned in short order that the request had been for financial backing for the entire expedition, he came across with a more solid contribution, and Amundsen was solvent again.

And thus it was that, three weeks after his statement that he was ready to depart *instantly*, Roald Amundsen left Oslo by train with his companion, Lief Dietrichsen. The date was June 16, twenty-five years to the day after the man who was to discover the South Pole left on his first polar expedition in 1903.

The long delay in starting was exasperating to Amundsen. But when he left, he had the satisfaction of seeing that many still believed in him, for several hundred people turned out to wave good-bye, along with many representatives of both the

Italian and the Norwegian press. The stolid old explorer stood at the window waving back. Then the train started with a jolt, and as it disappeared down the tracks, he must have wondered whether he would return triumphant, another mission accomplished, to the same cheering crowd.

In France, Amundsen and Dietrichsen joined forces with French pilot commander René Guilbaud, copilot Lieutenant Albert de Cuverville, radio operator Emil Valette, and mechanic Gilbert Brazy. The plane was a Latham 47 seaplane, not well equipped for polar exploration, and dangerously overloaded with the six men. It was equipped with a weak radio transmitter that could send signals barely one hundred miles, and then only when the wind was turning its generator propeller at high speed.

Impatient to be off, and knowing almost nothing about aircraft to begin with, Amundsen spent little time in preparation or making arrangements for keeping in contact with other rescue expeditions en route. All he knew was that he would head due north from France, across Norway and the Barents Sea. At some time they would pass over Bear Island, as Nobile had done with the *Italia*, halfway between the north coast of Norway and the islands of Spitsbergen. Then they would land near Kings Bay, refuel, and continue northward and slightly eastward in the search.

By June 19, when Captain Sora was embarking on the perilous venture from which he would be lucky to return, the Latham 47 was winging its way somewhere over the Barents

Sea. And, sweeping in ever widening circles, other rescue expeditions were engaging in the greatest search in arctic history.

But in Europe and America that day, few eyes or ears were
absorbing news of the drama taking place in the northern
wastelands. For newspapers were headlining the remarkable
story of an unknown young woman who was flying, more as a
passenger than copilot, from the United States to Europe:

AMELIA EARHART FLIES ATLANTIC;
FIRST WOMAN TO DO IT!

Back at the Red Tent, the reality of finally having radio contact had been a powerful tonic. Just the act of getting through
to the outside world, regardless of the contents of the message,
lifted the men's morale from deep depression to a state of jubilation. For three or four days after the contact on June 8, life
was filled with hope and good will. Even the wind cooperated,
veering to the southeast, so that it edged the ice mass back toward the position they had been in the week before. Once
again Foyn Island's welcome silhouette could be seen, this
time even nearer than it had been.

In the confirmation message to answer the request for Biagi's operator's number, to prove the message was from the survivors, Nobile had radioed:

We confirm longitude 280 E., latitude 800 301 N.
Giuseppe Biagi 86891. We only receive on short-wave.

> We are on the pack without sledges and with two men
> injured. Dirigible lost in another locality . . .

On the morning of June 9, Nobile again confirmed the coordinates of their position, to make sure of getting across that they were nowhere near the position originally estimated by the *Citta*. At this time, Biagi picked up a fragment of a message: "Be ready to make a smoke signal. Aeroplanes will be . . . "

To this, Nobile had answered: "We will make smoke signals and fire Very lights as the aeroplanes approach. Remember that our batteries may run out in a few days, but we shall still be able to receive."

Nobile also mentioned again the position, adding information on food supplies, the weather, visibility, and the fact that three of his men were marching east along the coast toward Cape North. Since Mariano, Zappi, and Malmgren had been gone now for ten days, it seemed reasonable to assume that they were somewhere along the coast itself, on land rather than still on the pack.

That evening, Nobile made contact once more, with the same information, since Biagi had picked up a message from the *Citta* at 10:27 that read:

> Call us again this evening at 6:55 P.M. G.M.T. We will
> call you at the fifty-fifth minute of every hour to give
> you news. Now there is a disturbance. Impossible to re-
> ceive from you.

To this evening message, he added more information especially for search plane pilots: the facts that the tent was dyed red for easier sighting and that they had no idea what had happened to the bag of the *Italia* after the crash.

At the height of this period of excitement and optimism, disaster almost struck again.

When Nobile told Viglieri to get the box of torch cartridges and pistol so they could shoot off a flare when they saw a search plane approaching, they discovered that the cartridges did not fit the pistol but were for another model that had been lost. Cecioni, assessing the predicament, suggested that he try filing the cartridge rims to fit the bore, using one of the files retrieved from his mechanic's kit.

He seemed close to success when all at once the head of the cartridge he was working on flew off, landed on the floor of the tent, and exploded with a flash of smoke and flame. A piece of fabric immediately caught fire. Nobile wrenched off his jacket with such quick instinct that he threw all of his weight on his injured leg and felt the sharp, searing pain run up it. But he was able to smother the blaze before it could get started, and there was no damage to the tent. Eventually, despite this upsetting experience, a sufficient number of cartridges were readied for use.

But this effort proved to be in vain. No search plane arrived, and, to make matters worse, radio communications lessened and vanished.

Now the days began to tick off slowly again and with them the flush of hope the survivors had experienced after making radio contact. The stress and strain of temperaments ran parallel to the stress and strain of the ice itself as it heaved and cracked with the ever warming weather. Biagi's communication with the outside world continued only intermittently. He sent out the daily changes in coordinates as their position moved southward. In return, he received sporadic messages that said little other than that help was on the way.

Which way? And what kind of help? No planes appeared on the horizon. On the clearest days no smoke from a ship was ever sighted. Yet, in anticipation of the time when a plane might possibly get through, Nobile radioed:

> It is important to help us hold out and make our position safer by sending aeroplanes at once to revictual us. Our provisions are now reduced to one hundred kilos. It would be most useful to send one hundred kilos of pemmican, or their equivalent; a rifle with ammunition; a packet of medical requisites for two fractured legs, with instructions and advice from a doctor; and a collapsible boat.

The boat was becoming increasingly vital as the ice deteriorated, and they faced the chance of being dumped into the ocean at any time. On June 13 and 14, strong west winds drove the ice eastward at the rate of five or six miles a day. A great heaving could be felt underfoot, and the air echoed with the sound of fracturing ice, as though the pack were peopled with unseen hunters discharging firearms.

"We may have to move soon, General," warned Viglieri on the 13th, after he had returned from an inspection trip. "The ice on all sides of us is broken by large cracks that grow wider each hour."

"Which direction would be the best?"

"It is hard to tell, but I'd guess we should go a little to the east." The winds had brought a dense fog, probably from sweeping over the open waters to the west. Viglieri had found it impossible to see more than one hundred yards when trying to inspect the ice, and at one time had almost lost his way back to the tent.

Everyone except the two injured men now began packing the equipment as best they could for the proposed move. During this, Behounek suddenly paused and held up his hand. "Listen. I think I hear a plane."

Everyone froze. There was, indeed, a humming noise that could be the sound of a distant engine. Then Biagi let out a groan and pointed to the radio antenna in despair. "It is nothing but that. No plane—nothing." Atop the antenna was a small pennant, attached to show wind direction. An increase in the speed of the wind had caused it to vibrate with a sound that was to deceive them several more times—just like that of a distant motor.

The packing continued until, all at once, Trojani shouted in alarm, "The ice! The ice! It's splitting right toward us!" At the same time there came a series of loud reports, like dynamite exploding, accompanied by a shuddering of the ice.

AGAINST THE ODDS

When it became evident that a dangerous canal was forming, Viglieri rushed into the tent to help the two injured men move out. The strain of the wind and current had opened a large canal, some ten yards wide, whose wedge-shaped end seemed to be headed directly at the Red Tent. The next move of the ice might swallow tent, supplies, and men if they did not move out of there fast.

With Viglieri's aid, Nobile hobbled out on to the ice, while Biagi, who was exceedingly strong, half-carried Cecioni into the open. For the first time in more than two weeks, Nobile had a chance to observe the utter desolation. In the tent, confined to a canvas prison, his world had been one of limitations and details. Now he sensed a sudden shock at the sight of the barren ice that rimmed them. He seemed to be on a gigantic white platter, with the Red Tent in the center and the edges determined by the icy white mists on all sides.

Moving turned out to be much slower and more laborious than anyone had anticipated. Though the tent was shifted only one hundred feet or so, it seemed like several miles. Everything had to be carried, rather than dragged, over the rough, uneven surface. Large puddles of dirty water had to be skirted. Dangerous crevasses had to be bridged. And every time supplies slipped into cracks, it seemed as though hours elapsed before they could be hoisted out again. Even Biagi's bearlike strength drained under the effort. The others became so utterly exhausted that they had to pause frequently to catch their breath.

For the first time since the crash, Nobile's nerves seemed to crack. He wished for nothing more merciful than to collapse and die on the spot. For one brief moment he blacked out as complete despondency swept over him. Then Viglieri was helping him on to a kind of crude sledge that had been pieced together from broken tubing but had never worked properly, and he was being lifted on this makeshift litter across the crevasses.

At the new site, the survivors appeared to be safer than before. But now Biagi was having difficulties with radio communication. During the period of heavy wind, contact had been cut off abruptly. Now it became difficult to send or receive. He worried about the batteries in the transmitter, having no instruments to determine how fast they were draining or when they might give out. If a search plane did not appear soon and at least drop supplies, including new batteries or a complete radio transmitter, they would be out of luck.

Nobile was equally worried about the radio, but his concern went further than the problem of communication. That in itself was serious because of the rapid drift of the pack and the need to keep giving new position reports. But he knew that once the radio became silent, his men would too, and a deeper depression than ever would settle over the camp. By June 15, the *Citta* was not reading Biagi's messages at all.

Then, in the middle of the afternoon of June 17, a shout suddenly went up from Behounek, "Planes! Planes!" His heavy frame seemed to bounce up and down with excitement as he waved and pointed. "There are two of them, coming from the south."

Nobile ordered Viglieri to break out the flare pistol and told Trojani to light the smudge fire—a pile of oily rags and bits of debris they had prepared for this very purpose, made flammable by the addition of oil, petrol, and bear fat.

Closer and closer the planes came, circling back and forth in a search pattern and evidently realizing that they were near the position the survivors had reported earlier. Viglieri fired his first flare, not sure whether it would go off properly. But Cecioni had performed his filing job well, and the cartridge gave no trouble.

"Surely they should see the signal," said Viglieri when he had fired two more flares into the air. The planes kept up their lazy circling, however, as though the survivors were a thousand miles away.

"Perhaps it is too bright out," said Nobile, trying to hide his discouragement. He knew the sun, reflections, and ice glare could very well absorb flares that had, by comparison, little contrast.

Then he turned to Trojani and urged him to try to make more smoke than seemed to be coming from the pile of rags. But all of Trojani's efforts failed, and all he could get was a thin wisp of sooty smoke that started to rise but was quickly dispersed by the wind.

When they were only an estimated two miles from the Red Tent, the planes wheeled ninety degrees and vanished to the west. It turned out later that they were navy seaplanes, fitted out with additional fuel tanks and piloted by Captain Hjalmar Riiser-Larsen, who had flown with Nobile on the *Norge* and now headed the Norwegian search party. With him was a Finn, Lieutenant Finn Lützow-Holm. They had taken off from Oslo Fjord that morning.

Nobile immediately tried to radio the *Citta*, praying that someone would be listening and the message would reach him:

> Today we sighted two planes heading in our direction. They came within two or three kilometers without reaching us. Weather conditions, especially visibility, are excellent. Take advantage of it to send the things we have requested. Ask the pilots of the planes to come back this evening before the weather changes. Let us know when they leave so that we can prepare our scanty signals.

The batteries were still strong enough so that this message somehow got through. Nobile was informed the next morning that the planes had been from the Norwegian expedition, and that they would set out that day (the 18th) as soon as an engine was changed in one of them. To this was added information that gave the survivors reason for great delight: "Riiser-Larsen reports that the ice is compact all the way to Cape North." This news meant that Mariano, Zappi, and Malmgren would not have found their path blocked by open water. They had undoubtedly already reached land.

In anticipation of rescue by plane, Nobile had radioed earlier asking that a message be relayed to Admiral Sirianni in Rome. In this, Nobile listed the order in which he and the other survivors were to be taken off the ice if small planes should land, and requesting approval. He placed Cecioni first on the list, then Behounek, Trojani, Viglieri, Biagi, and himself. This had been duly approved with one change: Nobile was relisted as next to last, and Lieutenant-Commander Viglieri last, since he was the only man who could continue to take position sightings, and Biagi could show him how to send them over the radio. Thus, if there were a delay, the last man would not be marooned with no way of reporting his position as the ice drifted farther to the southeast.

Nobile, always the engineer, precise and proper, according to formula, attached great significance to this list and to its official approval from Rome. He read the reply carefully to the others, noting that each man was satisfied with his position. But this theoretical order of departure seemed of little concern to the rest of the survivors. After so many days on the pack, what difference did it make—the few hours that would elapse between the rescue of the first man and of the last?

It is ironic that this order of departure, which Nobile, above all others, was so deeply concerned about establishing, and which not a single official in Rome really gave a plugged lira about, was later to become the most controversial issue in the whole disastrous affair.

The rescue operations were beginning to show results. On the 18th, the Italian pilot Umberto Maddalena, finally arrived at Kings Bay in his hydroplane. A second plane, flown by Major Penzo, had reached Tromsö, Norway, along with two trimotor planes, one Swedish and one Finnish. A fourth plane was also ready to leave Tromsö, the French Latham 47, piloted by Commandant Guilbaud and carrying Roald Amundsen.

Taking all convenient and logical precautions, it seems evident in retrospect that the four planes would leave the Norwegian city together and fly north to Kings Bay as a squadron. This was not the case. The rescue expeditions were separate missions under different flags. The Italians had not made the slightest effort to coordinate the search activities of the other countries. They had not even established an information center for keeping all nations informed about what each group was doing.

The omission would cause endless confusion.

From the first time it had appeared that planes might be on their way, Viglieri had scouted for a quarter of a mile on all sides of the Red Tent to locate a possible landing site smooth enough for a light plane. He had finally settled on a stretch of relatively flat ice about two hundred yards long, not far from the camp, which was free of large hummocks or hidden crevasses. In the four corners of this zone, he placed makeshift flags, and Biagi reported the marked-off area to the base ship.

On June 19, Maddalena, wasting no time, took off from Kings Bay in his Savoia-55 at 4:25 A.M., cruised along Cape North, and by 7:00 A.M. was within sight of the survivors. They watched him circle far to the northwest, never coming closer than about four miles. Then he turned back and disappeared. Nobile had refrained from using up his priceless flares and smudge fire at that distance, but he had Biagi radio to the *Citta:* "If you wish to make contact, start from Foyn Island and take a true course of 59 degrees. Go 20 kilometers in this direction; then turn back to within 8 kilometers of the island. . . . Observe with the sun at your back . . ."

Riiser-Larsen was also sighted once more that day but much too far to the east, which Biagi then reported to the base ship.

On June 20, Maddalena again took off from Kings Bay, first notifying Biagi that he was about to leave. A small wireless set had been installed in the hydroplane, so that Nobile could report to the pilot the instant he sighted the plane and direct its course to the camp. As soon as the general was informed that Maddalena was leaving, he ordered Viglieri to stand by with the flare pistol and cartridges. Trojani was again assigned the smudge pot, now filled with all the petrol that could be spared, along with additional oil, rags, scraps of wood, and some paraffin. At 7:35 A.M., Biagi was in touch with the plane by radio. And forty minutes later, they heard the first distant throb of engines.

"There she is!" shouted Behounek, from his lookout post, at which the smudge fire was immediately lit and the flare gun was readied.

With radio contact clearly established, Biagi relayed Nobile's orders to the pilot: "Turn ten degrees to the right . . . too much. Come back about three degrees to the left . . . You are now about 4 kilometers away . . . On course . . . Now head directly for us."

Within a few minutes the hydroplane was making a perfect approach. Larger and larger it grew. The survivors could see the head of the pilot now in his open port. At that instant a hand waved. They were sighted at last! Other arms appeared in various cabin windows as the rest of Maddalena's crew sighted the Red Tent and waved furiously.

Biagi had left his set and was joining the other survivors now, in a frantic demonstration of joy. Even Titina caught the excitement and dashed back and forth over the floes, barking wildly at the huge bat-winged shape that suddenly rushed by overhead with a tremendous and frightening noise.

Then the plane had passed by and was wheeling around again for another pass over the encampment. But the Savoia was a large and clumsy ship. She charged on for what seemed a couple of miles before completing the turn, and then she was way off course. Suddenly the survivors realized how difficult the camp was to spot from aloft. Maddalena—incredible though it seemed—was unable to find the place he had just passed over. Viglieri immediately fired a flare, and Biagi dashed back to his radio set to try to reestablish contact and guide the plane back again. But he could not raise any signal, and in the meantime the hydroplane was circling like a vulture, far off course.

It took almost half an hour to get through on the radio and guide Maddalena back again. As he was about to pass over the camp for a second time, Biagi sent out the signal "K-K-K." This was the code for "Drop provisions." Hands were seen reaching out of several ports, and small parcels rained down on the ice over a wide area. The plane made several passes over the camp, flying extremely low. Then it soared upward again and vanished to the south after radioing that it would be back soon, and that there was no possible area for it to land on the water anywhere near the camp. The sea was too choked with ice cakes for a plane the size of the Savoia to find enough room to set down.

All the rest of that day, Viglieri, Biagi, and Trojani searched for the packets that had been tossed overboard. It was a frustrating and difficult task. Many of the packets had fallen into crevasses or open canals of water or had just plain disappeared. When everything possible had been collected, Nobile took inventory. He found that they had six pairs of shoes, a few rations, two collapsible boats, some smoke signals, two sleeping bags, two rifles, and several batteries. However, the rifles and batteries had been severely damaged by the impact and turned out to be of little use.

Maddalena, upon his return to the base at Kings Bay, had two things to report. The first was that the condition of the ice was so bad and the surrounding waters so clogged with ice hazards that it would be impossible for any aircraft other than an extremely light ski plane to land. The second was that, even when given coordinates and directions, the camp was as difficult to spot as a pebble on a beach. And that, for this reason, all attempts should be concentrated on getting General Nobile off quickly so that he could assist with what was going to be an almost impossible task: locating the three men on the march and the missing men who had drifted northward on the bag of the *Italia*.

This choice, determined by the necessity of obtaining the most reliable information and guidance about further rescue operations, would prove later to have devastating effects.

13

MANNA FROM HEAVEN

When Maddalena and his crew flew out over the lonely arctic to search for the survivors, they did so with individual dedication to the task and with no thought of the risks involved. It was a strange and ironic fact about so many of the rescue operations that while brave men willingly risked their lives, much of what they might have accomplished was nullified by the deplorable planning and apathy of the officials to whom they were responsible.

A clear case in point was the nature of the supplies Maddalena had been given to deliver and the way in which they had been packaged. The batteries and rifles were vital, yet they had been so carelessly packed at Kings Bay that they could not withstand a drop from even a low height. The rations, too, had been thrown together as haphazardly as though the ship's junior cook had merely gone through the galley shelves picking out anything that happened to be handy. Instead of the hearty nourishment the exhausted and gaunt survivors needed, they received a packet of cocoa (the sight of chocolate was already almost sickening), a few oranges and lemons; a pot of marmalade (with nothing to spread it on); thirty fresh eggs, most of which smashed upon impact with the ice, and fifty bananas. Though the latter were welcome changes, they were hardly what any of the survivors would have recommended as proper fare for their condition of semi-starvation.

Nobile sent the following message to the *Citta* that evening:

> Today we see Foyn at 250 degrees of the compass. Send more batteries, better packed than today's, which arrived broken; also more boats . . . pemmican, cakes, a Primus stove, solid fuel, medicines, one pair very large shoes for Viglieri (the poor man has not been able to wear any of the ones sent), cigarettes, snow spectacles, handkerchiefs, and rifle butts to re-place the ones shattered. . .

He also informed the base ship that the rising temperature was steadily disintegrating the ice, preventing search parties with sledges from reaching them in time, and urged that they be removed by air, one by one, before the ice broke up, fog set in, and they drifted too far from land.

After getting ominous reports about Captain Gennaro Sora and his whereabouts, Nobile was worried about him and recommended that search planes look for him as well, since his perilous march across the ice would surely be endangered by large canals.

His messages to these effects were clearly received. Yet no action was taken, and worse yet the expected arrival of the Italian plane did not materialize. What could be wrong? The weather was, at that time, perfect. And the coordinates sent out were accurate enough that Maddalena should have had no trouble finding the tent's position again.

In order to make the camp as conspicuous as possible, the men had hoisted festoons of red and white strips of cloth to the peak of the antenna. In addition, they had spread out four unwanted charts, dyed them red with the coloring from the glass markers, and affixed them to the four triangles that made up the tent roof.

Early in the morning of the 22nd, Biagi picked up a message. Maddalena's Savoia seaplane was leaving Kings Bay, and when it reached Cape North, the pilot would contact him for directions. Equally welcome news was the assurance that the plane had been stocked with all of the supplies requested.

Once again Nobile ordered the men to their posts, all except Trojani, who was suffering from severe stomach pains, possibly as the result of eating the fresh fruit to which they were all so unaccustomed. Nobile and Cecioni again crawled outside the tent onto the ice. This time Nobile had a piece of paper, a pencil, and a compass. He had determined that the best way to keep track of the supplies thrown down was to list each one he saw falling, its compass direction from the tent, and a description of what it looked like.

There were two hydroplanes, the second one piloted by Penzo. They located the camp with no difficulty, circled the tent several times to estimate the wind direction and determine the best area for the drop, and slowed their airspeed almost to the stalling point. Then the bombardment began. Down from the sky came boxes, parachutes, sacks, and parcels tied with red flags. Nobile was hard-pressed to record them as the planes made their passes over the encampment. Some plummeted straight down, while others fell at an angle, caught by the wind, and a few drifted, dangling like pendulums, at the end of colored silk parachutes.

It was during this air drop that Nobile noticed something that both disturbed and shocked him at the same time. At the rear port of one of the planes, a motion picture photographer was stationed. His camera was halfway out, and his right arm moved rapidly as he turned the crank to record the scene below him. It distressed the general to think that within a few days those films would be in Rome, being processed for showing before theatre audiences all over Italy, and probably in other countries as well. As he envisioned it, he and his pitiful little band of men would be nothing but objects of curiosity, ragged, filthy, huddled in squalor and misery. He wanted to crawl back into the tent and hide from the prying eye of the press.

By the time the planes had flown off again, Nobile had counted eighteen packages in all. It took three hours to locate and retrieve all of them, but this time the smaller parcels were marked with red ribbons so they were easier to locate on the ice and in the crevasses. And this time, too, better planning had gone into the operation, providing enough tinned meat, powdered milk, biscuits, and cakes for about twenty days.

In addition, there were many items of wool clothing, which afforded a welcome change from the dirty, stinking garments they had on, but most of which were unfortunately too heavy for the mild weather they now experienced. The most welcome item was a pair of large-size shoes for Viglieri. And there were quantities of a luxury they had not enjoyed for almost a month, cigarettes, as well as stomach and fever medicines, splints, another collapsible boat, a new rifle, ammunition, two axes, and a portable stove with fuel.

That evening, the six men enjoyed another bonus: newspapers and letters from home. One factor disturbed them: not a word was mentioned about sighting Mariano, Zappi, and Malmgren. These worries were forgotten when, around 7:30 P.M., Biagi, who had taken a respite from his duties at the radio to serve as lookout and warn of changes in the ice, spotted two more planes on the horizon. He immediately told the others and put a match to the smudge fire to send up a smoke signal.

"They're Swedish," said Viglieri, picking out the markings when the planes had come close, "and they seem to have our location down perfectly."

The two seaplanes zoomed overhead, the pilots waving as cheerfully and casually as though they were at a flying meet. After they had performed a few unnecessary acrobatic maneuvers out of sheer exuberance, they flew in low. Red splotches appeared in the air, as though someone had suddenly splashed the sky with paint, and five crimson parachutes drifted slowly down on the ice. The Swedish pilots winged over gaily, circled three more times, and then headed south again when they saw that their aim had been right on target.

Viglieri and Biagi danced over the ice, chasing the pieces of red silk, and returned joyfully with new treasures.

"Tonight we celebrate!" laughed Biagi, holding up a bottle of whiskey that had been included in one packet.

The new supplies also included five dry-cell batteries for the radio, a sack holding a collapsible boat with oars, a rifle and ammunition, two medicine chests with splints and other fracture supplies, oranges, and more cigarettes.

On the brown paper wrapping of one packet, a note was printed: "From the Swedish Expedition. If you can mark a landing area for planes fitted with skis (minimum 250 yards), arrange the red parachutes in a T-shape on the leeward side."

Since Viglieri had already scouted the area and selected a landing zone, he had only to place the red parachutes as directed and inspect the ice to see that no cracks had formed in it during the interim. This done, Biagi was given the following message to relay to the Swedes:

> To the Swedish Expedition, Virgo Bay: Cordially thank you for your visit and for all the useful supplies dropped. A landing area suitable for ski-equipped planes exists southwest of our tent at a distance of about 150 yards. The red parachutes will be laid out as a T on the leeward side. The length of the field is 325 yards, and the width 250 yards. It is absolutely flat, but we suggest coming before the weather conditions, which are now so favorable, change.

To everyone's dismay, it now turned out to be impossible to transmit the message, despite the arrival of the new batteries. The *Citta di Milano* did not answer the call. Either it was blocked by interference or—what was more likely—the base ship was again blithely sending out personal messages and minor news reports without bothering to monitor the *Italia's* frequency. There was only silence, hour after hour after hour.

Although there was no longer any problem about food, the situation of the ice had worsened, and the chances of moving quickly in case of its break-up had lessened. Trojani was definitely an invalid now, with acute stomach trouble. And Behounek, who had found physical exertion a heavy drain because of his weight, inadvertently revealed now that he had hidden from the others a serious injury to his right arm. When

Biagi accidently stumbled against him, he cried out in pain so great he could not stifle the outburst. He could not hide the seriousness of the injury when his arm was inspected by the others. So it was now evident that, if they should have to move camp in a hurry, the amiable Czech could not be counted on for much assistance. That left only Biagi and Viglieri to bear the brunt of the work.

The next day, the 23rd, Nobile and Viglieri held a brief conference to determine what alternatives they would have when the ice really started to break up. The only feasible course would be to take to the boats as soon as they could, and thus it was imperative to start loading them right away with provisions and all necessary supplies so they would be ready if the situation got that desperate.

"We'd be lucky to get them into the water without capsizing or smashing," said Viglieri. "And once in, we would still be faced with the Herculean task of trying to buck the wind and currents to reach land."

He was right, but they all knew they would have no choice if the ice should start to crumble. So, with these somber thoughts in mind that evening, Umberto Nobile started silently munching on the new rations, in contemplation of what to expect next. The others, too, seemed lost in meditation. It was in the midst of this gloomy silence that they heard a distant humming sound that seemed to be increasing. Of all the noises they had heard, or imagined, this was to be the most significant.

14

A DECISION IN DOUBT

L ieutenant Einar Lundborg was, at thirty-two, a soldier
of fortune who had fought in three wars for countries
other than his native Sweden. Handsome, dashing,
and dramatically heroic, he was decribed by one journalist as
"fearless, a quick thinker and fast actor." His childhood background was completely out of keeping with his later life, for he
was the son of a Lutheran minister and trained so that his in-
clinations would lean also toward the ministry.

In 1914, Lundborg joined the Swedish army as a cadet, at
nineteen, the youngest in the school. He was on the one hand
classified as "irrepressible" and "behind every practical joke
perpetrated" and on the other described as one of the finest
skiers, horsemen, and all-round athletes in the army. Despite
his weakness for horseplay, his good sense of humor and

willingness to sacrifice himself pulled him through. Later on in World War I, he joined the German army, won the Iron Cross, and was discharged as a captain. Not content with sitting idle while there was a good fight brewing, he next joined the Finns to fight the Russians, winning the White Rose of Finland and emerging as a colonel. This was followed by a hitch with the Latvians and Estonians in their fight against the massive might of Russia. Lundborg liked, in his own way, to be fighting for the underdog. When he finally ended up where he should have been all along—in the Swedish air force—he became known as a flyer with "no sense of personal danger," a great stunt pilot and a man who always made snap decisions.

Such was the character and personality of the man who decided that, while the Italians played a stealthy game of politics and the Russians plodded doggedly onward in their icebreaker, he would rescue Nobile. He had no trouble getting proper approvals from his superiors, who assigned him a plane and copilot of his choice and all necessary supplies and equipment. His commandant even insisted on assigning a support hydroplane, which could land on open water in the event that the ski plane should crash on the ice.

For his aircraft, he selected a small Fokker CVD military plane with ski runners. It was a light, maneuverable ship with room for a mechanic (usually as necessary as the engine in those days) but hardly room for the man Nobile had radioed was in bad need of being the first to be rescued from the pack: the bulky and heavy Natale Cecioni. At about 10:00 in the evening on June 23, Lundborg took off from the base camp on Danes Island, near Virgo Bay, and, accompanied by a fellow pilot, Lieutenant Birger Schyberg, headed northeast toward the position of the survivors, closely followed by the hydroplane.

As he zoomed low over the pack, rose and circled under full power, Lundborg could see the pitiful little tent, streaked with fading red dye in an attempt to make it conspicuous. Two men, obviously incapacitated and unable to move far, balanced themselves by the tent entrance and looked up with great smiles on their faces: the general and the mechanic, Cecioni. Two others raced, slid, stumbled, and hopped their way across the ice in the direction of the markers laid out on the ice, showing where the best landing spot was located. Lundborg looked down and shuddered. He would sooner have set his ship down in a brickyard. Behind him he could see Schyberg clutching his head as though to keep what blood remained in it where it was. His face was deathly white. But Lundborg was not one to pause and deliberate. He eased the throttle in and circled lower, trying to gauge the wind from pieces of fluttering cloth below.

The skis touched with a hiss, clattered across rough ice as brittlely as a pair of milk bottles tumbling downstairs, and the plane gradually sank on its shock absorbers and glided to a safe but bumpy stop. It was just 11:00 P.M.

In a few minutes two dirty, unshaven, and sickly looking fellows sprinted the final distance across the ice and came up against the plane gasping for breath. They were Biagi and Viglieri.

Lundborg climbed down, leaving Lieutenant Schyberg in the plane to keep the engine idling, and was warmly clutched by the two walking skeletons who smelled of gasoline and rancid grease. In the meantime the hydroplane circled lazily overhead, unable to find a safe stretch of nearby water on which to land. "Can the general walk?" asked Lundborg.

The two men shook their heads, still too much out of breath to do more than gasp.

"Then we shall have to go and help him."

"I think Cecioni is going back with you first," said Biagi. "Trojani is to help him on a sledge."

It was a difficult, though not long, walk across the ice to the Red Tent, and when Lundborg arrived, he was horrified to see the condition of the camp, one he talked about later as being "indescribable." Perhaps it was the general's appearance as he went up to him and embraced him. Tears were in the general's eyes and his face was masked by a greasy, scraggly beard that made his thin face seem even more gaunt.

"General, I have come to fetch you. The field is good. I shall be able to take away all of you during the night, but you must come first."

"That is impossible," said Nobile, indicating Cecioni, whom he had already told to dress warmly for the flight. "Take him first. That is what I have decided."

The pilot stood his ground. "No, sir. I have orders to bring you first because we need your instructions about looking for the others."

A DECISION IN DOUBT

This made sense. Only two days before, Captain Romagna had radioed Nobile to say that he needed "data and instructions to search for the airship," and Nobile had been unable to transmit these because of consistently poor radio contact. Aware of this need, Lundborg insisted that it was logical that the base camp should want Nobile there in person to help chart a plan of rescue, not only for the six lost men on the bag of the *Italia*, but also for Mariano and his small group.

But Nobile, still the orderly engineer ruled by the formula that he himself had written as "The Order of Departure," kept insisting that he would not leave first. To the impatient Lundborg, who had no stomach for the repugnant setting to begin with, this petty matter of politesse was both ludicrous and exasperating.

Finally, he could contain his annoyance no longer. "Come, General," he barked, "this is not grand opera."

Lundborg's position—that of a junior officer countermanding a general—was bizarre, to say the least. He was a dedicated officer and as such was accustomed to carrying out orders—and there can be no doubt that he had been given precise orders. Besides, his dashing nature could never have submitted to the idea of flying out a mere mechanic on this first historic trip when he could have the distinction of rescuing one of Italy's top-ranking officers and aviation experts.

"I cannot take Cecioni anyway," he persisted. "He is too heavy, and it is impossible to take him without leaving Schyberg behind, whom I'd need in an emergency. Later tonight I will fetch Cecioni. But we have no time to lose. Please hurry, General."

Still Nobile hesitated. Though weakened and sometimes delirious with fever, he could not relinquish the instinctive idea that he was not just an army officer leading his men, but a father to the group. "What do you think, Biagi? Do you not think Cecioni should go first?"

"You had better go first, General," replied the radio operator. "It will set our minds at rest."

Nobile did not budge. He consulted with the others—Behounek, Viglieri, Trojani. They all felt he should leave first. Even Cecioni, who had been the most fearful of being left behind, sat up as far as he could and urged, "You go. Then, no matter what happens, there will be someone to look after our families."

Nobile turned to the impatient and by now thoroughly annoyed pilot. "I am ready."

Biagi had brought the general his Iceland wool jersey for the flight, but Lundborg interrupted, "Please leave everything you can. Make yourself as light as possible to minimize the danger of our takeoff. It is not cold." Nobile set aside the jersey and also removed his headgear and high reindeer boots. The only excess baggage he took was the radio logbook, which he felt would be of value in reconstructing their positions and the general movement of the ice pack.

Viglieri grasped the general around the waist and Biagi took him by his good leg, and they started the ponderous trek across the ragged ice to the flat strip where the plane stood. From time to time Nobile struggled to put his good foot down and assist his two men and the pilot as all three panted at the hard going. Sometimes they sank in slush up to their knees. After a while, Lieutenant Schyberg ran back to give assistance, and Lundborg hastened toward the little Fokker to warm up the engine and check it for the hazardous takeoff. Then Nobile heard a thin bark and saw his little terrier perched in the cockpit, looking joyously over the rim as though this were a great adventure.

"Titina, come down," said Nobile.

"It's all right," said Schyberg. "She ran up to the plane, and I put her aboard. She will go too. She weighs nothing."

After Nobile had been laboriously lifted into the plane, he leaned out and gave a last order to Viglieri. "Take command for these last few hours—I'll be waiting for you."

The plane was pushed around until it headed into the wind. The engine roared to life, the skis bounced protestingly over the lumpy ice, and then they were in the air safely. As Nobile sat cramped in the cockpit with Schyberg, he looked down on the pack that had meant so much misery to him. At first he could not even locate the tent, then Schyberg pointed it out, a wretched little object, a scrap of dark material almost invisible against the whiteness of the ice. He could understand now how planes could have flown up almost within a mile of the site and never observed a thing.

Lundborg circled, then headed for Foyn and Broch islands. What were these barren islands really like? wondered Nobile.

They had served so long as possible objectives that it seemed absurd they could in reality be only the jumbled piles of gray rocks and white snow he saw below him.

Schyberg thrust a small chart toward Nobile. "Here," he said, indicating a spot south of Foyn, "we caught sight of human footprints. These went on for several miles, then they suddenly disappeared, and in their place we saw numerous tracks of polar bears."

Nobile shuddered. Could it be possible that Mariano, Zappi, and Malmgren had gotten that far, only to be overwhelmed by animals? He remembered how he had asked that the pistol and ammunition be left with the group at the tent, because Malmgren had been so certain he would not encounter polar bears.

Then the plane passed beyond the islands, and the general was left with his disturbing thoughts.

It was colder now, and he wished he had kept the heavy cap on his head. He was dressed only in a gray knitted jacket. His legs were encased in light gray sports trousers. On his good foot he wore a light summer shoe and on the other a wool stocking and a reindeer sock. His broken leg was wound round and round with a dirty puttee. Schyberg pushed him lower into the cockpit, out of the wind, and drew a small rug about his shivering shoulders.

"Well, we are here now!" shouted Lundborg a short while later, trying to be heard above the engine. Nobile, unable to see over the coaming, heard the propeller whine eerily as it slowed down, then felt the sensation in his stomach that they were dropping. In a few moments there was a bump and the swish of skis on snow. They were on the ground.

As Nobile raised himself painfully upward until his head was over the coaming, he expected to see a base camp and a flurry of activity. Instead, the spot was deserted, the ground thick with snow and to all appearances not a great deal different from the pack where the Fokker had recently taken off. Three strangers ran forward, tall, lean men dressed in pilot uniforms. They greeted the general with delighted smiles, hoisted him easily into their arms, and began carrying him about four hundred yards toward the sea, where two large hydroplanes were moored.

"Where are we?" he asked.

"This is Ryss Island."

Along the shore the snow had melted, and the rubble of the beach stood out darkly. At one point, a tremendous fire of driftwood was blazing. Several more young airmen were in evidence, one of them cooking food on a small gasoline stove. There were sleeping bags and provisions scattered about, and the men carried him toward one of the bags, while others converged on the spot to help him slip in between the warm furs. One man handed him food and a hot beverage. Another offered him a cigarette, which he took eagerly and somewhat curiously. He had not smoked in seven years.

Lundborg introduced them as some of his fellow pilots, explaining that they had flown aloft to greet the *Italia* when the airship had flown over Stockholm early in May.

Nobile recalled taking photographs of the planes in flight around him then and promised to send some prints when he eventually located his film at the base camp.

Then Egmont Tornberg, the leader of the Swedish group, introduced himself and assured Nobile that his rescue team was now much better organized and would shortly be able to get on with the search for Mariano's party and begin looking for the lost airship. "Your presence will make everything easier," he asserted. "The *Citta di Milano* is on her way to Virgo Bay, and in a few hours the *Quest* will arrive here." The *Quest*, Nobile learned, was the Swedish base ship, a 400-ton sealer, which had been assigned by the Swedish government as a support vessel for the search planes.

But the general could not get the five men on the ice pack off his mind long enough to concentrate on the others. "When are you going back?" he asked Lundborg.

"Very soon," replied the Swedish pilot absently. Then, after the general had shown his impatience, he rose and said with a great smile, "I'm off!" and he wandered back across the ice toward his small plane.

Tornberg and the other officers then slid into their own sleeping bags and were sound asleep almost before the sound of the Fokker's engine had disappeared out over the frozen wastes. But Nobile was unable to sleep, despite the fact that for the first time in many days rescue was for him a reality and for the others a sure thing.

A DECISION IN DOUBT

After the departure of General Nobile with Lundborg, Lieutenant-Commander Viglieri was in command for the "few hours" the survivors were told they would have to spend on the pack before their own rescue. Before departing, Nobile had given him orders to get the bulky Cecioni to the landing area so that he could quickly be flown off when Lundborg arrived for the second time. This was no easy task. Biagi, who was still the strongest of them all and in the best condition, was elected to help his comrade. But Cecioni stubbornly refused help, assuring them that he could make it on his own. He then stood up, partially supported by one of the crutches that had been dropped by plane and equally by a makeshift crutch that he himself had fashioned.

The venture turned into an ordeal, complicated by the rough ice and many pools of water, into which he slipped several times. His triumphant arrival at the appointed rescue spot was gradually dimmed as, shivering, miserable, and pained by his exertions, he waited . . . and waited . . . and waited. The hours went by. Viglieri and Biagi paced back and forth up and down the length of the section that had been marked out as a landing place, looking for any new cracks to warn the approaching pilot about. Back at the tent, Behounek continued his pastime of jotting down scientific observations in his logbook, while the sickly Trojani lay inside with a high fever and stomach cramps.

"What could be wrong?" asked Viglieri time and time again. "The weather holds clear. The Swedes know our exact compass position, and the general certainly would not let the rescuers delay returning to us."

After three hours had elapsed from the time of Lundborg's departure, Biagi returned to the tent and tried to make radio contact with the *Citta*, to relay a message to the Swedes asking what was wrong. He was unable to get through. So after half an hour of trying in vain, he returned to the landing area and continued pacing up and down with Viglieri.

It was almost six hours before Viglieri paused in his nervous pacing and shouted, "I hear it—the plane!"

There was now no mistaking the sound. They sighted a tiny speck, growing larger, then watched Lundborg circle high in the air until he had sighted the camp and then started his glide in low over the ice to the strip marked out with the red parachutes. Lower he came and lower, but he did not seem to be judging the distance properly. He was going to overshoot the mark.

Biagi waved his arms wildly, trying to signal the pilot that he should go up, circle, and try again to hit the mark. But it was too late. Lundborg was setting down in the center of the marked area instead of the end—so he would have only half the length to land in before hitting rough ice.

They watched in consternation as the skis touched, the engine was cut, and the plane went bumping erratically across the ice, still at extremely high speed. It was difficult for the three onlookers to tell exactly what happened next. Cecioni thought that Lundborg had deliberately flipped the plane over to avoid ramming large blocks of ice. Viglieri thought the skis had caught on a crack in the ice and thus made the ship up-end on its nose. At any rate, in a matter of seconds the plane was upside down, the propeller smashed and a couple of struts bent, but otherwise without too much apparent damage.

Viglieri and Biagi rushed over to rescue the pilot, fearful that the plane might at any moment burst into flames. But the engine was still. A little puddle of oil leaked darkly onto the white ice. There was a violent sound of swearing in a foreign tongue, and Lundborg wriggled from the cockpit and lowered himself to safety.

"Are you all right?" asked Viglieri, with great concern.

There was no answer except more profanity. As Viglieri walked over to the Swedish pilot, the swearing subsided and Lundborg's face reflected his anguish and mortification at having failed in this critical moment when he had expected to be a savior. Viglieri was relieved that the pilot seemed unharmed by the crash, and now faced the task of trying to help Cecioni dry off, find a place to lie down, and get out of his misery.

The decision was to leave Cecioni where he was, provide him with a sleeping bag, and later move the Red Tent to the vicinity of the plane. But it was almost thirty-six hours before the tent was moved to the new position. Moving camp proved to be a far greater project than Viglieri had anticipated. Lundborg, though in no way injured, was in a despondent frame of mind and thought it was ridiculous to go to all that trouble. "There are other pilots and planes, you know," he kept saying. "They will arrive any time now."

"Perhaps," said Viglieri firmly, "but the welfare of all of you is in my hands, and I am ordering a move. The ice is much safer near the plane, in case your friends do not arrive as quickly as you think. And I want everyone ready to leave at a few minutes' notice, without having to struggle two hundred yards across the ice to reach the takeoff point."

As he pointed out, in case Lundborg did not understand, Cecioni, who was suffering from snow blindness now as well as his injuries, was not the only problem. Trojani was too feverish and weak to do anything more than move himself, and Behounek's arm injury handicapped him.

On Ryss Island several hours went by, and Nobile began to worry. What had happened to Lundborg? Another hour passed. Then came the sound of an airplane in the distance, its engines growing louder as it approached. As it came in sight, he saw that it was a lone hydroplane, the same one that had accompanied Lundborg on both trips. It made a quick landing. Nobile woke an officer next to him, a man named Christell, and said that Lundborg must be coming back too, with the injured Cecioni aboard. He would need some help getting across the ice to the shore.

Christell rose and walked to the water's edge, near the spot where the hydroplane was taxiing to its mooring. There was an exchange of conversation, most of which Nobile could not understand; then the officer returned.

"There has been an accident," he said calmly. "The Fokker has overturned on the ice pack near the red tent."

Nobile gasped and tried to say something, but all that came out was a stammer.

"Oh, it is nothing to worry about," said Christell, noting his alarm with good humor. "Nobody hurt, and I imagine the damage can be repaired soon. Lundborg is rather indestructible." Christell turned away, not impolitely but as though he did not want to bore the general with minor details, slid once again into his fur bag, and was soon asleep.

Nobile was now in despair. Then he noticed with some relief that the leader, Tornberg, who lay in a sleeping bag on the other side of him, had awakened.

"What are we to do?" asked Nobile. "Has your expedition any other planes with skis that could land there?"

"No," said Tornberg slowly and thoughtfully, "although there is a Finnish plane—a trimotor—that could be adapted. The best thing is to send for some small sporting planes. The British Moth would be a suitable type." These planes, he explained, could be obtained from England. Tornberg advertised Nobile to ask the Italian government to send for several at once. He added, too, that Nobile could count on the Swedish government to do everything in its power to assist.

Nobile agreed and began analyzing what the situation would be like on the ice floe and what his companions would need most, now that they could not be removed immediately. He told Tornberg that the men would need pemmican to eat right away, since he had asked Romagna for a supply of it several times, but the *Citta* did not include it with the other provisions in Maddalena's air drops.

Tornberg said he would take care of this request immediately, asking Nobile at the same time if he would like to wait for the arrival of the *Quest*—a bit late but expected within a few hours—to see what she might have aboard in the way of supplies. The general declined, eager to leave for the *Citta* at once, now that the accident had occurred, to radio for the Moths at once and give other necessary instructions for rescuing his men and searching for the others who were lost.

Tornberg wakened Christell, and together they helped him to a small boat and thence out to one of the waiting hydroplanes. Within a few minutes they were winging their way out over the barren wastes toward Virgo Bay. It was a gray, desolate spot, with ragged mountains piercing the snow here and there, the place from which the ill-fated Salomon Andrée had disappeared in the first historic balloon attempt at the North Pole. In the center of the bay was the *Citta*, lying idly at anchor with little signs of activity aboard.

When the plane landed, the deck of the little ship became immediately crowded with sailors. A motor launch put out to meet the hydroplane, and the general was lifted aboard it and carried on deck amidst the cheers of the crew. Photographers and reporters crowded around and wanted words from him and pictures.

It was for them a memorable and historic occasion—the end of an ordeal for an injured and exhausted explorer. But for Nobile, the real ordeal had just begun.

15

PRISON WITHOUT BARS

Looking at himself in the mirror in the cabin where he was now confined, Nobile was stunned to see the change that had come over him. His skin was tanned dark from the constant sun and had the texture of old leather from the accumulation of dirt and grease. The lower part of his face was completely hidden by a grizzled beard. When a crew member helped him remove his clothes, Nobile was ashamed to have anyone see their filthy condition or smell the stench that began to permeate the cabin as layer after layer was peeled off. It surprised him to realize that he had not once given serious thought to the matter of cleanliness after the first few days on the ice floe. Although he knew that he would need to have his injured arm and leg treated soon, they had healed remarkably well and no longer gave him the pain he had experienced for many weeks. But now there was only one thing in the world he desired—a hot bath.

Before bathing himself, the general sent word to Tornberg, Christell, and Captain Romagna, asking them to meet in his cabin to discuss rescue plans. Tornberg and his pilot came in first, and Nobile again mentioned the need of the stranded men for more food, which the Swedes promised to air-drop immediately. The next step would be to have the Finnish tri-motor plane Tornberg had mentioned equipped with skis for a rescue attempt. The plane was too large for the small landing area staked off on the pack, but a skilled pilot might be able to make it and take off all the men, including the stranded Lund-borg, in just two trips. "I think it can be done," said Tornberg.

"Good," said Nobile. "It should be done at once. In the meantime, I'll radio to Rome to have several Moth sporting planes shipped here immediately, in case the trimotor cannot land."

Heartened by the discussion, the general then sent a message by radio to his men:

> Don't be anxious. I am on the Citta. A Finnish plane is being equipped with skis, but as a precaution we have ordered three small planes from England. You will receive six more batteries from the Swedes, smoke signals, a tent, various medicines, and some solid fuel. I think

you have plenty of petrol. But I hope all this will not be needed because I am reckoning on seeing you all again very soon . . . and keep your spirits up, as always.

Your Nobile

The Italian officers aboard the *Citta* were sympathetic, warm hearted, and eager to do everything they could for the general. Perhaps, thought Nobile, he had misjudged the Italians at the base camp. Perhaps there had been serious reasons for the delay and inactivity on the part of his own countrymen while the Norwegians, Swedes, and Russians were so aggressively conducting rescue and search operations. But where was Romagna?

Finally, the captain did go down to Nobile's cabin. His greeting was cold and reserved, completely different from that of the other officers. Well, it was, perhaps, just the man's nature.

"You must help me organize rescue operations," Nobile told him emphatically, "not only for the men on the floe, but to locate Mariano, Zappi, and Malmgren, and to search for the *Italia* and the men who drifted north with her."

Romagna, however, was not concerned with rescues. "People might criticize you for coming first, General," he said coldly. "It would be well to give some explanation."

Explanation! Nobile was astounded. Wasn't it the base ship that had sent out orders via, Lundborg that Nobile was to be brought back immediately to help supervise the rescue operations? And had Lundborg not been put in the embarrassing position of almost having to force Nobile to leave first, only succeeding when he assured him he would make quick return trips for the others?

Romagna denied giving Lundborg any such orders and said if they came from any source, it must have been the Swedes.

"Well, however that may be," replied Nobile, "the fact is that I did not leave by personal preference. I am here only because I was told it was of great importance that searchers use my directions to find Mariano and his companions, and for the six who disappeared on the bag of the *Italia*."

Romagna was so insistent on this incredible matter of explanations that finally Nobile gave in and sent to the naval secretary a message that he would never have written if he had not been weakened by his long exposure and injuries and confused by the attitude of the *Citta's* captain. The message, a kind of lame apologia in defense of a nonexistent cowardice, served no purpose other than to discredit Nobile further.

The meeting with Romagna left Nobile confused and bitter. He had felt a great urge to level criticism at Romagna for his inaction, his hesitation, and his failure to post a twenty-four-hour watch on the radio receiver to try to pick up the SOS signals. But he had held himself in check, feeling that this was a matter of minor import now, when compared with the life-and-death matter of searching for the missing men.

Romagna's attitude was just an indication of the greater treachery being perpetrated in Rome. Almost at the moment Nobile had arrived on board the *Citta*, after being transferred from the Swedish hydroplane, the government in Rome had

released, via the Stefani news agency, a communiqué announcing that the Italian government could not understand
why the general had been rescued first. This report by implication alone portrayed Nobile as a coward. And just to make
sure the damage was done thoroughly, Italo Balbo—annoyed
that Nobile had actually reached the Pole in the *Italia* and disappointed because he had turned up alive, after all—dreamed
up a story for his own newspaper, *Corriere Padano*: that the
general had not been injured in the crash itself but had broken his leg running to get on the Swedish plane first.

This was disputed by other press reports, especially in the
Scandinavian countries, that Nobile had acted courageously
in all matters and was, in fact, a heroic figure who had in no
way abandoned his men.

From that day on, Balbo never hesitated, during cabinet
meetings and press conferences, to stir up public sentiment
against Nobile. It would have been dangerous to the air minister's prestige to give the public time to think about the most
significant fact of all: that the *Italia* had actually reached the
North Pole and ventured far into unknown territory on preliminary trips. Or that Nobile and his officers had made valuable meterological observations about the polar regions.

To discredit Nobile, his enemies in Rome did not hesitate
to use methods that dishonored the name of Italy as well.
Knowing that the French press had anti-Italian elements,
they saw to it that reporters in Paris had slanderous inferences
leaked to them, since there was growing concern in France

about the lack of communication with Amundsen's Latham 47 and a fear that it had crashed in the north. The Fascists aimed their barbs at escalating the rancor of the Norwegians, already sensitive to the bad feelings between Nobile and Amundsen, and more than ever concerned since Amundsen's disappearance. While there was no way anybody could blame Nobile for the loss of a search plane, it was easy to stir up resentment by implying that the searchers had sacrificed their lives to save a coward rather than a hero.

Nobile's bitterness was such that he decided he would leave the ship and return to the forward base camp of the Swedes at Ryss Island. To carry out this plan, he talked with a pilot named Sarko, the observer on the Finnish trimotor, to ask to accompany him to guide the plane down on the best landing area. It was agreed that Sarko would let Nobile know the minute the plane was equipped with the skis. Nobile was jubilant and radioed to the men on the floe that he would shortly be flying to the camp in the ski plane.

However, when it became evident that Nobile had intentions of leaving the ship, Romagna was afraid that he might accomplish what the Italians had thus far failed to do: find the missing Mariano, Zappi, and Malmgren and possibly even the men who had drifted off on the bag of the *Italia*. So the ship's captain had members of the *carabinieri* posted in the corridors, supposedly to prevent the general from being hounded by newsmen, but actually to keep him from leaving. The general had been invited to go aboard the Russian icebreaker, *Krassin* and the Norwegian *Braganza*, but Romagna saw to it that he got nowhere.

The pressure from the Fascist government was now constant. Romagna would not even permit Nobile the dignity of helping to supervise rescue plans. Orders were given that when Nobile sent messages to his stranded companions, the words were to be censored and sometimes the signature changed so the men would not even know their commander was trying to contact them. Reporters were not permitted access to the general's cabin unless they represented the "right" publication.

Going through his notebooks containing the records of the endless and frustrating attempts Biagi had made at radio communication before finally getting through, Nobile decided that, if he could accomplish nothing else, he could at least see that radio communication was improved so the men on the floe would no longer face the long hours of silence. He called Romagna and spoke to him quietly and firmly: "Commander, it is necessary that your wireless operators stay on duty at the receiver around the clock."

"They are doing their duty," came the cold reply. "They listen frequently."

"But frequently is not enough. It must be constantly."

Romagna was silent. Nobile went on to describe how Biagi had listened, day after day, to the endless chitchat of personal messages from the *Citta* to Rome and later the flow of reports for newspapers.

"Do you remember," he added, "that in the days following the crash every two hours, at five minutes to the hour, as a pure formality you transmitted your message: "We imagine you are near the north coast of Spitsbergen, between the 15th and 20th meridians east of Greenwich. Trust in us. We are organizing help."

Romagna gave a slight, indifferent nod.

"Well, we were east of Cape North—much farther east. You didn't hear us. You didn't attend to our signals as you ought, and so you made us exhaust our batteries for nothing trying to warn you that your deductions were all wrong."

Romagna muttered something unintelligible, and Nobile continued, now greatly agitated. "And get it into your head that the three [Malmgren, Mariano, and Zappi] would never have left if they had not been convinced that our SOS would never be heard. If you had concentrated all your efforts on listening, you would certainly have picked up our signals before May 30th, even if only fragmented. You would have let us know it, and then we should have been hopeful and the three men would no longer have insisted on going and risking their lives."

Discussion was frustrating. Romagna simply came up with all kinds of excuses—mainly implausible—as to why the radio operator on the *Citta* had come to the conclusion that the radio on the airship was dead and attempts at communication useless.

Later, Nobile heard another story, this time from wireless operator Ettore Pedretti, who had accompanied the *Italia* on all trips except the one to the Pole. "On the afternoon of May

29th I was at the earphones in the wireless cabin of the *Citta*, sitting next to chief operator Baccarani. Suddenly I leaped out of my seat. I had intercepted the single word *"Italia,"* and a little later the distinct message: *"Reply via Ido 32K."*

"That was Biagi," said Nobile. "The code word *Ido* was for San Paolo, to show we could receive from there clearly, and the *K* means urgent, as you know."

"I was certain of it. So I grabbed Baccarani by the arm and exclaimed, 'The *Italia* is calling us!' He did not believe me. He thought it was probably Mogadiscio, [*Italian spelling of Mogadishu, in Somalia, formerly Italian Somaliland.*] a relay station we used in communicating with San Paolo."

The conviction aboard the *Citta* that the *Italia* could not transmit was so strong that neither the chief radio operator nor Romagna would believe that the SOS had really come from the lost airship. Nor did they even bother to radio the Mogadiscio station to see whether one of its operators had tried to make a contact a short while before. Nobile was dismayed that Romagna paid such little attention to his plea and when Romagna heard about Nobile's plan to take off in a Finnish plane to direct rescue operations, he hastily went down to the general's isolated cabin.

In an accusatory manner, he said he had heard that Nobile intended to leave and go with the Finns. Nobile responded in a perfunctory tone that this was true, since he could not get any action from the Italians and so had to turn to other nations that seemed more interested in attempting a rescue.

Romagna warned him that he had orders from Rome to prevent Nobile from taking part in any rescue missions whatever. Furthermore, he threatened, if necessary to obey that order, to post guards at the door of the general's cabin.

Realizing that he was a virtual prisoner, Nobile urged the two Italian pilots Maddalena and Penzo, to set out immediately to look for the six men who had vanished on the bag. Although they were both highly capable aviators, with initiative and daring, Maddalena seemed strangely hesitant. He expressed doubt about the feasibility of carrying out extensive exploration. He mentioned the grave risks attached to it, said that large hydroplanes were not as suitable as small light planes, and ended with the remark that his engines had already had too many hours of flight and needed to be replaced.

Nobile was surprised by Maddalena's attitude when he learned that the Italian pilot was misinformed about the size and condition of the landing area on the ice pack near the little red tent. Then the Finnish aviator, Sarko, came to him with a worried look and mentioned Maddalena's opinion. Did the general really think landing would be as dangerous as all that?

Nobile was upset. If the Italian Air Ministry wanted to order its fliers to use extreme caution and take no chances, that was one thing. But it was quite a different matter when the fliers discouraged the pilots of the other nations. He called for the young airman Penzo and had a confidential talk with him, unbeknownst to either Maddalena or Romagna. Penzo was greatly distressed. He had personal reasons for wanting to get the survivors off the floe and would have risked his life to do so, but thus far he had been prevented from action by orders from Rome.

After talking with Nobile, Penzo agreed to try to fly in close to the ice pack with his hydroplane. "Is there any kind of long canal near the tent?" he asked. "Even one twenty or thirty yards wide will do."

"There was a large canal some sixty yards wide when I was there. And it extended out of sight. So there is good reason to expect a suitable canal exists, especially now that the snow is melting."

Despite this optimism, little action was taken. Another spell of bad weather arrived, bringing with it thick fogs that made air search impossible. And when Nobile urged Romagna to steam toward the north coast of Northeast Land, near where the Swedish rescue expedition had landed from the *Quest* to look for the Malmgren group, and possibly the six men lost on the airship when it rose in the air after the crash, he was quickly rebuffed.

Romagna asserted that it was far too risky to take the old vessel into a sea of unknown depth and scattered ice floes.

If that were so, responded Nobile, then why not at least let Maddalena and Penzo move forward with their planes so they could operate from the same base as the Swedes?

That was not possible either, said the captain. They were under his jurisdiction, and he was not about to relinquish control. Repeating that he had his orders, he turned and walked away, as he had done so many times before, leaving Nobile frustrated and despondent.

At six in the morning of June 29, a radio message was received from Viglieri at the Red Tent:

> Weather variable but now seems to be clearing up. The sun sometimes pierces the clouds. Visibility from five to ten miles. Light wind from the northwest. Clouds about 500 meters high. Landing area still good, but you should come as quickly as possible for it might get worse in parts.

The moment had come for another attempt at landing. But by this time the fears and criticisms of the Italians had rubbed off on the Finns. They no longer were eager to try to send in the trimotor plane, though she stood ready with skis. The two Italian hydroplanes and the Swedish machine were also ready to start. But precious time was wasted as delay followed delay.

Finally, on July 1, the three hydroplanes took off again, headed in the direction of the little band of men on the ice floe. By then, however, the weather had worsened. They ran into a heavy bank of fog and were forced to wheel around and head back for the base, defeated once more.

As the few hours that Lundborg had predicted would elapse before his fellow pilots would arrive turned into days and not a plane was sighted, the discouragement of the men became even more pronounced. Only Biagi seemed able to cope.

Every morning, he would look up cheerfully from his radio set and announce that he had just picked up good news: planes were departing from Kings Bay, or from the Swedish base at Virgo Bay, or from the advance encampment of the Norwegians. Then heavy fog would start rolling in until visibility was reduced to less than half a mile, and the weather would remain heavy the rest of the day.

In this manner, another week passed. Lundborg, who had proven to be such a fearless flier and cited often for bravery in his many years of military service under various flags, was a complete enigma to Viglieri. He was obsessively restless. He refused to eat anything except an occasional piece of chocolate. Having come from the clean, organized camps of the rescue expeditions, he was almost pathologically revolted at the smell and sight of the filth that the survivors had grown gradually accustomed to. Furthermore, he was not conditioned to the torment that the others seemed to take for granted: having hopes lifted high one moment, then shattered the next.

Lundborg's depression was infectious. It spread easily to Trojani, who was moody to begin with, and to Cecioni, who was not only in pain physically, but also in a surly state of mind. Behounek tried to escape moodiness by focusing on his scientific notes, thus depriving the group of his former good humor. Biagi and Viglieri alone retained their morale, the former because he was a born optimist, the latter because of his training as a military leader and because he realized that, in this crucial period, he must not fail.

It was especially unnerving then when Biagi collapsed with a high temperature. Although he refused to let the fever interfere with his duties and his constant monitoring on the radio, his condition had the ultimate effect of plunging the company deeper into doubt.

On June 29, Viglieri completed a new set of solar sights and radioed that their position was off Cape Leigh Smith, which they could see nine miles away. In his opinion, this would now make it easier for another rescue flight to reach them. But he was caught by surprise when Lundborg—who had been so outspoken in his assurances that another plane would arrive—now began insisting that the only hope left was for them all to make a march across the ice. He was motivated by several factors in addition to his increasing discouragement over the non-arrival of the expected planes: first, and most serious, was the fact that the ice was not only cracking but showing signs of crumbling everywhere. Often the feet of the men would sink into soft spots. Second, the landing strip itself was becoming saturated with water, so that a landing—if any plane did show up—would be extremely risky, and takeoff might be impossible.

Later on the 29th, Viglieri allowed Biagi to send a message from Lundborg directly to Nobile quite contradictory to the earlier one:

> Parts of field have today become very bad. There is water under the snow making the surface very bad . . . Also,

the weather is so warm, the ice will become even worse as a landing place. So I ask you, sir, if we can begin walking to Grosse Island and have a pilot drop food to us till the icebreaker can reach us.

On receipt of this, Nobile was greatly dismayed. He knew that such a march would be suicidal. So he radioed back that the group at the Red Tent had to be patient, that four rescue planes were ready to start, as soon as visibility improved, and that, furthermore, the *Krassin* was also on the way and might be unable to locate them if they started any kind of march across the ice.

A day later, Viglieri radioed that the time was ideal for the rescue planes: "Visibility excellent. Wind calm. Clouds at 5,000 feet. Weather perfect." This message was relayed to the Finnish, Norwegian, and Swedish pilots, the only ones with planes light enough to land on the pack. One plane took off from the vicinity of Kings Bay immediately but flew only as far as Virgo Bay to rendezvous with three other planes for a mass flight to the Red Tent. By the time they were ready to start the next day, the weather had done its usual about-face. They flew less than fifty miles when they found their way blocked by an advancing front of heavy fog, topped by an umbrella of dark storm clouds.

For five days, there was no activity at all. Cyclonic winds raged high over the Arctic Ocean. Sleet, hail, and snow pelted the small group of survivors viciously without relief. And underfoot, the ice groaned and shuddered.

On the fifth, as quickly as it had formed, the storm vanished and the sun returned. During the blow, the ice pack had reversed its drift, moved in a counter-clockwise position, and was now only four and a half miles from the coast at Cape Leigh Smith. Through his glasses, Viglieri sighted what he thought were men moving along the shore. He radioed the estimated position of the Red Tent at this time, reported a clear sky with excellent visibility, and urged immediate flights in order not to let this chance slip.

As soon as he received this message, Nobile communicated with Commander Tornberg, chief of the Swedish expedition. Two seaplanes were promptly dispatched to fly over the Red Tent and drop supplies but, more importantly, to evaluate the condition of the landing area.

The next day, Viglieri sighted a small plane approaching and awakened Lundborg to ask if it was from his flight group. The Swede identified it as one of the small British Moths they had ordered for searching. Unhappily, he added, although it was light enough to land in a very small space, it would hold only two people.

The tiny plane seemed little larger than its name as it circled overhead and then gingerly sideslipped in for a landing on the ice, barely using one third of the field. The plane taxied toward the tent, sending up sheets of water on both sides of its delicate little skis. The men ran out to meet it, with Lundborg well in the lead.

"Schyberg!" he exclaimed, as the man in the cockpit removed his helmet. The two embraced each other as though they had been convinced they would never see each other alive again. Lundborg had tears in his eyes.

Viglieri had expected to ask that Cecioni be taken off prior to anyone else. But when he saw Lundborg's emotional display and assessed his despondent state during the past days, he decided it would be more untroubled all around if Lundborg were to leave. This seemed to be what Schyberg had in mind anyway, for he asked Lundborg whether he had anything to bring with him.

While Schyberg was checking the outside of his Moth to see whether ice or water had done any damage, Viglieri questioned him about the immediate plans of the pilots to return to the pack. Schyberg spoke evasively. His face was pale and drawn, his hands shaking, his voice unsteady.

It was then that Viglieri realized the truth: the strain of polar flying, the uncertainties of the weather, the dangers of landing were beginning to tell on the overwrought and physically exhausted the pilots. Schyberg would not be back. Lundborg certainly would not be back, given his uncontrollable reactions. And their colleagues were undoubtedly just as reluctant to risk their necks as long as so few Italians had gone out of their way to help their own countrymen.

Back on the *Citta*, Nobile applauded the rescue of Lundborg, convinced that now other small planes would be sent to pick up his own men, one by one. Then he heard the discouraging news: the Swedes were not going to attempt to land anymore planes on the ice. On the afternoon of July 6, in fact, Tornberg flew to the *Citta* with the rescued Lundborg to speak frankly to the general.

"We are willing to fly over often and drop supplies," he said, "but quite bluntly, I am reluctant to risk the lives of my men with further landings, now that I have a report on the exact condition of the ice." In place of landings, Tornberg proposed that all effort be made to reach the survivors by ship, and to speed up the work that was already being done in that respect.

Nobile agreed, but with one reservation: that Tornberg authorize just one more attempt to land on the ice in a light plane. If even Cecioni alone could be brought off, it would ease the tension and give the others a large boost to their morale. "Lundborg knows, even as I do," said Nobile, "that the state of mind of the men is perhaps more important than the state of their physical health."

Although the Swedish commander agreed to one more flight, it was never to come about. The condition of the ice degenerated so that even those at the Red Tent discouraged any further flights. They would only end in tragedy and with no chance of rescue.

16

THE ICE TORTURE

How long it was after setting out on the disputed march across the ice that Malmgren realized his tragic error, no one will ever know. But it became evident to commanders Mariano and Zappi that the meteorologist was having an inner stuggle with himself as soon as the second day after leaving the Red Tent.

Finn Malmgren was both wise and experienced in the ways of the arctic. He had served for three years on the renowned *Maud* expedition, from 1922 to 1925, and knew what to expect when traversing the ice on foot. So it came as a surprise to Mariano and Zappi to see that their companion and guide was beginning to falter so early in the struggle. Amundsen and Riiser-Larsen had not only referred to Malmgren as "the best meteorologist available" during the *Norge* flight over the Pole in 1926, but had also considered him always ready for a joke and enough of a prankster to be nicknamed Imp. Now, however, he had become glum and moody, plodding onward with no heart and troubled to the point of being mentally sick over what he considered his failings.

This inner struggle ran a close parallel to the physical one, as the three men trekked westward. Although Malmgren had been known for his humor, he also reflected a fierce Nordic pride. He had made several mistakes that were not only disastrous in themselves, but that he felt were serious reflections on his nationality—particularly since he was the lone representative of his country in the midst of so many Italians.

Malmgren first reproached himself for having been wrong about the weather. When he and Nobile had discussed plans on reaching the North Pole, and given thought to the alternative of continuing, with the wind, on a course to Alaska, he had been certain the winds would die down. As it turned out, the wind did die down, but too late to be of any help to the doomed airship. Malmgren's prediction had been as accurate as possible under the conditions.

Nevertheless, this first error weighed so heavily on him that his next mistake also became greatly exaggerated in his own mind. This was his estimate that he could march an average of eight to ten miles a day over the pack. When, after three days of marching, they had averaged only one third of that distance per day, Malmgren grew despondent. Several other unhappy facts became evident as the three men slipped and stumbled over rough ice with their heavy supplies and equipment between them. Mariano was not in good condition to begin with. Large of frame and unaccustomed to long hikes, he gasped and puffed and showed obvious exhaustion on the march. But his lack of stamina was nothing compared with Malmgren's poor condition.

When they set off, it had been an accepted fact that Malmgren would have to favor his wrenched shoulder by carrying a lighter load than his two companions. But it was not realized then that he had apparently also suffered a serious kidney injury during the crash. The pain in his side had seemed inconsequential during the relatively inactive days at the Red Tent. Now, however—only two days on the march—it became so acute that every step was torture.

When Zappi offered to relieve him of some of his load, Malmgren protested and stumbled on. Though they did not know it that second morning, they were in for a respite—a forced one. During the day, the wind increased with every hour, whipping loose snow into clouds that obscured all vision beyond a few hundred feet and propelled sharp slivers of ice against the men's poorly protected faces. By the end of the afternoon they were caught in a howling blizzard.

It was obvious they would have to stop their march and make some kind of shelter. Zappi unfastened his small axe and began hacking away at a large chunk of ice. As he broke it into smaller blocks, the others piled them around a shallow depression in the ice. In this the three men huddled together.

Zappi broke out the rations of pemmican and a small oil stove that they had been using to heat the mixture, both to improve its taste and to provide meager warmth. Try as he could, he was unable to light the stove in the wind. Then, seeing that he would use up all the matches in vain, he shoved the stove back in his pack and they ate the pemmican just as it was.

It was almost two days before the storm let up sufficiently to let them proceed. If they had been discouraged before, the situation was now even more gloomy. When the clouds lifted, Foyn Island was farther away than ever. The incessant drift of the ice pack to the southeast had more than cancelled out any progress they had made walking westward. It was then that Malmgren's morale snapped completely. All at once, he threw himself down on the ice, sobbing and muttering incoherently. Though his words made little sense, it was obvious to the others that he was mouthing self-accusations for having gotten them all in an impossible situation.

"Finn, Finn!" shouted Zappi. "Get up off the ice. This is no way to act." He shrugged off his heavy pack quickly, bent down, and tried to lift Malmgren back on his feet.

"You two go on. Leave me here," begged Malmgren, his eyes wild and staring blankly off into the distance.

Mariano broke out the stove, managed this time to get it lit, and boiled some pemmican in melted ice. He offered it to Malmgren, who then began to calm down and speak more coherently. Within a few minutes his depressed mood seemed to have passed, and he apologized for his conduct. He then shouldered his pack and continued the march as though nothing had occurred.

The next few days were without incident. The men walked continually, sometimes for fifteen hours at a stretch. Then they would flop down in some protected position among ice hummocks and rest. Since there was no period of darkness, it was almost impossible to keep any regular routine.

On the tenth day of the march, particularly grueling through slush and pools of water and jagged fields of sharp ice, Malmgren began lagging behind, at first only a little, then farther and farther. The others would stop and wait for him to catch up. Sometimes Zappi, the strongest of the three, would unhitch his pack and retrace his steps to give encouragement to his infirm companion, assuring him they were making good progress in the right direction. But Malmgren could never be fooled into thinking they were making any progress at all. On some days the drift would carry them as much as six or seven miles in the wrong direction, while they would be lucky to cover two or three over rough ice in the right direction. Zappi finally relieved him of the small pack, leaving him with nothing to carry but a blanket. He also abandoned some of the supplies, such as the stove, which was useless.

Finally, Malmgren was in too much pain to speak. His only words were occasional pleas for the others to go on and to leave him behind. "I can't go on," he would say. "There is nothing left for me but to die." His words were not empty heroics. He had been brought up in the rigid codes of Nordic tradition. During the flight, he had once said to Nobile, "If one member of an expedition is sick or injured, and because of his infirmity endangers the others by hindering their progress, he should be left behind, even if it means he must thereby die." This was an inflexible code, which Malmgren had not only preached but was willing to practice.

On the twelfth day, Finn slumped to the ice in a semi-conscious state. He was unable to rise again until Zappi and Mariano lifted him gently. Then he began to protest once more that be should be left behind. When the others insisted that he keep on, he finally continued the march again, numbly taking one step after the other as though each would be his last. Two days later, he collapsed again, and this time it was impossible to get him back on his feet. He took off one shoe to show that his feet were red and raw with frostbite. He held up his compass. "Give this to my mother as a remembrance. And tell them in Sweden why I did not return."

Zappi took the compass from him gently and placed it in his pocket. Then, remembering that Finn had never shown any deep religious faith and that he had once remarked that scientists have no religion, he decided that he should at least be baptized before he died. So he knelt down on the ice, dipped one finger in the wet snow, and made the sign of the cross on Finn's forehead, pronouncing slowly the Latin words spoken by priests, as well as he could remember them. When this rite was finished, Malmgren made two pleas—one for protection from the wind, and the other for a yellow icicle to suck on. They had discovered that much of the pack ice was too salty to use for drinking water, but if they could find yellowish icicles, these would be potable.

When Malmgren had been made as comfortable as possible in an icy trench that Zappi hollowed, covered with a soggy blanket, and left with his drinking supply and a little pemmican, the two navy officers wearily trudged westward for several hours before themselves stopping to rest. Zappi expressed the thought that Finn might recover some strength and follow them. But Mariano shook his head despondently. "I do not think so. He said he felt no pain any more. That means he is near the end." He could not forget the sight of the raw, frostbitten foot, or the dead fingers of Finn's hands, so swollen that he had not been able to remove his ring to send home to his mother. He knew that, even if they were lucky and discovered within a few days, it would be too late to save Finn.

Malmgren was never seen again.

It was now the 15th or 16th of June, they thought. Although they had tried painstakingly to keep track of the days in order to ration their precious food supply accurately, it was becoming increasingly difficult. Neither Mariano nor Zappi suffered much from hunger as yet. In fact, the reduced rations served to make each man's mind extremely clear and active, as near starvation will often do. Mariano later described his mental state at one point as "something like nirvana," though his numbed, tired, and pained body seemed often to be something half detached from his mind—a kind of nightmarish presence that intruded upon this keen mental condition.

By now, both men were suffering acutely from the glare. Before leaving on the march, they had at least been able to enjoy periods of comfortable semidarkness inside the Red Tent. But on the open ice pack, there was no escape. Though both men wore snow glasses, the intensity of the whiteness seemed to penetrate right through the glass, or knife its way through the slits at the side, or strike the eyes like a blast of sand whenever the glasses were removed for brief periods. After the end of the third week, Mariano suddenly clutched at his eyes with both hands and cried in agony, "I can't see. I can't see!" He yanked the glasses off and began frantically rubbing his eyes.

Zappi rushed to him in alarm and forced the snow glasses back in place. Then he took a strip of dark cloth and began wrapping it around Mariano's head in the form of a blindfold. "You'll be all right. You must keep your eyes in darkness until the attack passes."

For several days, Mariano was unable to see. The pain in his eyes was intense. During that time the two men shuffled forward, with Zappi leading his companion by the hand. If Mariano suffered the agonies of snow blindness, Zappi suffered perhaps even more agonies at being able to see. Foyn Island often seemed to be only a couple of miles away, standing out darkly against the mists, its crags bare from the heat of the summer sun. Yet no matter how they struggled westward, the island was always just as far away at the end of their daily march.

As the supply of pemmican dwindled, it became more urgent than ever to reach Foyn, where there would be birds and small game, and at the very least seagull eggs. Zappi tried time and again to creep up on the few birds they encountered on the ice and kill them by lashing out with his ax, or by hurling pellets of ice at them. He never once succeeded in making a kill.

Mariano's snow blindness had one serious side effect. Since he could not see where he was being led, he frequently splashed through water he would otherwise have avoided. As a result, his feet began to suffer from frostbite. At first this was agonizing, then numbness took over. Before long, he would be unable to walk.

One afternoon—it must have been about the 21st or 22nd of June—Mariano held up his hand and cocked his head. Had he heard a plane? Zappi dismissed it as just the distant wind. Then he too heard it, cupped his ears, and turned his head slowly, trying to determine the direction. Then he saw it—a black dot against the white horizon.

"A plane! It is a plane!" He undid his pack and began frantically searching through it. "The matches! We must light a signal fire so the pilot can spot us."

Mariano threw his own pack on the ground and began feeling through it with intense excitement, swearing because he could not yet see. As the sound of the engine grew louder,

Zappi located his matches, a piece of cloth, and some oil. He struck one match after the other. All sputtered briefly and went out when applied to the cloth. The material was too wet, even with the oil. And by the time he had started the fabric smoldering, it was too late. Already the plane had passed far off to the east and was disappearing back into the mists.

The two men stood silently, then dropped to their knees and began to pray. If one pilot had passed that close, others might soon follow.

This turned out to be true. For the next four days planes were sighted, but too far to the east to do any good. Zappi would study them through his binoculars to try to determine their type and nationality. But they were too distant. He speculated that they must have located the Red Tent, since there was so much activity toward the east. If that were so, the general would by now have indicated the direction in which the three of them had gone.

Just as everything seemed more hopeful and Mariano's eyes started to improve enough so he was ready to take off the blindfold, another accident happened. Mariano slipped on the ice, twisted his right leg, and gave a gasp of pain. Zappi rushed over to him and cut the right trouser leg away with his knife. The flesh was swollen and pallid from frostbite, but there was no break evident.

When Mariano tried to get to his feet and stand on the injured leg, he gasped again with pain. It was no use, he said. He would be unable to walk any further. He would—like the ill-fated Malmgren—have to remain where he was until he were rescued or died. At this point, Zappi expressed the conviction that any further march across the ice would be useless anyway, as well as totally enervating. It was possible that the drift of the ice pack might take them right up against the shore of Foyn Island, since the wind and currents seemed more westward and favorable now.

Mariano was now able to remove the blindfold for short periods, trying to accustom his eyes again to the brightness. This was fortunate, since they now had to make hazardous transfers from one section of ice to another as the floes disintegrated. They moved to the very center of the most solid floe they could reach and made camp—such as it was—among hummocks that served as windbreaks, affixing a soggy blanket to act as a partial windbreak. Come what may, they would now have to remain here until they were picked up or died of exposure and starvation.

It was now the end of June. All hope of reaching Foyn Island was given up, for the current that had carried them temptingly close suddenly reversed itself and sucked the floe far away from land. Zappi tried to make a kind of walled enclosure with blocks of ice, but it required so much energy that he gave up in exhaustion. As an alternative, he and Mariano struggled to pull on all of the clothing they had, hoping that its very bulk would keep them warm despite the fact that most of it was soaked through.

On June 30, they divided the last ration of pemmican and settled down to wait for what seemed like certain death. Of

water they had enough, in the form of yellowish drinkable icicles, but the taste was so foul it almost made them throw up
what little food was still in their stomachs. At about this time,
Mariano was certain he heard the distant barking of dogs. He
said nothing, however, since Zappi apparently had not noticed it, and he was certain he was having delusions.

Zappi's only attempts to attract attention were the flying of
the brightest-colored rags he could find atop a pinnacle of ice
and laying out strips of cloth on the surface to spell the words:
"HELP FOOD MARIANO ZAPPI."

A week went by as the men grew weaker. Mariano began
having spells of fever, during which he would peel off his
clothing in delirium. At first Zappi was able to persuade him
to put them back on, but with the passage of time both men
became completely inactive. They did not sleep except for a
few minutes at a time. As though in dreams, they thought
about the past, from days of earliest childhood right up to the
present.

Zappi had a fitful dream in which God had permitted him
to return to Rome for a brief visit, but only on condition that
he would return to the ice pack again. So he went feverishly
from restaurant to restaurant sampling all of the finest food
in Italy and cramming a bag with supplies that he would take
back to sustain himself in the arctic. Then he was back on
the floe again. And all the fine delicacies he had packed had
vanished.

THE ICE TORTURE

During this time, too, he heard several planes. Some he decided were purely his imagination. But two or three were real. He could see them as tiny specks growing larger and larger, always veering off to the east or north before they reached the floe. Then, on July 10, one of the dots in the sky did not veer. Instead, it came straight on. It grew and grew until Zappi was roused from his state of semi-death and seized his binoculars with shaking hands.

"It's a German," he croaked in a voice that seemed to come from inside a can, "a Junkers."

Mariano stirred slightly and looked up. Zappi staggered to his feet and tried to climb up a small hummock of ice. Now, as he sighted through the glasses, he could make out Russian markings on the wings and fuselage. "The Russians have come to help, too." He waved his hat feebly. The plane flew a short distance to the north, then turned and made a wide arc directly over the floe. Mariano was half on his feet now. He could see the hand of the pilot waving out of the opened cabin window.

"They have seen us!" screamed Zappi like a wild man. "We are saved!"

The plane circled several more times, the pilot seeming to be trying to come in close enough to drop supplies. Having no proper equipment for this, however, he was forced to give up. The plane disappeared again in the direction from which it had come.

That afternoon there was a flurry of activity as more planes appeared on the horizon. "They are bringing supplies now," said Zappi. "We shall eat and drink at last." But no planes came close, and for the next two days there was utter silence. Not the slightest speck appeared in the sky. Now the two men knew that death was staring them full in the face, and they were afraid. Before being sighted, they had lain in what they considered their grave, resignedly awaiting the end and praying from time to time. But now, having had a sign of hope, it was a bitter way to die—with rescue just out of reach. Zappi thought of what it must be like to be a drowning man, to reach up with a final desperate effort, enough to touch the fingertips of a would-be rescuer, then to slip back into the black and silent depths.

Mariano was critically ill now. He could not last more than a day or so, thought Zappi, staring at him and wondering if he would look as deathly within a few hours. Why was it that the Russian pilot in the German plane did not come back?

17

FOOLS FORSAKEN

Captain Gennaro Sora's prospects were not particularly bright as he and the Dutch Sjef van Dongen and the Danish Ludvig Varming coaxed, cursed, and badgered their dog team eastward across the slushy snow on June 18, after landing from the *Braganza* in Beverly Sound. The chances of his finding the *Italia* survivors were slim. The odds were about even that he would not come back at all. And it was a sure thing that if he did return, he would be court-martialed. But his opinion of the *Citta*'s captain, Giuseppe Romagna, was such that he would willingly have gone to hell if need be, in order to tell Romagna to do likewise.

"That weak-kneed, yellow-livered little bastard!" he muttered on several occasions to his Dutch and Danish companions. "I am ashamed to admit such an incompetent and timid boob is my countryman." Well, let the little man institute a court-martial recommendation, if he wanted! Sora could tell the trial board a few blunt facts about Romagna's conduct in backtracking from his responsibilities as a ship's officer.

Although the snow was soft in many places from the summer sun, and crusty in others where surface water had frozen into a thin shell, the three men and their dogs made good time at first. But only fourteen hours after leaving, when they reached Cape Wrede, Varming complained about severe pains in his eyes. He had an attack of snow blindness, which bothered him a great deal on the trek and slowed their progress somewhat. He also complained of stomach pains. So around midnight on June 19 when they reached Cape Platen, where they made a temporary camp, it was decided to leave Varming near the depot that had been set up by another searcher. Rolf Tandberg on June 16 for the Malmgren group.

Varming had been demanding, with increasing firmness, that he be left behind. "With a sleeping bag and food," he insisted, "I will be all right, and after a couple of days' rest, I'll start back toward Cape North, where I can surely find the *Braganza* again, or some other ship."

"We will leave you, then," agreed Sora after further discussion. "However, it is my responsibility still, and my orders are that you should go directly back to the ship. No matter how improved you may feel, under no conditions are you to try to follow our trail and catch up with us."

After Varming agreed to this stipulation, Sora scouted the area until he had found what he considered the most protected spot for an emergency camp. They were on land so there was no problem of ice disintegration. Sora found a depression, protected by rocky outcroppings on three sides yet with enough drainage so that water from melting snow could not form in the pocket. Van Dongen stretched a piece of canvas between two rocks and secured it tightly to protect Varming from the sun, and to some extent from sleet and snow if there should be a storm. Under this the sleeping bag was rolled out on top of another piece of canvas to give protection from dampness.

"Whatever you do," warned Sora, "wear your snow goggles at all times—even when you go to sleep. If you should contract blindness out here, alone and miles from any possible search party, it would be certain death."

The next morning, on June 20, after leaving a two-weeks' cache of provisions with their sick comrade, Sora and van Dongen hitched the dog team and headed east. Now they would be crossing directly over a large bay, risking the dangers of decaying ice, crevasses, and the chance of being marooned on an isolated floe surrounded by water in the event that a storm should break up the pack. This was Dove Bay. Once across it, they would reach land again for a brief interval and then head out to the northeast toward Foyn and Broch islands. This last leg would prove far more dangerous than crossing Dove Bay, since it would mean venturing over the drifting ice pack of the open ocean.

DISASTER AT THE POLE

Halfway across the bay, where the ice was so fractured and jumbled that the sled often had to be lifted over obstacles, van Dongen pointed to the north. "I don't like that sky," he said grimly. "It means nothing but trouble."

The Dutchman was right. Within a few hours, the two men were trapped in a snow squall, which roared around them so solidly they could see only a few feet in any direction. They found a large hollow for the dogs and a smaller one for themselves, each somewhat protected from the wind by jagged blocks of ice. The dogs, in characteristic fashion, huddled together so closely for protection and warmth that they looked like a single, huge mound of fur. The two men crawled into their sleeping bags, laid out in the lee of the sledge, and were half successful in securing strips of canvas overhead to fend off most of the wind and snow.

For more than two days, the men huddled helplessly, eating nothing but two bars of chocolate, which they could nibble without getting out of their sleeping bag. Sora was not worried about their own nourishment, however. He was much more concerned over the dogs. They had been fed just before the storm, but they would become ill-tempered—even vicious—if forced to go long on empty stomachs. However, on the afternoon of the third day, the wind shifted slightly and died enough so that the two men could crawl out and attend to the animals. Two of the dogs were in critical condition. One had injured a leg so badly he could barely hobble; the other was seriously ill with an unknown ailment. There was only one course of action to take: the men led the dogs as far away from the others as they could and shot them. Then they broke camp immediately.

With the remaining seven huskies, they set off again to the east, their progress impeded by the wind and lack of visibility, but with the sledge riding somewhat easier wherever the snow had not been blown away. By the 29th, with clearing weather, the two men had made their way as far east as Cape Bruun. On that day, while climbing to a high point, they heard the sound of a plane to the west heading straight for them. They pulled off their jackets and waved them until they were sighted and the aircraft flew low over them, circled, and came back. It was the Norwegian aviator Lieutenant Finn Lützow-Holm.

On the next go-round, the pilot heaved out a small packet with a red marker, which landed about fifty feet away. Wrapped around a wrench was a note, which puzzled them: "Do not leave the mainland and venture over the ice." Since it gave no further information or instructions, they could only assume that it was some kind of warning. As it later turned out, in a report by Captain Hjalmar Riiser-Larsen to his commander, he and Lutzow-Holm had been on a scouting flight the day before and had noticed that the ice was in such bad condition that "it would be risky for the Sora team to start out on it, and under those circumstances they would not be able to render any assistance anyway."

When the plane circled once more to get their reaction, Sora—thinking that Romagna might have influenced the

Norwegians to cancel some of their search efforts—made his opinion known by thumbing his nose at the pilot. The plane then veered back toward Kings Bay, and Sora and van Dongen continued their plodding way, with no intention of turning back.

The two men then began the last, most perilous, leg of the search. Getting out onto the pack proved disastrous. Where the ice touched the shore, it had been smashed into great jagged blocks far too high for them to cross with even the lightest equipment. In other places, where there was no barrier and the ice was flatter, there were treacherous crevasses and cracks showing open water. For half a day they scouted the coastline, vainly looking for an out. Finally, almost in desperation, Sora selected the most likely spot.

"There is where we will try," he said grimly.

Van Dongen looked with dismay at the place Sora pointed to. Several large floes had been pushed together, like giant stepping stones. Each was large enough to support them all— sledge, dogs, and men—but most were surrounded by water and continuously in motion as the sea heaved underneath and the currents whipped them back and forth. He could see why the ice pack was popularly referred to as "the white hell."

Somehow, with great effort and considerable whiplashing of the dogs, they managed to get out onto a large, flat cake of ice, which would eventually have to drift out to the edge of the jagged, but more solid, pack. Suddenly, the ice shuddered from a surge of water underneath, and there came a loud report as it split in two.

All at once, Sora, the sledge, and two of the dogs were on one side of the crack, while the rest of the dogs and van Dongen were on the other. The Dutchman grabbed the harness of the lead dog and tried to yank him back. Then he leaped over the widening gap to join Sora, who was desperately trying to hold the sledge and keep it from sliding off the floe. Now all of the dogs were in the water, two of them still attached to the sledge, the others floundering at the end of the broken harness.

"Pull it back!" screamed Sora.

"I can't! Can't get a grip in ice."

The front end was hanging over open water as the two men tried to dig in at the rear. But the surface was wet, smooth, and far too slippery. In horror, they watched the sledge and all their equipment slide off the crumbling edge of the floe and into the dark water.

"Take this and make for the shore." Sora handed van Dongen a line, which was attached to the sledge and which he had grabbed at the last moment. "I'll try to reach another one." The sledge was partially floating, buoyed up by the sleeping bags, which had retained some air. As van Dongen plunged from the shore side of the floe into water up to his chin, Sora lay flat on his stomach at the other end and reached out for the floating equipment. His hand grasped a piece of rope and he tugged at it. This was a mistake, however, for all he succeeded in doing was loosening the lines that secured the equipment to the sledge. As he yanked, one of the sleeping bags bobbed loose, and the sledge sank lower in the water. He called to the dogs, trying to get them to swim toward him, but they were entangled in the harness and almost pulled under the load.

Farther out, three dogs were struggling vainly to rid themselves of the harness and of each other. The more they clawed and tugged, the more desperate their situation became. Sora could see that they were quickly becoming exhausted, and there was nothing he could do.

Finally, from the shore, van Dongen managed to exert enough strength on the line that the sledge began moving sluggishly toward him. Sora plunged into the water to help him, and within a few minutes they were making progress. But the accident had been costly. Many of the supplies had disappeared. When they finally heaved the sledge onto land and dragged two half-drowned dogs from the water, the men found that they had only the light packs each of them was wearing, with first-aid kits, chocolate, extra snow goggles, matches, water, compasses, a change of socks, one sleeping bag, Sora's pistol with fifteen rounds of ammunition, and one sealed package that held a week's supply of pemmican.

As they watched in horror, they saw that there was too much current to save the other dogs. One had already vanished, and the others had all but ceased to struggle. Within a few minutes they were gone.

The rest of the day was as miserable a period as either man had ever experienced in a lifetime of ventures in polar regions. Cold, soaking wet, hungry, and discouraged, they had to keep continuously on the move for warmth. The two dogs recovered and dried out much more quickly. In the course of moving about, van Dongen discovered some birds' eggs in crude nests in the rocks. Rather than break open their precious supplies of pemmican, the men ate the eggs raw. They had a strong, fishy taste, which only caused van Dongen additional misery by making him throw up. "Well, there's no choice now," said van Dongen, trying to spit out the fishy taste that clung to his mouth. "We'll have to go back now and try to reach the *Braganza*."

"No way," said Sora firmly, to the Dutchman's surprise. "We must go on, to Foyn Island."

"That would be suicide."

"To go back would be even worse. First, we'd have to cross Dove Bay again, which is almost as bad as crossing to Foyn. Then we'd have a two-week hike back to Cape North." As he pointed out, Foyn Island had become a landmark for the pilots in their searches. "If we get to it, the chances are good that we can signal a plane and get supplies dropped to us."

"Why not stay here?" pleaded van Dongen. "Lutzow-Holm found us once. When we don't show up at Kings Bay, as ordered, he'll come back."

But Sora was adamant. He not only considered Foyn the better alternative, but also was still determined to try to find the *Italia* survivors. Turning back would be an admission of failure.

After a day on the shore, the men were ready to set out for a second time across the ice. They took with them the two remaining dogs, too few to pull the sledge which was left behind. Just before starting, they built a small cairn of loose rocks, and inside the top Sora inserted a note, wrapped in a small scrap of canvas: "We are heading NE across the ice to Foyn Island. 1 July, 1928. Sora and van Dongen."

By July 2, they were well out on the pack, having navigated the dangerous crossing from shore with surprisingly little difficulty, moving from floe to floe and thence on to more solid ice. Hour after hour they kept on, too uncomfortable to stop for rest or sleep. They had slipped in shallow pools, broken through shell ice into pockets of water, and waded up to their hips through slush so many times that they were as soaked as though they had been swimming.

"When we get to Foyn we can dry off," said Sora hopefully. "As soon as we hit land, we can collect dry moss. At least enough for a small fire to heat pemmican soup on. It will bring us back to life quickly."

Somehow just the idea of a tin of hot liquid gave them new strength. Van Dongen pictured this as an event of great significance. "Pemmican soup . . . soup . . . soup," he kept muttering. Sora realized, with alarm, that his companion was running a fever from the constant immersions and was beginning to fall into a mild delirium.

On the afternoon of July 3, the two dogs wandered away from the men and soon could be heard barking furiously. At first, they decided the dogs had found bird nests, since one of the dogs had earlier been seen with a few pieces of feathers on his fur. Sora climbed up on a hummock to look in the direction of the barking. But what he saw was not welcome.

"What is it?" asked van Dongen, seeing the look on his companion's face.

"Bears—two of them." Sora stumbled down from the hummock. "Huge ones. The dogs are worrying them. We had better get out of here." He took the pistol out of his pack and checked it carefully. It was damp but not yet rusted and seemed to be in working order. He did not want to use any ammunition yet. The barking subsided. Fortunately, the bears were not in an aggressive frame of mind. They simply ambled off over the ice, and the dogs were too cold and tired to follow.

On the evening of July 4, they reached the edge of the ice at Foyn Island. Separating the ice from the shore, however, was a kind of moat, at least forty yards across, choked with cakes of ice of all sizes but only a few large enough to bear the weight of a man. For several hours, Sora tried to locate one close enough to the pack so they could ride it shoreward like a raft. Using a piece of line he had retrieved from the sledge and kept in his pack, he made a grapple by tying a jagged chunk of ice the size of his head at one end. His idea was to swing this, like a bolo, out on to a floe and drag it to him. All he did, however, was exhaust himself.

"Games, games, more games," mumbled van Dongen almost incoherently from a position on the pack where he had flopped down. He was now in a high fever and constantly muttering words that made little sense.

Sora decided there was only one course of action: to jump into the water where it seemed most shallow and swim or wade ashore. He called the dogs and managed to lash them to his line. Then, half supporting van Dongen, he slipped in among the ice cakes, and the two staggered shoreward in water that was in places up to their chests. Overhead with one hand he held his knapsack, containing the precious matches and pistol.

Two more days passed, more miserable even than any that had gone before. The moss and lichens Sora had expected to find were not only rare, but too damp or green to be used for a small fire. Van Dongen was seriously ill now. He lay in the wet sleeping bag with alternating attacks of fever and chills. Every time he was given a little pemmican to swallow, he would throw it up, gagging and shaking with dry heaves because there was nothing else in his stomach to regurgitate.

Sora moved about continuously to keep warm, pausing only occasionally to throw himself down in a depression between outcroppings of rock where he was protected from the wind. Though he was utterly exhausted, he could not sleep for more than five or ten minutes at a time. Shortly after coming ashore, the dogs had disappeared, and he did not see them again, though once or twice he thought he heard barking.

FOOLS FORSAKEN

On July 8, Sora heard another sound, a distant humming like a gathering wind. At first he thought it was a storm approaching. Then he perceived it was a plane. He immediately started scrambling up a rocky rise, scraping his leg twice in the process but being rewarded by sighting two planes. One was to the north and too far away, but the other seemed headed straight for Foyn. Sora removed his soggy jacket and waved it violently. Surely he would be seen. He started to yell, then realized the foolishness of it. The plane passed near the northern end of the island but headed at full speed toward the east, without once veering or slowing down.

When it disappeared beyond the misty horizon, Sora put his jacket on dejectedly and stumbled back down the hill to where van Dongen lay in his feverish delirium.

Three days went by. Van Dongen seemed, surprisingly, slightly improved. He sat up and talked and was able to eat some chocolate. But Sora was growing noticeably weaker. They were down to a handful of rations each day and a little brackish water, which he managed to make by melting snow. On several occasions he tried to catch birds but managed only to tire himself with no results. The pistol would not fire. And, though he knew there must be bird eggs somewhere on the island, he never discovered any nests.

Then, on the morning of July 12, Sora spotted something that suddenly gave him hope: smoke. It came from somewhere out on the pack, beyond the high hummocks. Was it the camp of the *Italia* survivors?

He watched for ten minutes, finally deciding it must be a ship. Then he painfully dragged himself up the slopes until he could see that it was indeed a ship. It was the *Krassin*. "We must move more to the north of the island—that is where she will pass by, and we can signal to her easily if she continues on the same course."

During the morning, the ship came closer, passing about half a mile off the island as she ploughed laboriously through the ice. The two men could actually hear the hollow sound of the ice crashing against her steel hull. They stood up and waved every piece of clothing they thought might show up.

Their efforts were not in vain. From the *Krassin* there sounded the blast of a siren, and a man was observed waving a flag from the bridge. The ship turned and for the next half hour came directly at them. Then, for no apparent reason, she turned again and headed eastward, charging at full power into the ice. The man on the bridge waved some flags in the air, as though trying to say something that Sora could not interpret. And soon the ship was nothing except what it had been when first sighted—a column of dark smoke rising beyond the white hummocks.

"Why are they leaving us?" moaned van Dongen in a kind of stupor. "How many days do they think we can hold out?"

"I don't know. I don't know," replied Sora weakly. He had not the heart to tell the Dutchman that all they had left between themselves and starvation was half a bar of chocolate.

18

BREAKING THE ICE

The battered old icebreaker *Krassin* had weighed anchor and chugged out of the harbor at Bergen, Norway, in a cold drizzle at an hour past midnight on June 24. She was given several rousing cheers by curious spectators who had remained all evening for the dubious pleasure of giving her a send-off. The Russian ship had been out of service for two years and looked it. She was encrusted with the soot of her last voyage, which was overlaid by a velvet mantle of coal dust that settled when she took aboard some three thousand tons of Welsh coal. The drizzle had not been hard enough to wash this off but had merely converted it into an inky paste that rubbed off on the clothing of all on deck.

Whether topside or below, there was barely room for officers and crewmen to move. Deck space was cluttered with ancient lifeboats strung on rickety davits, and with a gigantic crate formed of thick planks of wood, in which nestled a three-engine Junkers aeroplane, which was to be used in the search. On board the ship were 138 people, including four radio operators, the pilots and mechanics for the plane, seven Russian journalists, and one Italian journalist, the only non-Russian representative of the press aboard.

This antediluvian vessel, heavily armored with steel to resist the ice, and distinguished by two of the tallest smokestacks that—proportionately—perhaps any ship ever bore, was under the command of Captain Karl Eggi, formerly of the icebreaker *Lenin*, who had been given the challenging assignment of gathering crew, fuel, and supplies for an extended expedition in less than five days. Eggi, a powerful Estonian in high jackboots and tightly belted jacket, had the rough, confident manner of a man who had worked his way to a command from the very lowest seaman's rating. When Eggi gave an order for action, there was no nonsense.

Superior to Eggi, and in charge of the entire expedition, was Professor Rudolf Samoilovitch, forty-five, president of the Institute of Arctic Studies and well qualified for the job, both because of a sympathetic personality and because he had experienced thirteen other arctic explorations. He was distinguished by a bald head, which from the front looked almost as though it were on a platter, set off at the bottom by a wide walrus mustache.

BREAKING THE ICE

Despite her looks, the 10,000-ton *Krassin* still carried an effective punch. With two bows and three engines capable of developing 10,500 horsepower, she was considered the most powerful icebreaker in European service and could make a steady, if not speedy, eleven knots. Hardly designed for comfort with a normal complement, she was even less luxurious with the added entourage, for whom the only resting places at night were the sofas in the tiny saloon and the cushions on the decks of the passageways.

By June 27, as the ship lumbered through the seas and crossed the Arctic Circle, most of the expedition members were wretchedly seasick. With many ports and hatches closed to keep out heavy seas, the interior became as fetid as an animal pen. But after this first ordeal, the seas quieted, the sun came out, and lookouts were posted. They had to cling to ladders running up the tall iron stacks, whence they could scan the seas. Though too far south as yet to worry about the *Italia* survivors, the men on the *Krassin* had hopes that some sign of Amundsen and his missing French plane might be found.

Two days later, near the southern tip of Spitsbergen, the first ice floes were sighted, looking like a loose flotilla of large white rafts but solid enough to force the icebreaker to reduce speed to six knots. Then began an experience quite terrifying for those who had never traveled via icebreaker. Captain Eggi resolutely maintained a straight course, ignoring the floes. As the high bows of the ship came into contact with the ice, they would rise with an upward surge, seemingly about to lead the whole vessel out of the water and onto the pack like a stranded whale. Then the ice would shatter with an explosive report. Great chunks would slither off the steel sides with an ear-splitting clamor, sometimes bouncing high into the air and plunging into the water to send up geysers high enough to splash the bridge. It was hard enough on the eardrums of those on deck, but for those below it was like living inside an oil drum on which a strongman was beating with a sledgehammer.

On June 30, the *Krassin* received the first estimated position report of the *Italia* survivors, which came from Viglieri via the radio on the *Citta di Milano*. During the exchange of messages an incident occurred that Professor Samoilovitch could not account for at the time. He received a request from General Nobile asking permission to join the *Krassin* expedition in order to help find his men. Samoilovitch readily agreed. But when he proposed that the *Citta* should proceed north to Virgo Bay to effect the transfer, he received a cryptic answer from the general: "Impossible to come." Not until many days later did he learn that Nobile was virtually a prisoner in his isolated cabin and that all of his outgoing messages had been strictly censored and often changed entirely.

The *Krassin's* radio, powered by a unit that had been on board since World War I, was less than satisfactory and often almost useless. Its maximum range was about three hundred miles, and transmission was slow and laborious. There were periods when reception inexplicably went dead or was too garbled to understand. And there were always the usual problems of language barriers and erroneous information. Despite all of these difficulties, the chief radio operator proved to be a dogged, patient man who could eventually get the report required or send out the message handed to him. Typically, it was an accepted fact that all messages going and coming were subject to rigid censorship so that the Russian exploit would be presented favorably to the outside world.

In this bizarre communistic world, life seemed to plod rather than progress, with all around it the white, noisy scatteration of the ice pack stretching as far as the eye could see, and farther than the mind could grasp. To the Russians, the monotony of the scene and incessancy of the noise were an accepted adjunct to the occupation of icebreaking. But to Roman journalist Davide Giudici, it appeared to be the prelude to going mad. This was particularly so when Samoilovitch decided that the ship was nearing the possible position of Mariano, Zappi, and Malmgren and ordered the ship's ear-splitting siren to be sounded every ten minutes.

On July 2, however, even the steady plodding stopped. Off Scoresby Island, far to the west of the supposed position of any survivors, the Krassin's forward motion ceased. Here the ice was either solid or jammed in giant blocks one on top of the other, so the heavy steel bow could not break it up and make even the narrowest of passages. On a number of occasions, the ship wedged her way so far into the ice she was almost unable to back away again, despite the reverse action of her three heavy propellers.

When Captain Eggi advised Samoilovitch that they'd be better off heading north, their progress improved slightly, and they passed a group known as Seven Islands, where they sighted their first polar bears. However, after proceeding laboriously for one hundred miles, they had to change course abruptly to the east. There was no choice. With a limited amount of coal remaining, Samoilovitch had to head for the position in which the survivors had been last reported. Now the going really became rough. The ice was softer, but the ship's steel bow kept pushing it into mountains of freezing slush, which brought all motion to a halt when the accumulation built. Only a clever feature of the *Krassin's* design permitted progress at all. When the ship was frozen solidly into one of these masses so she could move neither forward nor backward, the crew used her ballast tanks. The forward tanks would be flooded until the weight forced the bow loose from the slush that froze to the steel. Then the bow tanks would be emptied and the stern ones filled, which not only shifted the position of the hull in relation to the ice, but also set the propellers deeper in the water, where they had a stronger bite. An additional maneuver was that of rolling the vessel from side to side by filling and emptying the port and starboard tanks alternately.

In this manner, the old vessel rocked, buffeted, and forced her way against the stubborn pack. But there was always the question: How long can this go on before the coal runs out? In one four-hour period, for example, while bucking extremely tough ice, the *Krassin* advanced exactly one mile by burning twenty tons of coal.

On the evening of July 3, a conference was held aboard the *Krassin*. The situation looked dismal. The ship was now almost directly north of Cape Platen. Even when motionless, her drift with the pack was about half a mile per hour, carrying her relentlessly away from civilization. When the time came to make a return, she would have to fight even harder to make headway. It was decided then to stop the engines completely and make an examination of the propellers, which did not seem to be performing effectively any longer. A diver was put over the side, and when he surfaced, he had a woeful report to make. A blade was missing from one propeller, the blades on the others were all damaged to one degree or another, and the steering gear braces had been so battered and weakened that they might soon give way altogether.

There was no alternative, said Samoilovitch, but to radio Moscow and inform the government that assistance was urgently needed before the ship could proceed. A day later he got his answer. The government was more willing to take a chance on losing the *Krassin* in the arctic than it was to risk losing face at home, as was evidenced by the radioed reply:

No return. Locate ice smooth enough for aeroplane takeoff and descent without serious danger. Airman

Chuckhnovsky to be allowed to attempt rescue of
Viglieri group by air. Continue work of rescue with utmost activity until only 1,000 tons coal left aboard for
return voyage.

Steam was built up quickly, and for the rest of the day the
old icebreaker nosed through the ice pack until a suitable
stretch of flat ice was located that would serve as an airfield.
Then, eleven miles north of Cape Platen a halt was made, and
the pilot Boris Chuckhnovsky and Samoilovitch went over
the side with skis to determine whether the field was properly
surfaced. Although Chuckhnovsky approved the site after
only the briefest of inspections, it was anything but safe for a
ski plane, potted with depressions and lumpy with ice ridges
and mounds. However, he was eager to get on with the air
search for which he had joined the expedition.

Boris Chuckhnovsky, thirty, had already built up a remarkable record as a flyer and had earned a reputation for exploration in the northlands around Novaya Zemlya. Yet his build
and nature seemed anything but those of an aviator or explorer. Slight of physique and with a sensitive face, he gave a
first impression of being somewhat effeminate. He had studied
as a naval engineer, however, and possessed a natural aptitude
for handling aircraft and other machines of almost any kind.

All during the nights of July 6 and 7, the seamen from the
Krassin labored to unpack the Junkers from its massive crate
and to build a plank ramp from the ship's deck to the ice,

some thirty feet below. Down this the plane's fuselage was carefully and laboriously slid, then skidded across the ice two hundred yards to the point where it was to be fitted to the wings.

Within another day, the aircraft was ready. No one knew better than Professor Samoilovitch how much depended on the performance of this plane. His engineers had just informed him that the total amount of coal left in the bunkers was 1,700 tons, 700 of which was the absolute maximum available for a further sea search before heading for home port.

Chuckhnovsky and three crew members squeezed through the plane's narrow door into the cabin, and within a few minutes the ice pack echoed with the sound of the engines. The men shoved the plane out onto the flattest stretch of ice; there followed a deafening roar; and the Junkers began lumbering heavily across the so-called airfield on its fragile skis. Now it was apparent that Chuckhnovsky had been overly optimistic about the condition of the ice. What looked like flat snow in many places turned out to be pockets of water. The plane skidded and bumped and dipped first one wing, then the other, as it gathered speed precariously.

A crash seemed imminent as the plane, now traveling at high speed, suddenly lurched into a pocket. There was a great flurry of snow and splashing of water. Then somehow the plane recovered itself and the skis were seen to lift from the ice, plunk down hard, lift again, and then begin to soar upward.

Few aviators besides Chuckhnovsky could have wrenched the ship into the air.

The Junkers circled several times over the *Krassin* to get bearings, then disappeared westward, toward Charles XII Island. Samoilovitch returned to his cabin to study his charts and nervously await a message from the pilot that he had spotted some sign of the *Italia*'s crew. Hours went by, and the only reports were negative. Even with a crew of four aboard the plane, all observing the ice intently, it would be an exacting task to pick out the tiny speck that would be what the Red Tent looked like from the air. Then came the message that the plane was returning, and Samoilovitch laid aside his charts. They would have to hope for better luck the following day.

Then he heard the sound of shouting outside. "Signal him not to come down!"

He rushed to the deck. Because of the rough takeoff, one of the skis had become detached from its rear strut and was hanging vertically from the front strut, as though on a hinge. When Chuckhnovsky settled lower, he saw the warning wave-off and zoomed upward again to circle around and around until he had ascertained what all the commotion was about. Then he planed down so gradually that the loose ski settled back into place as it was dragged over the ice. The plane touched gently, slowed, and came to a stop as perfectly as though it had landed at a municipal aerodrome.

As the pilot reported, the search had been discouraging. They had flown far beyond Charles XII Island and sighted nothing but endless stretches of ice as far as the eye could see—no evidence of any human beings or equipment.

"We will push on past Cape Leigh Smith tomorrow," said Chuckhnovsky hopefully. "I think we may find something there. But we had better take supplies for an air drop. I am not certain what kind of ice we shall find. In most places it would be impossible for a landing."

On the morning of July 10, Chuckhnovsky prepared for his next flight by loading aboard all possible supplies—both for the men in the Red Tent and for himself and his crew in the event of a forced landing. With him on the trip would be copilot Georgij Straube, a mechanic, a navigator, and a cameraman—to make sure the Russians could develop some useful propaganda of their part in the search and rescue operations. That afternoon, the plane took off and disappeared again in the general direction it had taken the day before. Now, however, Samoilovitch had a new worry. No sooner had the plane vanished over the horizon than a fog bank was seen rolling in from the west, hanging low over the ice and looking more like a fast-moving glacier than mist. Locating and returning to the ship might be a problem for the plane when the fuel was getting low.

At 5:20 that afternoon, Chuckhnovsky reported by radio that he was passing over Great Island, east of Cape Leigh Smith. Then followed thirty-five minutes of silence, broken by the brief message: "Have not yet found Viglieri camp." Soon it became evident that Chuckhnovsky must have expected weather trouble, for an hour later he radioed that he was returning. Aboard the *Krassin*, the observers could barely see two hundred feet ahead now. So the captain ordered the engine room to stoke the fires heavily in order to send up large columns of black smoke from the tall stacks to act as beacons.

As the time drew near for the plane's approach, all ears strained to catch the sound of the engines. Yet nothing was heard. Samoilovitch requested that rockets be sent up and the powerful bow searchlight turned on and beamed skyward in a futile attempt to pierce the fog.

As hope began dimming, all at once the radio operator reported a message—an unexpected one—from the plane: "Cannot find *Krassin* in fog. Have discovered Malmgren trio. Will attempt to land in Seven Islands area."

Malmgren, Mariano, and Zappi found alive! It seemed too good to be true. But, even if it were, could Chuckhnovsky possibly find a place to land in this fog without cracking up?

The hours passed endlessly, one after the other. Crew members began jamming the passageway leading to the radio room, silently listening for the crackle from the earphones that would signify a message coming through. The *Krassin*'s operator tapped out message after message: "Come in CH . . . Come in CH. . . ."

But the hours went by in silence.

19

LIBERATION

The long period of silence that followed Boris Chuckhnovsky's report of sighting the three lost men, Malmgren, Mariano, and Zappi, meant only one thing to the anxiously waiting crewmen aboard the *Krassin*: tragedy.

Professor Rudolf Samoilovitch, however, refused to give up hope. His optimism was justified when, around midnight, while he was holding his vigil in the radio room, the operator suddenly held his hand up for complete silence. "Wait! Here is something, I think. It is very faint." He pressed the earphones tighter with one hand and began to jot down letters tediously with the other. He held up the notepad for the professor to see:

Have . . . landed . . . Cape Wrede or Platen . . . Aircraft damaged, but we are safe . . .

The professor exhaled vociferously with immense relief. The plane was damaged, but if repairs were possible, Chuckhnovsky and his crew could be counted on to get it airborne again. Now too came a more detailed report on the *Italia* survivors who had attempted the march over the ice. Two of them had been sighted waving some kind of handkerchiefs, while a third seemed to be lying on the ice some distance away. The position was exact: 80°40' latitude north and 25°45' longitude east, or about five and a half miles east-southeast of Charles XII Island.

Rescue was imperative with all possible haste, because the three men were marooned on an ice floe surrounded by open water. Its surface had the slushy, soft look of floes about to crumble. Chuckhnovsky had circled low five times but had been unable to hit the floe with any supplies. "They seem in poor condition," he reported of the three men. "You must get to them as soon as you can, since the *Krassin* is now their only hope."

Later on, after urging the icebreaker to start on the rescue attempt, Chuckhnovsky reported what had happened to the Junkers. Realizing that he would become hopelessly lost in the fog if he attempted the return flight to the *Krassin*, he had elected to risk a landing and thus save enough petrol in the tanks so they could complete the flight after the weather lifted. They had selected the smoothest section of ice they could find, about a mile from the coast at Cape Wrede and somewhat south-southwest of Cape Platen. But in landing, the skis had struck a hummock of snow and flipped the nose low enough so that the propellers had been smashed and the fuselage damaged.

"We have enough food for two weeks," he radioed, "and can hold out until you complete urgent task of rescuing Malmgren group."

Aboard the Soviet icebreaker, everything had become active. Charts were laid out and pinpointed; the stokers built up steam; deck crews started hauling in the ramp and all supplies that had been laid out on the ice for the plane; and others heaved away at the ice anchors to get them aboard.

Captain Eggi estimated that the lost men could be within three sailing days if the ship did not encounter any unusual blockages. So within hours the familiar shipboard sounds were in everyone's ears: the headache-inducing boom of ice against hollow steel, the labored beat of the engines as they strained at full power against the constant rebuffing of the ice, and the piercing scream of the siren at regular intervals futilely trying to signal the marooned men that help was on the way.

By this time, the news of the sighting of the three men had been relayed to other rescue expeditions and in turn broadcast around the world. In Stockholm, it was a moment of rejoicing, for Malmgren had become something of a national hero as the anxious Swedes followed the course of rescue operations in newspapers and over their radio sets.

But aboard the *Krassin* optimism was not shared by all. No matter how Eggi belabored his engine crew, the battered old ship could barely reach a speed of half a mile an hour—and then only at great sacrifice to the coal bunkers. Also disturbing, an increasing number of polar bears were sighted as the terrain grew rougher, a sign that the men on foot might be in danger of attack by one or more of the beasts, against which they could put up almost no fight.

After the *Krassin* had cleared Charles XII Island, however, the ice was more broken and channels of open water more frequent. The ship was now in the position where Chuckhnovsky had sighted the men drifting on the large floe. The number of lookouts was increased, and the captain even offered one hundred rubles to the first man who sighted the survivors.

At exactly 5:20 that afternoon, Second Officer August Brejnkopf, peering through his binoculars, shouted, "There they are!" His hand pointed, with fingers trembling, but nothing could be seen. Was it just a dark shadow in the ice? Brejnkopf kept insisting, and about twenty minutes later the figure of a man was indeed seen, dark against a hummock of ice. But there was only one—not three.

Engine speed was reduced, and the ship edged forward, painfully slow so as not to split the ice too far ahead and risk tumbling the survivor into the water. A quarter of a mile away, the *Krassin* came to a halt. Rope ladders were quickly tossed over the side, and a rescue party descended onto the ice, led by the ship's surgeon. Now the figure could be plainly seen, a pitiful wreck of a man who, through the ship's glasses, looked as though he had been burned black by fire, and whose hair and beard were matted like mud-caked straw. Beside him lay a second man who painfully tried to raise himself on one arm, then sank back in exhaustion, too weak even to watch his rescuers approach.

"It is one of the Italians," said the surgeon. It was Captain Zappi. The pitiful-looking survivor stumbled forward, hand outstretched, and almost fell into his arms. The surgeon then hurried to the prone figure on the ice, who lay half in a puddle in a blanket so soaked with water it was worse than none at all. He kneeled down and placed one arm under the man's head to lift him up so he could see. Mariano's agonized, fever-racked eyes stared blankly. He mumbled something, but the words were incoherent. Quickly the sailors placed his water-logged form on a stretcher and began picking their way carefully over the ice blocks to the ship. But soon the question on everyone's lips had to do with the third man in the search team, Malmgren—where was he?

At this question, Zappi broke down and began to sob. Malmgren had long since died, he said. The figure of the third man Boris Chuckhnovsky had seen had been nothing but an abandoned sleeping bag.

The rescuers picked up the few remnants of the camp, which were little more than bits of clothing and the strips of dark cloth laid out on the wet snow to spell the words "HELP FOOD MARIANO ZAPPI." Then they returned to the ship.

For some time it was feared that Mariano would not survive the ordeal, after all, and that rescue had come too late. He was not only gripped with fever but was near starvation and badly frostbitten. Only his willpower carried him through. Zappi, on the other hand, had enough reserve strength that he was able to climb the rope ladder to the ship's main deck, where he immediately asked for "coffee, very hot coffee."

During the next few hours, both men were given small amounts of food, carefully administered, since, according to Zappi, it had been thirteen days since they had eaten. Then they were bathed in hot sea water, wrapped in blankets, and placed in the ship's hospital under sedatives. In addition to this treatment, Mariano was given a series of massages in an attempt to save his frostbitten arms and legs. Only after Zappi had awakened from a deep sleep was the story of the ordeal brought out, along with an account of Malmgren's death.

An hour after the two men were brought aboard, the *Krassin* got under way again and headed due east. A new position report for Viglieri and his group had just been picked up, which placed the Red Tent slightly more to the north than previously imagined. While passing at some distance off Foyn Island, and to the north of it, one lookout suddenly called to the officer of the deck to report sighting two men on the shore of the island. From the location and clothing he could see through the ship's glasses, Captain Eggi decided the two must be Captain Gennaro Sora and the Dutch engineer, van Dongen.

LIBERATION

Now a critical choice had to be made. It would take several hours to approach this part of the island and send a party ashore in a small boat. On the one hand, the men looked to be in good condition and were on an island where there surely was game and where their position could not change. On the other hand, the Viglieri group was on treacherous, disintegrating ice, in a position that was constantly changing as the currents swept the ice pack eastward.

"We will push on," decided Samoilovitch, "and return for these two later."

By the end of the afternoon, the *Krassin* had reached a position where some sign of the survivors should have been seen. Yet nothing appeared in the glasses except the endless white expanse of ice. Captain Eggi ordered an erratic course, certain that his lookouts would spot the Red Tent beyond some sheltering hummock. This strategy paid off, for within an hour more a shout went up simultaneously from two lookouts. They had spotted a thin spiral of smoke, and within a matter of minutes the strange sight of Lundborg's plane, upside down, with its nose pressed into the ice and its tail up in the air.

By nine that evening, the rusty old vessel had worked her way to within 150 yards of the famed Red Tent. First to rush forward from the camp was the tall figure of Viglieri, followed closely by Trojani and the lumbering Behounek. Within a few minutes the gangplank had been lowered, and Samoilovitch raced down it to embrace the three men. He then walked toward the tent, from which Cecioni now emerged, limping along on crutches. He took both of these in his left hand and gave an awkward salute with his right.

Last to appear was Biagi, a ludicrous sight, his face framed by a preposterous, dirt-caked beard, his short figure topped by the air force general's cap, which Nobile had left with him.

One of the most wondrous things about the meeting, recalled Samoilovitch later in an interview with a Norwegian journalist, was the fact that the survivors were so buoyed by their long-awaited deliverance from their ice floe imprisonment that they seemed to have more animation and energy than the liberators themselves. And this *joie de vivre* continued for more than an hour before they finally collapsed and wanted nothing more than showers and soft bunks in which to rest.

It was a strange meeting. The haggard and hungry survivors were eager to go aboard the ship, where they could have hot drinks and a real meal. Yet they were just as interested in showing their crude encampment to the curious officers and men of the rescue expedition who crowded around. So they lingered for well over an hour, explaining how the radio antenna had been set up, displaying some of the supplies that had been dropped from the air, and showing how they had used parts from Lundborg's wrecked plane to improvise necessities of life.

"Water, water, water . . . ," chanted Cecioni, who had been, more than any of the others, threatened by the rapidly deteriorating condition of the ice. "If you had taken any longer to come, we would all have been swimming."

His words were not completely in jest. Had the *Krassin* arrived many days later, it would have been too late. Viglieri had already prepared an emergency plan for the time the ice should break up and had stocked the small, collapsible boats with food and clothing in the event that they should have had to abandon the crumbling ice pack. Each bundle of food inside the boats had been securely bound and fastened with line in the event the boat should turn over during the perilous transfer from ice to sea.

At the time the *Krassin* first reported sighting the column of smoke, General Nobile had radioed from the *Citta* to request the Soviet officers to salvage everything of any scientific value, such as instruments and relics from the *Italia*. This was performed in such a thorough manner that there was hardly a scrap of anything left on the ice by the time the ship backed away into the gathering mists.

Although Viglieri pressured Captain Eggi to continue north to search for the men who had disappeared on the bag of the airship, his plea was to no avail. The *Krassin* had barely enough coal left in her bunkers to make the voyage back to Kings Bay. If that had not settled the matter, the condition of the weather would have, for a thick fog settled in to blanket the area so heavily that any kind of search was out of the question. Reluctantly, the officers of the *Krassin* headed the vessel for Kings Bay, under as full a head of steam as possible.

Fortunately, word was received on the morning of July 14, that the *Krassin* would not have to put in at Foyn Island on the return trip. Sora and van Dongen had just been rescued by Finnish and Swedish aviators who had effected a landing on the island.

Now at last the many loose ends were being tied together. Chuckhnovsky and his crew would soon be picked up by the *Krassin* on her return trip. Perhaps word had even been received about Amundsen and his companions in the missing French plane.

20

REVERSE RESCUE

When the icebreaker slowly began to get under way as it left the scene of the long ordeal, Giuseppe Biagi stood on the deck, looking back at the now barren ice marked only by a few remnants of tattered cloth, his eyes wet with emotion. He was thinking of that horrifying moment forty-nine days earlier when the ice-encrusted *Italia* started its fatal plunge from the storm-ridden sky to the craggy ice below. As journalist Giudici stood beside him, the little radio operator suddenly gripped his arm and pointed back into the mists toward where the Red Tent had been. Almost without realizing it, he pronounced the name of his friend and colleague who had been killed in the stern engine gondola: "Pomella."

Then he knelt down simply and unashamedly on the cold deck and bent his head in prayer. It was the only tribute he knew to the men who would never return from the Arctic.

"Giuseppe," said Giudici to him a little while later, "would you ever return to this part of the world if given a chance?"

"With the general, yes," replied Biagi, taking off the battered air force cap that had been given to him by Nobile when he was flown to safety, and looking at it absently. "With him I would return, despite the dangers."

Contrary to what the officers in the *Krassin* had thought when they passed by Foyn Island two days before and decided, temporarily, to bypass Sora and van Dongen, the two courageous, if foolhardy, searchers had been almost at the end of their own endurance. Thus it was fortunate that a Finnish plane and two Swedish ones had landed on Foyn Island in the evening of July 12 and flown the two men back to Kings Bay, where they were taken aboard the Swedish expedition's base ship, *Quest*. The pilots had been guided to their position by a report from Lutzow-Holm, stating that the duo was continuing toward Foyn and ignoring the order not to cross the disintegrating ice pack.

Sora's return was, on the one hand, a moment of triumph and, on the other, a time of personal trial. He had contradicted many experts who had asserted that an attempt to cross the ice to the islands would be impossible, but the rescue mission had proved a near-fatal, wasted effort. There was also the blunt fact, which Captain Romagna would allow no one to forget, that he had deliberately disobeyed orders when he set out on his own.

The machinery for a court-martial was actually set up and the charges against him pressed. But when Sora's commanding officer heard about the young captain's courage and exploits, he acknowledged that he was indeed a brave soldier, served him with a reprimand that was strictly a technicality, and found that there was a lack of evidence sufficient to build a case against him. Van Dongen, for his part, was astounded that the Italians should even consider such proceedings against a man who was an acknowledged hero.

This political infighting was not known to the officers on the *Krassin* and would have been dismissed as asinine if it had been known. They were too concerned with trying to find and rescue the lost pilot Chuckhnovsky and the men who were down on the ice with him.

Now the *Italia* survivors had a chance to see why rescue by sea had been so slow in coming. The old icebreaker resounded once more with the clash of steel against ice as she pounded her way off the capes. On July 15, she was further hindered by a blizzard that wiped out all visibility in every direction. By four that afternoon, heavy winds had swept the blizzard away enough so that a dark, ragged coastline could be made out, its sharp features broken by expanses of white glaciers.

"There is the plane!" shouted a lookout, pointing through a gap in the storm. About three miles away a shape could be discerned, dark against the ice. It was Chuckhnovsky's aircraft, without a doubt, though no human life could be seen anywhere near it. Foot by foot, the *Krassin* crunched her tedious way toward the plane, until the captain decided a rescue team could do much better on skis. One of the Russian journalists and a radio operator volunteered to go and within a few minutes were on their way. Their progress was observed for about a quarter of a mile; then the mists and snow flurries swirled in, and all sign of men and plane was lost.

After three hours had gone by, Samoilovitch began to worry. It was possible the two men had lost their way in the fog while following the erratic course necessary to get around cracks in the ice. Just as he was about to dispatch another rescue party, a dark figure could be seen coming through the mists—and another and another and another.

Samoilovitch was counting half aloud as he watched the number grow to five, then seven. "That must be Chuckhnovsky," he said. "With our two skiers and his crew, there would be seven in all."

"But there are more than seven, Doctor," said one of the officers. It was true.

"Is it Amundsen and his crew from the Latham?"

For a few minutes there was intense excitement. Amundsen had not been heard from for four weeks. If his plane had been forced down, it could very well have been somewhere near Cape Platen. It was impossible to tell until the heavily clothed figures came within shouting distance.

"Is it Amundsen . . . Amundsen?" shouted a voice from the deck.

"No. Sucaini . . . Sucaini."

The faces of those on deck looked puzzled, until the journalist Giudici explained that *Sucaini* was a name commonly given to members of the S.U.C.A.I. (*Studenti Universitari Club Alpino Italiano*) and hence to any experienced graduates of Alpine schools—in this case the Italian alpinists who had been assigned to the small steamer *Braganza*.

After the *Braganza* received the radio message that Chuckhnovsky had been forced to land, engineers Albertini and Matteoda, Sergeant Major Gualdi, and a Norwegian guide, Hilmar Nois, had set out to attempt a rescue on foot. The two engineers and Nois had explored much of the northwestern coast of West Spitsbergen and then gone on to much more difficult terrain, the coast of Northeast Land, from Beverly Sound to Cape Leigh Smith.

Within a few minutes after he was sighted striding through the mists, Chuckhnovsky climbed aboard the *Krassin* as briskly as though he had just returned from a training flight. He and his men had not, in fact, undergone any real hardship during their five days on the ice. The plane had been stocked with supplies to begin with, and they had managed to shoot two reindeer along the coast of Cape Wrede. Since the plane was also stocked with clothing and other supplies that they had intended to throw down to Mariano and Zappi, these came in handy in their own emergency.

The next day, Chuckhnovsky supervised repairs to the aeroplane, then taxied it across the snow to a point where it could be lifted aboard the *Krassin* and stored once again on deck.

Now the greatest problem was Mariano. Having recovered from the numbing effects of his rescue, he was now tortured by extreme pain in his gangrenous right leg. On the 16th, the *Krassin* made contact with the *Braganza* off Cape North, and when the two ships came together, Lieutenant Elido Cendali, an Italian navy surgeon, came aboard to consult with the ship's doctor about a possible leg amputation.

After examining the patient, Cendali said emphatically that they would have to operate at once, and since there were no suitable facilities on the *Krassin*, they would have to head full speed for the *Citta di Milano* in Kings Bay. But it was not until three days later that the ship reached the port and anchored near the immobile *Citta*, which seemed the very symbol of inactivity. From the Italian vessel a small launch was sent, while Commander Mariano was placed carefully on a stretcher to be lowered over the side in a sling.

As the launch approached, it could be seen that Captain Romagna was aboard. For the first time perhaps since the fateful expedition had begun, he showed signs of impatience as his launch circled several times waiting for the *Krassin's* boarding stairs to be lowered so he could come on deck and give an "official" welcome to his countrymen brought back from the icy jaws of death.

This done, he scrambled on board and was soon engaged in an emotional display of affection—hugging the survivors so-licitously and proclaiming loud thanks for the salvation he had himself done precious little to bring about.

"Where is the general?" asked Biagi.

"Yes," echoed Viglieri, his voice cold and his eyes flashing. "Why didn't you bring him here with you?"

There was a moment of embarrassed silence. Then Ro-magna hastily turned aside and mumbled something about having to hurry to get Mariano back to the ship's hospital for the operation.

Where, in fact, *was* Umberto Nobile?

The type of suffering Nobile was going through could not be alleviated either by anesthetics or amputation. Physically, his injuries from the crash of the airship had long since started to heal. But his mental anguish had not. He greeted his res-cued comrades with mixed emotions when he was finally per-mitted to visit them after they boarded the *Citta*. Biagi, Viglieri, and Behounek had only the warmest signs of affec-tion, as though they were lost sons returning to a father. Tro-jani was not certain quite how to greet the general, torn by his loyalty to his leader, on the one hand, and the puzzling ani-mosity displayed by Captain Romagna, on the other. As for Mariano, Nobile expressed a natural, and sincere, feeling of sympathy for the navy officer, which was reciprocated by a cordial, though slightly formal, friendliness—as one ranking officer to another.

But an unexpected dispute occurred when Nobile met with Zappi and shortly discovered that he had taken it upon himself to express the opinion to Soviet officers on the *Krassin* that there was no doubt that the missing *Italia* crew members had perished instantly because the bag of the airship had exploded and burned shortly after vanishing to the north. After telling him that he had no justification whatsoever for making such a statement, Nobile now requested, and somehow managed to get, permission to talk with Professor Samoilovitch. When the two met, the general was relieved to find that Samoilovitch had every intention of recommending a further search for the missing six men.

Samoilovitch informed Nobile that he intended to keep the *Krassin* at Kings Bay only long enough to refuel with coal and undergo needed repairs to the rudder and propellers, which had all been badly chewed up during the search cruises. But this plan was not to be. Inspection during temporary repairs showed that the damage was far greater than expected. The Soviet ship would have to steam to her home port for an extensive overhaul and would not be able to return to Kings Bay for many months.

The best Nobile could do (while still confined to quarters) was to secure the aid of the pilot Boris Chuckhnovsky, who began making aerial reconnaissance flights in the Junkers from Kings Bay. He was limited in the amount of terrain he could cover in the northern areas, however, until the *Krassin* could return to transport him closer to the position where the airship had gone down.

In the meantime, the *Braganza*, with the Italian flyer Penzo steamed several hundred miles east of Cape Leigh Smith, where the ice was somewhat broken up but survivors could have drifted on a large floe. A small whaler, the *Viking*, also cruised in somewhat the same area. A ship from the French relief expedition, the *Veslekari*, mainly concerned with trying to locate the French Latham seaplane, scanned the area between Victoria Island and Northeast Land, as did a second ship belonging to the French, the *Heimland*. And the small *Hobby* continued its relentless pursuit, venturing far to the east, toward the unknown territory around Franz Josef Land.

Despite the determination of their captains and crews, none of these vessels sighted anything of importance, and one by one, depending upon their size, power, and position, they were forced to retreat in the face of stormy weather and return to their respective bases.

Nobile's final—but futile—hope was the *Citta di Milano*. His efforts to talk, harass, or threaten Captain Romagna into making a search cruise to the north were totally rebuffed. The ship was not even going to remain at Kings Bay, said Romagna, but was about to return to Italy.

"But there is still hope," persisted Nobile.

"I have no authority to remain longer or let you do so," replied the captain. "You can radio Rome if you like."

Nobile sent the message. But even before the answer came back, the *Citta* was already being prepared for the return voyage, steam was being built up in the boilers, and the seamen were preparing to weigh anchor. Everyone but the general seemed to know what the answer would be.

Two days after the message went out, the reply from Rome crackled harshly over the air: *"Request denied. The general is to return at once."*

21

VOICES MUZZLED

ICY SILENCE GREETS NOBILE IN NORWAY

On July 26, this newspaper headline characterized the reception the *Italia* survivors received on reaching the Norwegian mainland on their way home. Their arrival was greeted with animosity, an attitude that was understandable on the part of a nation that had lost a national hero in the search while the Italian government sat on its duff.

After Nobile had received the blunt answer to his request to continue the search with Samoilovitch and the *Krassin*, Captain Romagna was ordered to head immediately for Italy, but first to leave the survivors at the port of Narvik, in northern Norway, where two railway cars would be awaiting them. No explanation was given for this unusual arrangement. The

Citta had adequate accommodations for taking the men to Italy. Why was the Fascist government in such a fret to return the survivors more quickly after having paid so little attention to them previously?

At Narvik, a mute crowd was on hand to watch the *Citta* arrive in port. Not a Norwegian hand was waved in friendly greeting, and even the stevedores barely made a move to assist the Italian ship in docking. There were no Norwegian officials on hand to welcome the men, and not a single Italian flag flew at the scene, though the arrival had been made known many hours beforehand. The focal point of this hostility was a large poster, conspicuously placed, which stated, "Reward: 10,000 kronen [about $3,000] for any information leading to the location of the missing explorer Roald Amundsen." Not only was rancor directed at Italy's failure to send any search expedition to look for Amundsen, but the Norwegians now recalled the bitter feud between the White Eagle and the Fascists after the *Norge* expedition.

Almost before the ship had touched the dock, an agent of the Italian Consulate was scrambling for the ship's ladder, hastily thrown over the side, to come aboard and give official orders. The gangway would be lowered in such a manner, he told the survivors, that they could pass directly from it to the waiting railway cars on the dock. There was to be no speaking to anyone en route, and particularly not to any representative of the press. Once in the railway cars, no one would be permitted to go to other parts of the train that would soon connect with them. Furthermore, no written messages were to be sent to anyone, journalists or otherwise.

A great silence hung over the docks, broken only when the *Citta* rasped harshly against the pilings. It was all the more strange because of the sizeable crowd on hand, which kept increasing while the gangplank was slowly lowered and the survivors were shepherded down it. The men trudged in silent file to the waiting railway cars, which had been specially sent all the way from Paris.

Once inside, Nobile and his men found themselves in an almost prisonlike atmosphere. The curtains had been drawn, and the men were told to leave them that way until after the train had pulled away from the city. They were not actually prisoners. There were no guards or constraints. But the implication was that this was a touchy international situation, in which it would be best to follow the suggestion of the Italian Consulate. As for the survivors, they were too exhausted to care much one way or another and not inclined to try to escape from this morbid atmosphere to mingle with the hostile onlookers lining the docks.

The train pulled out slowly, left the city behind, and began rolling through the rugged Norwegian countryside. Though the survivors perked up at the sight of picturesque villages and country scenes en route, they became depressed again each time the train rolled to a stop at a station. For there would again be the curious crowds, standing in silent and sullen condemnation to glare at what the Norwegian press was now referring to as "the sealed railway carriages" carrying the Italians, who were described as "broken in spirit."

After crossing the border and reaching the first Swedish station, Videln, one small act of friendliness suddenly shone like a beacon on a dark night. Here the crowds were sympathetic and open in their greeting, so much so that the blinds were opened and the men looked out on people who responded to them with smiles and warm-hearted greetings. As Umberto Nobile stood on the platform of his railway car, a little girl approached. She could have been his own daughter, except that she was typically Nordic, with fair hair and blue eyes. She smiled sweetly, mumbled something shyly that the general did not understand, and held forward a bunch of summer flowers.

Choked with emotion, Nobile reached down and took them from her, stammering his gratitude and asking for her name. He never forgot it—Ebba Haggstrom—a name that revived his faith in humankind at a time when he and his companions felt as deserted and miserable as though they had still been lost on the ice pack.

Throughout most of Sweden and Denmark, the gathering crowds were in a hospitable mood. Ludvig Varming, the Dane who had begun the search with Gennaro Sora and was something of a hero in Denmark, having been rescued and treated for his snow blindness, was on hand to greet the Italians with respect. But as soon as the train crossed the border into Germany, the attitude of the onlookers changed abruptly once more. This time the animosity was more overt than it had been in Norway, with some of the people screaming jeers at the two railway cars. Here the accusations seemed to be directed more against the two navy officers who had survived the march than against their leader.

It was with a heavy sense of dread that they approached Italy. If people in other countries had been worked up to such hysteria, what would be the situation at home, where some of Nobile's bitterest detractors controlled elements of the press? It was rumored that in Italy Premier Mussolini had forbidden receptions or any public gatherings that might acclaim the survivors and that certain members of the government had actually organized mobs that would shout down any expressions of welcome small groups might extend on their own.

Into this vale of the unknown they sped, trying to detect signs of what they might expect. To their surprise, at the very first stop on Italian soil, the bystanders swarmed onto the station platform to greet them, displaying a most enthusiastic welcome. If the survivors were skeptical at first, they were reassured when, at station after station, the townspeople turned out to hail them and bring flowers. Even the newspapers, so commonly stifled by Fascist censorship, spoke of the acclaim and the welcoming receptions.

Thus it was that when they reached Rome on the evening of July 31, 200,000 people were waiting in the station area—and this despite the decree that there should be no public ovations. Mussolini's ban had been issued under some pressure, brought to bear by men like Balbo and Valle, who would lose face if public opinion should upend their whispering campaign that the *Italia* expedition had been a national disgrace. Thus, when it quickly became apparent that the public was paying little attention to the ban, the Fascist leaders knew there was little they could do but wait for public sentiment to die down and try another approach. To enforce the decree would simply antagonize the crowds and goad the people into proclaiming Nobile as a martyr.

The general returned to his wife and daughter, with his faithful dog, Titina, and for a few days it seemed as though he would be able to resume normal life again. He was certain that the issue of his own rescue would be a thing of the past. But it was not to be. What he wanted most was to be able to get back to his designing, to incorporate into a new airship improvements that might prevent any recurrence of the kind of tragic accident suffered by the *Italia*.

The fact that there had been accusations, and that there were forces in the government trying to use him as a political wedge, gave Nobile the disturbing impression that he was always caught in some great, relentless glare. He began to find that he could not focus on his work and his goals until he had explained his side of the catastrophe and until someone in authority satisfactorily explained to him why he had been so continuously slandered. With this in mind, he requested an audience with Premier Mussolini. And so it was that he was ultimately given an appointment at Viminale Palace on

August 10. He was greeted cordially by the official secretary and with equal warmth by Il Duce.

"How are you, my dear Umberto?" Mussolini waved him informally to a chair near his desk and took another seat a few feet away. "I see that you are still limping." In an affable way, he asked a few questions about the expedition, the events leading up to the crash, and the condition of the men while lost on the ice pack.

After half an hour, with Mussolini always steering the conversation in the direction he chose, the premier said, "I think this will do." He rose to indicate that the appointment was over. "If I need more details, I will call for you."

Nobile rose also but stood firm, indicating that he was not quite ready to be expelled like a schoolboy who has finished his recitation. He had come to find an answer to his personal enigma, and he meant to say what was uppermost in his mind. "Excellency, now I have something to say on my own account."

Mussolini, at first taken aback, recovered his poise and responded with a slight smile. "Go ahead."

Slowly, one by one, the general took from his jacket several documents. These showed how poorly he had been treated by the Italian press for his "cowardice" in leaving the pack first, with Lundborg. One was a Stefani communiqué in which the Italian government declared not to know the reasons, or the conditions under which, he had left the ice pack. "It sounded," said Nobile bitterly, "as though I had never sent a long radio message giving full details."

"Well, that came later," replied Mussolini, with a show of annoyance at being thus forced into giving an explanation.

"That could not be," insisted Nobile, pursuing the matter doggedly. "The Stefani communiqués and my own declarations appeared in different sections of the Italian press at the very same time." He paused, seeing that Il Duce was not going to stoop to further explanations. "And even if my message had come later, the government's duty was to wait for information before releasing such a damaging communiqué."

Mussolini turned his back and moved over to his desk. "It was hardly necessary," continued Nobile, "to broadcast throughout the world a declaration that could do nothing except make the foreign press aroused against me. Even if some member of the government had lowered himself into accusing me of leaving first out of a desire to save my own skin, it would have been more charitable to this nation to shield me in the eyes of the rest of the world until . . ."

Mussolini leaned over the chair at his desk, and as he turned to sit down, his face was no longer affable, but hard and square, like the caricatures of him in the foreign press. He said nothing.

"Who is there in the government who is qualified to call me a coward, when I have faced the risks of a polar flight once, and then returned steadfastly to face them all over again a second time?" All of the fury and frustration that had been building up within Nobile since the end of May now exploded. Without even noticing it, he raised his voice sharply, forgetting that the man he was addressing was not accustomed to being criticized to his face. Mussolini reached out for a glass of water on his desk and quickly took a swallow. Nobile could see that his hand was shaking in anger.

Then Mussolini pressed a button, and an aide appeared immediately. "See the general out." Il Duce's features were pale and tense.

Umberto Nobile made a polite bow, turned, and strode quickly down the long chamber and out the door. It was his last meeting with Mussolini but not the last time he was to feel the wrath of the Fascist Party.

His next setback came in early September, when General Arturo Crocco, who was then in charge of the Aeronautical Engineers, came personally to inform him that he was not to try to leave the city, write articles, speak to groups, or even go to public gatherings such as the theatre. At about the same time, another incident occurred that evidenced how much political pressure was being directed against him. He arrived in the morning, as usual, at his office at the airship factory. Not only was it locked, but official state seals had been attached to the door, making it a criminal offense to enter, even with force. When he made inquiries among the people who worked for him, they all expressed ignorance as to how, when, or why the door had been sealed. Nobile did not bother to inquire further. From the looks on their faces, he could tell that their lips were sealed by fear, and by the knowledge that they could be locked out of their jobs and livelihood just as easily and quickly.

From the 10th of September on, Nobile was a man without an assignment, though he was still technically a general in the air force. Even when at home, he could look out and see members of the secret police surveilling the building, ready to shadow him when he came out to the street. This situation continued throughout September and October and into November.

Even more distressing, it now became apparent to Nobile that the few men who had continued as his friends were avoiding him, out of fear for their own independence. This situation worsened when, in late fall, it was announced publicly that there would be an official inquiry and trial. However, general opinion was that a trial would be unjustified. For never in the history of global exploration had men been formally accused of a crime simply because they had failed to return victorious in the battle against those forces of nature that had sent many of the strongest, bravest men in the world to their deaths.

22

AN ABUNDANCE OF
ENEMIES

By the end of the year, a commission had been set up to make investigations and conduct the inquiry. There was doubt, in the opinion of many Europeans, as to the impartiality of the group. As Captain Willy Meyer, the noted German aviator, expressed it, "Alas, almost all the men appointed as members of the commission were Nobile's avowed enemies." Cappelletti, director of the Stefani News Agency, reported, "This is pure formality. The conclusions are already written." And to make certain that the dice were properly loaded, General Italo Balbo cautioned the entire commission beforehand that Nobile was "an ambitious man and a dangerous subverter."

The president of the commission was Admiral Umberto Cagni, a man with some polar experience but no knowledge of airships. The only member, in fact, who had any acquaintance with lighter-than-air craft was Admiral Salvatore Denti Amari di Pirajno, who had flown off and on, a few years earlier, in older models of World War I vintage. Another member, General Francesco de Pinedo, not only had no knowledge of either exploration or airships, but was also an outspoken critic of Nobile and a favor seeker of Balbo's. General Nicola Vacchelli was also hostile. The remaining three members, who were perhaps the most impartial, were Senator Francesco Pujia, General Pietro Molinelli, and Michele Vocino, the secretary.

However, as Pujia admitted, "A commission thus formed was bound to be hostile to Nobile." It looked as though the cards were stacked in the characteristic Fascist manner.

By the beginning of 1929, little had changed. Nobile was still a virtual political prisoner, the loneliest man in Italy and constantly in the eyes of the secret police. The other survivors had returned to their pre-expedition duties, for the most part, but were reluctant to talk to the press or to give out opinions. They, too, lived under the shadow of the inquiry. When they did speak, it was only when brought before the commission and questioned about various aspects of the flight and the weeks on the ice floes.

Despite this dismal outlook, Nobile began to take heart that the inquiry would, in the end, prove to be beneficial to Italy and to all the men concerned. One day Giunta, the undersecretary of the council of the Italian government, called him in to explain the workings of the commission and to give him some personal reassurance.

"Don't worry about this commission," said Giunta privately. "The chief [Mussolini] has told me that, in accordance with his instructions, the commission is charged with ascertaining the facts about Malmgren's tragedy and the work of the rescue expeditions, but must not bother you at all. You will not even need to enlarge fully upon details." There was not, it was stressed, the slightest intent to brand the expedition or any of the members of it. No formal charge was being made against Nobile at this time, he was assured.

During February, while the investigation was being concluded by the commission, Nobile noticed that a change in attitude seemed—at least on the surface—to be taking place. Government officials were friendlier to him. The secret police appeared only occasionally, and there was considerable relaxation in the blanket of censorship that had been thrown over the members of the expedition. He was even told that Mussolini's office had given him approval to go ahead with the preparation of several articles he had in mind about the expedition. Yet he was surprised a short while later, when he was ready to send them off for publication, to receive a request from the premier's office to withhold them temporarily. The excuse was that they would be much better received by the public once his name had been fully cleared. Nobile was not an impatient man. He was willing to wait, particularly in light of the favorable developments he had heard about.

On March 3, Nobile went to lunch at the home of a friend of long-standing, General Moris. He was in good spirits, for this newfound freedom was like a draft of fresh air to a man who has been down in a dark mine for days on end. In the middle of the meal, he was called to the phone. The voice at the other end was that of Prefect Beer, chief of Mussolini's cabinet. "I have good news for you, General," he said. "The commission has just presented its conclusions to the chief of government. The findings are wholly favorable to you. I present my heartiest congratulations!"

When Nobile returned to the table, his dark eyes sparkled with gratitude and relief. "I knew the report would have to be favorable," he said.

"I knew it, too," replied General Moris. "And I had heard rumors, not only that it would be, but that you were in line for a promotion for what you suffered and accomplished."

On that day, the lock and seals were removed from the door of Nobile's office at the Aeronautical Factory, and he was given complete freedom to come and go as he wished.

The next day, the official findings of the commission were reported in the newspapers of Rome. Nobile arrived at his office early, to start catching up on the work he had been forcibly kept from for so many months. He had given little thought to the report itself once he had been told the outcome, for the details seemed unimportant.

AN ABUNDANCE OF ENEMIES

Suddenly the door burst open and his aide rushed in, a newspaper in his hand and his face as pale as the paper on which the news was printed. He held it up and the black headline struck Nobile in the face like the lash of a whip:

NOBILE BLAMED FOR ITALIA DISASTER!

Equally damning, he was further headlined as a coward for having "deserted" his own men and as incompetent for having piloted the ship in such a manner as to cause a crash that was avoidable. One account described the moments before the crash as a time of "utter panic," in which the general lost his head, issued conflicting orders, and made it impossible for any of the men in the pilot cabin to carry out their duties in trying to regain control of the airship.

"But, Umberto, what about the news you received yesterday?" asked the aide, aghast at what he read. "What about the phone call from Beer that you had been completely exonerated? And the report to you, directly from Mussolini himself, that you were not being charged with any dereliction of duty?"

"Empty words . . . just words," muttered Nobile in cold shock, staring right through the headlines and into space. He could see the whole vicious scheme clearly now—the reason Mussolini had granted permission for him to write his articles, why he had been accorded more and more freedom of late, and why he had been treacherously informed that the commission's report was favorable to him. Even the rumors of a "promotion" had been cleverly planted and the seals removed from his office for a deliberate reason.

It was all a plot to throw him off guard. Fearful that he might get wind of the real report and its implications, and knowing that his popularity with the public was strong enough so that he could demand open hearings before the re-port was printed, signed, and approved, the commission had done every underhanded thing possible to keep him ignorant of what was going on behind the scenes.

One of the more ludicrous findings of the report regarded the praise given to the Italian government for its involvement in rescue operations. "The commission considers with regard to rescue work," it said in part, "that everything possible was done with the utmost speed toward the location, aid and res-cue of survivors, as well as toward searching for the airship. . . . This work, which was undertaken with energy and devotion by Italians, with the important collaboration of other countries, constitutes a remarkable example of solidarity . . ."

When the numbness had left him after reading the newspa-per report, and the flush of anger shocked him back to life again, Nobile wrote to Premier Mussolini to protest, and to ask that he be given a chance to answer the charges that had been leveled by the commission but never before revealed to him.

He received no answer to his letter. Nor did he receive one when he wrote a second time on March 14, and again a little later, but this time to Augusto Turati, secretary of the Fascist Party.

Shortly after the first letter, however, Nobile received a personal visit at his home from Commander Pellegrini, who was then chief of the air minister's cabinet. The man was troubled and seemed unable to speak at first, apologizing and extending profuse regrets over what had happened. But when Nobile finally insisted that he say what he had come to say, Pellegrini seemed to find his tongue.

"I have been sent by Il Duce," he began, "because the air minister has recommended that, in light of the results of the investigation, you put in for retirement from active service."

"I do not wish to retire," replied Nobile, emphatically. "I am hardly at the age for such an action."

"Well," stammered Pellegrini, "Premier Mussolini has already promised to see that you get a pension—a good one."

"I refuse to make such an application for charity," replied Nobile, his anger mounting. "You may inform the air minister that the proceedings against me are without precedent, and that I never even heard the charges against me until reading them in the newspapers."

Pellegrini tried further to remonstrate that retirement would be in Nobile's favor. But he made no impression and finally left with Nobile's comment, "My written reply to the chief of govermnent will be ready before the evening."

Nobile's reply was not the expected request for retirement but a blunt, outright letter of resignation, as a measure of protest. This action was not only a direct slap at Mussolini's plan of benevolent compromise, but also cut off any chance of benefits or pension.

As expected, the resignation made Mussolini violently angry. Several of Nobile's friends considered his action rash in the extreme and deplored the fact that he had not forced the government's hand by simply doing nothing and awaiting whatever step the cabinet might take. But the act was done, and there was no reconsidering. Men had been hanged, shot, or reported as having mysteriously disappeared after far less serious clashes with the Fascists. Nobile was saved by two factors. The first was that there were still strong pockets of pro-Nobile sentiment in the country, among them elements of the Church, echoing Pope Pius XI's tribute to Nobile as "Crusader of the Pole." The second was that Italy was being severely criticized throughout Europe for the handling of the *Italia* investigation.

Many of the people with the most expert knowledge of airships, the polar regions, and the extreme difficulties of exploration sided strongly with Nobile. Professor Gerard de Geer of Stockholm, a polar authority, wrote in a magazine article that responsibility for the disaster should be placed on the nature of the unequal struggle for survival in the arctic, and not on the victims hard hit by the catastrophe that overtook them. He pointed out, too, that the Italian government had, astonishingly, completely ignored the value of the scientific data gathered by the expedition.

Professor Behounek, in a book about the expedition, described Nobile as a leader who "rested less than anybody else, an exemplary commander, always at his place in the captain's cabin, supervising, steering, and charting, allowing the whole crew the maximum possible rest, while he himself was always on his feet."

Einar Lundborg reiterated time and again, in speech and in print, his strong defense of the man. The noted Vilhjalmur Stefansson, one of the greats of arctic exploration, stated, "Few men have ever been so outrageously railroaded as General Nobile has been." And Trygave Gran, the Antarctic explorer and aviator, said: "The judgment against Nobile makes me rebel. It is unjust. In this case, Italy took recourse to finding a scapegoat and created a new Dreyfus affair. To say that Nobile has not conducted himself wholly honorably is preposterous impudence."

But even among those who were his strongest supporters, few people in any country could discern Nobile's real anguish. The outcast of Rome, ostracized by society, shunned by timid friends, censored in speech and print, restricted in everything he tried to do, he was nevertheless so devoted to Italy, his native land, that he preferred a life of virtual imprisonment and daily abuse to seeking the solace of voluntary exile in some other nation. It was his ultimate tragedy that he was out of place in the world that existed in the 1920s and early 1930s as Fascism grew stronger and stronger under the Mussolini dictatorship.

EPILOGUE

I t is reasonable to surmise that the crash of the *Italia* might have caused a sharp decline in aviation's confidence in the dirigible for both peacetime and military service. But such was not the case. Particularly in the United States, the navy was convinced that dirigibles were ships of the future, as evidenced by the construction of the *Akron* and the *Macon*, which saw extensive service before they, too, crashed in the mid-1930s. In Germany, the belief in these giants of the sky was portrayed by the construction of the *Graf Zeppelin*, which saw long and reliable international passenger service before finally being decommissioned, and the *Hindenberg*, whose fiery crash at Lakehurst, New Jersey, in 1937, decisively wrote "finish" to airships as commercial carriers.

Strange things happen in the world, not the least of which was that all the survivors of the *Italia* flight, despite their ordeal, were still alive in the late 1950s when I began research for a major article on the crash, whereas most of the other principals in this international saga were dead and had been for many years.

No signs of Malmgren or the six men who vanished on the bag of the *Italia* were ever found. As for Amundsen and the French pilot and crew members, the only clue to what had become of them was a blue-green seaplane float discovered in the rocks of the Fugloe Islands, near Tromsö, Norway. It was identified as having come from a seaplane of the Latham type, in which Amundsen was a passenger. From its condition it was deduced that it had been "wrenched from the fuselage with great force," suggesting that the plane had nosedived to earth or the sea.

The dashing Captain Einar Lundborg was killed in a plane crash in an unidentified location while flying on a Swedish military mission in February of 1931. The heroic Umberto Maddalena, at the time a colonel, was killed one month later in a bizarre accident when one of the propellers of his plane flew off in midair, ripped through the fuselage, and cut the craft in two. Sergeant Axel Svensson, also a rescue pilot, died in May of the same ill-fated year, and so did Captain Karl Eggi, of the *Krassin*, under mysterious circumstances. Though reported to have been fatally injured in a tramway accident, rumor had it that he was executed by the Russians for some political crime.

Captain Gennaro Sora, after his gallant venture, was reprimanded for disobedience but eventually attained the rank of general, served through World War II, and was able to enjoy a brief retirement before he died in the late 1940s. His companions, Ludvig Varming and Sjef van Dongen, were not so fortunate. Both died in the 1930s. The Russian pilot Boris Chuckhnovsky and the *Krassin* expedition leader, Professor Samoilovitch, are among the multitudes of Soviet citizens who have inexplicably vanished in Communist purges.

As for the Fascist leaders, little need be said about the death of Benito Mussolini. Yet he did not go to his violent end unmourned. He had a strong rapport with farmers and the poor and was actually more fond of dressing casually than in resplendent uniform, despite the many publicized photographs of him to the contrary. Even Nobile felt that he had some good in him and might have been a great leader of the Italian people, had he not been too weak to overthrow the vicious Fascist elements that really manipulated the political strings.

General Italo Balbo died early in World War II, in a mystery that was never solved. Leading a flight over water off the North Coast of Africa, he was reported to have been fired on and downed by the guns of Italian ships. An accident? Or a purposeful error? It was said by many that he had become too big for his breeches—and in the Fascist regime that was a great offense.

Arturo Crocco retired after World War II and, before he died, admitted to Nobile, face to face, that he had actually been shocked at the verdict of the board of inquiry, but for his own personal safety could not take any action or question the outcome.

At least three members of the Scandinavian rescue teams were still living in the early 1960s, at which time I had some correspondence with all of them. One was Hjalmar Riiser-Larsen, who was with the Swedish air force and had accompanied Nobile on the *Norge* flight across the North Pole. Another was Rolf Tandberg, who searched areas near the route of the Sora team, with whom I had correspondence and who sent me a booklet he wrote in 1977 about subjects and places he had encountered in his own explorations.

Last, we come to General Umberto Nobile. After his condemnation by the board, by the Italian press, and by many of his professional associates, he went into a period of semiretirement for two years. During that time, he was constantly under surveillance by the Fascist secret police, an ordeal that he was able to withstand but that hastened the death of his ailing wife in 1930. A year later, he accepted an invitation from the Soviet Union to serve as a consultant in airship design and construction, an assignment that kept him away from Italy for almost five years.

In 1936, on returning to Rome, he was permitted to teach aeronautics at the University of Naples for three years, until he was invited to the United States to teach at the Lewis Holy Name School of Aeronautics in Lockport, Illinois. Even though he became an enemy alien when America entered World War II, he was allowed to remain in the United States until the summer of 1943, when he voluntarily returned to Rome, feeling that his daughter needed him there. This was a period of extreme mental anguish for Nobile. On the one hand, he was anti-Fascist, but on the other hand, he was, emotionally and spiritually, an Italian. And he was deeply disturbed by the death in action of one of his beloved nephews.

At the end of World War II, Nobile was automatically restored to rank and promoted to major-general in the Italian air force. Somewhat against his wishes, he was talked into running for office and was elected to the Deputy Assembly in 1946. Once again he became a target for criticism, this time being labeled a Communist because of his long service to the Russian government prior to World War II, which caused him to lose any taste for further political involvement. He was far more productive and fulfilled spending his later years in writing and research, and teaching on the faculty of the Aeronautical Institute of the University of Naples. His love of aeronautics, his engineering integrity, and his desire to pass along to a younger generation his own technical knowledge sustained him and helped him to bear his personal ordeals during more than three decades.

The last time I saw him was in 1962, when my wife and I were visiting Rome. We had dinner with him and his second wife, and during lengthy interviews over a period of three days discussed revisions and additions to the biographical material I was writing about him and about the *Italia* expedition. After that, we continued an intermittent correspondence between Rome and New York throughout the 1960s and early 1970s. He died in 1978, and although he had long since learned to live with the torments and agonies of his ordeals, I had the impression that he never quite understood how history could place a person whose intentions were so honorable in the role of martyr.

ACKNOWLEDGMENTS

My warmest acknowledgment goes naturally to the late Dr. Umberto Nobile himself, who for years patiently put up with my relentless demands for information, documents, photographs, letters, sketches, maps, and a bulging file of other material. And who answered, with directness and thoughtfulness, the hundreds of questions that my researchers and I put to him over the years, no matter how personal they may have been. I am grateful also to the many stringers of *Life* magazine abroad, whom I persuaded to interview survivors and rescuers whom I could not visit with personally. In this manner, we had the good fortune to interview every single *Italia* survivor and many members of search parties.

I am particularly grateful to the late Rear-Admiral Alfredo Viglieri and Giuseppe Biagi, both of whom visited me in New

York City and furnished me with innumerable photographs, as well as with factual information and personal impressions. Excellent recollections from their diaries also were sent to me by three other survivors, long since deceased: Admiral Adalberto Mariano, Commander Filippo Zappi, and Sr. Natale Cecioni.

A great deal of the personal interviewing was done by my chief researcher on the project, Ann Natanson, of Rome, who took hundreds of pages of notes and never seemed to tire of uncovering new material. In Rome, I was also grateful to have the temporary services of two others: Mrs. Nelson (Jean) Fry and the late *Life* photographer Thecla Haldane, who photographed Dr. Nobile in his study, along with many mementos of the ill-fated expedition.

From an old friend of the general's, Mrs. Vera M. Schuyler, came a good many of my original impressions of the man. She had met him shortly after his return from Spitsbergen and recalled with great warmth and understanding the way he reacted to the sudden and unexpected judgment against him. Another who gave me an intimate personal impression of Nobile was C. H. Zimmerman, of Akron, Ohio, who contributed many newspaper clippings from the mid-twenties and described what the Italian aeronautical engineer was like when he spent several months in the United States in 1922 as a consultant to Goodyear.

After intensive inquiries to locate surviving members of the many search expeditions, I learned from Dr. Nobile about Einar Christell, who at last report had been a major in some

ACKNOWLEDGMENTS

branch of the military in Sweden. Taking a gamble, I wrote simply to "Major Einar Christell, Swedish Air Force, Stockholm, Sweden." It is to the great credit of the Swedish postal service that within ten days I received a reply. Major Christell mailed me a whole packet of photographs a few weeks later, along with caption material running to eight typewritten pages of valuable data.

Since my knowledge of arctic lore was limited, I drove to Hanover, New Hampshire, to examine the finest assemblage of polar studies in North America, the Stefansson Collection of the Baker Library at Dartmouth College. I am greatly indebted to the late Dr. Vilhjalmur Stefansson, one of the most noted arctic explorers of this century, not only for his perusing dozens of books, letters, documents, and photographs pertinent to the subject, but also for his many hours of personal discussion and comment. Further data on the nature of the North Pole, northern ice packs, and arctic currents came from the late Sir Hubert Wilkins, who wrote to me while he was on his final expedition in the Antarctic, in the winter of 1957–58. He sent me a long report, which I had requested for a chapter on him that I was including in my book on submarines, *Challengers of the Deep*.

Many others have contributed—directly and indirectly—to the material that appears in this book. While I cannot possibly hope to credit all who have had a hand in the work, I at least express the hope that my organization, interpretation, and writing have done justice to their fine assistance, and to the subject.

BIBLIOGRAPHY

The following list covers only those books published in English and does not include about triple this number published in Italy, France, Germany, the Netherlands, and the Scandinavian countries. Many books and articles were authored by survivors of the *Italia* crash and members of search and rescue teams.

Amundsen, Roald. *My Life as an Explorer*. Heinemann, London, 1927.

Botting, Douglas. *Shadow in the Clouds*. Kestrel, London, 1975.

Cross, Wilbur. *Ghost Ship of the Pole*. Paperback, Young Adult. Sphere Books, London, 1972.

Dither, Elisabeth. *The Truth about Nobile*. Williams & Norgate, London, 1933.

Giudici, Davide. *The Tragedy of the* Italia. Benn, London, 1929.

Grierson, John. *Challenge to the Poles*. Foulis, London, 1964.

Hogg, Garry. *Airship over the Pole*. Abelard-Schuman, London, 1969.

Lundborg, Einar. *The Arctic Rescue*. Viking, New York, 1929.

Montague, Richard. *Ocean, Poles, and Airmen*. Random House, New York, 1971.

Nobile, Umberto. *With the* Italia *to the North Pole*. Dodd, Mead, New York, 1931.

―――. *My Polar Flights*. Putnam, New York, 1961.

Simmons, George. *Target: Artic. Men in the Skies at the Top of the World*. Chilton, Philadelphia, 1965.

Stefansson, Vilhjalmur. *Unsolved Mysteries of the Arctic*. Macmillan, New York, 1939.

Tandberg, Rolf. *The* Italia *Disaster: Fact and Fantasy*. Privately printed, Oslo, 1977.

Toland, John. *Ships in the Sky: Great Airship Disasters of the World*. Holt, New York, 1957.